Options
Made Easy

Second Edition

Options Made Easy

Second Edition

Your Guide to Profitable Trading

Guy Cohen

Library of Congress Number: 2005923851

Vice President and Editor-in-Chief: Tim Moore
Associate Publisher and Director of Marketing: Amy Neidlinger
Executive Editor: Jim Boyd
Editorial Assistant: Susie Abraham
Development Editor: Russ Hall
Marketing Manager: John Pierce
International Marketing Manager: Tim Galligan
Cover Designer: Alan Clements
Managing Editor: Gina Kanouse
Senior Project Editor: Kristy Hart
Copy Editor: Chrissy Andry
Indexer: Lisa Stumpf
Interior Designer: Sue Lamble
Compositor: Major Productions
Manufacturing Buyer: Dan Uhrig

Printed in the United States of America

Seventeenth Printing   April 2012

ISBN 10: 0-13-187135-8
ISBN 13: 978-0-13-187135-9

Pearson Education LTD.
Pearson Education Australia PTY, Limited.
Pearson Education Singapore, Pte. Ltd.
Pearson Education North Asia, Ltd.
Pearson Education Canada, Ltd.
Pearson Educatión de Mexico, S.A. de C.V.
Pearson Education—Japan
Pearson Education Malaysia, Pte. Ltd.

To Geoff, whose genius and contrarian outlook gave me the stomach to perform one of his reasonable miracles.

Contents

Acknowledgments

It's amazing how many parts of your mind go into writing a book like this. As a result, there are a number of people I must thank for both their direct and indirect influence.

First to my friend Geoffrey Glassborow to whom this book is dedicated and whose wondrous skills enabled me to prove modern medicine wrong. In 1994 I was diagnosed with ulcerative colitis, an intensely debilitating condition of the lower intestine. The condition was serious enough to lead doctors in both the UK and USA to recommend surgery as the only means of "relief." At this time I was in constant pain and fear, such that even venturing out of my home became an achievement in itself. Through Geoff, I not only made a full recovery, but I also learned how to think, something we don't really get taught at school. It may sound a bit trite but because of what was achieved, I can now look on every obstacle in life as a challenge and every challenge as an opportunity.

I also need to thank my MBA Finance options lecturer from City University (Cass) Business School, Professor Gordon Gemmill. It was his enthusiasm that got me hooked in the first place.

Alpesh B. Patel, the renowned financial journalist and author, has been another source of inspiration. From our first meeting where I demonstrated OptionEasy, he has encouraged me and introduced me to other important people in this industry. It's a rarity to find his sort in any industry once they become well established.

Finally, to my friends, particularly those who stuck around during the darkest days when it was almost impossible for me to even go out. I will always remember who you are...particularly Dominic and Lulu who went way beyond the call of duty.

The publisher is grateful for permission to use charts created on Worden Brothers TC2005 and TradeStation®, the flagship product of TradeStation Technologies Inc. http://www.tradestation.com.

About the Author

Guy Cohen is the creator and originator of *OptionEasy* and *TrendSearcher* and

has extensive experience of both the US and UK derivatives and stock markets.

Specializing in trading and analytics applications ranging from real estate to derivatives, Guy has developed some of the most comprehensive business, trading, and training models that are all expressly designed for maximum user-friendliness.

Guy has an MBA (Finance) from City University (Cass) Business School, London. He is a successful private investor and trader in his own right and also teaches individuals, specializing in trading psychology, Technical Analysis, and options strategies.

For more information about Guy and *OptionEasy*, go to **www.optioneasy.com**.

If you have any comments regarding this or *OptionEasy*, please contact: **enquiries@optioneasy.com**.

Executive Summary

Have you ever wanted to trade stocks and options but didn't know where to start? Now you can with this easy-to-read yet comprehensive and *practical* guide to options trading.

Options Made Easy is designed to steer you through the entire trading process, from how to select thrusting stocks right through to safely implementing specific stock and options strategies. *Options Made Easy* is engineered to *simplify and accelerate* the learning process to give you *increased confidence* for making *consistent profits*.

Using *plain English*, dynamic pictures, and *real-life examples* throughout, *Options Made Easy* demystifies the world of options and, whatever your current knowledge level, you'll be amazed at how quickly you'll learn:

- options basics on a *realistic* level, right through to the most *advanced* strategies;

- facts and myths of technical and fundamental analysis;

- how to filter for moving stocks;

- how to select your optimum strategy;

- your trading plan for high-probability trades and consistent profits; and

- secrets of trading psychology, how to increase your confidence and eliminate the gambling mentality from your investment decisions.

As you read this book you'll discover that you're learning with an interactive guide that you can reference time and time again. By now you'll appreciate that you have the potential to feel truly confident in making your trading decisions. Keep *Options Made Easy* with you as your essential companion for both stocks and options trading.

Preface

This book can be used by any options trader, although it is fair to say that it is most specifically targeted toward novices and intermediates. Simplicity is the name of the game here, and I have made it my mission to enable anyone and everyone to learn and apply the benefits of options trading simply and easily. By giving you a grounding that is second to none, we look to give you the solid foundations required to give you the confidence to enable you to become a dynamic and successful trader. And we want it to be a fun and pleasurable experience too!

You'll find during the course of this book that much of the teaching is done through use of charts and diagrams. Even the "non-visual" among you will appreciate the power of this approach. Options is frequently taught as a stodgy, theoretical subject, and I have often been bewildered as to how people can "teach" this fascinating area of finance without the use of a single chart, diagram, or illustration. So much of my own knowledge is based on the understanding of simple diagrams.

You'll also discover that I ask you the reader lots of questions during this book. It's a technique I also use during my other teaching. Learning is at its best when it is interactive. So get ready to have some fun while learning at a rate and speed that you couldn't have imagined possible before now. The writing style is as close to a relaxed speaking style as possible.

Another important aspect of this book is that the examples we use are designed to facilitate your learning experience. You'll discover that we don't try to make this too much of a mathematical obstacle course for you. The numbers are reasonably straightforward because we want to keep your focus honed on the specific learning points; besides, there are software products that will help you with the math anyway. Even now I still use my own *OptionEasy* application just to be sure before I place any spread trade.

People often ask me how I got involved in options trading and training. Well, with my commercial real estate background, I'd always had a passion for finance and during an enforced sabbatical in 1995, I decided that once I had fully recovered I would pursue all the things in life that terrified me! That included a finance MBA at City University Business School, and once there it meant opting for the options specialist module. I was completely hooked, and that was the advent of the *OptionEasy* software package, initially just for my own benefit.

That doesn't quite tell the whole story. Just weeks before taking the options exam I could barely explain the difference between a call and a put! However, by the time I got into the exam room I had brought my knowledge level from zero to getting over 80% in the exam, the fifth highest mark in a big class. As you'll see later, though, learning the academic material did not necessarily prepare me for the practicality of actual trading....

In the meantime, during those frantic weeks of revision, I developed the silliest and most outrageous techniques for learning about options in simple and eccentric ways. I drew pictures in my mind, invented silly phrases and used "junko" logic to piece things together. The way I learned is now the way I teach. It's a little unusual, but it's fun, fast, and highly effective. No one forgets what a call and a put is when I teach them. And because we build everything on such solid foundations, you'll find that the *OptionEasy* way is the simplest, most effective, and fastest way of learning about options. Wherever a picture can be used to explain even the most complex of topics, we use it and combine it with the logic too. We are constantly and simultaneously using different techniques to facilitate the learning process. *If you don't remember the logic, then you will remember the picture; if you don't remember the picture, then you will remember the logic.* Either way, you'll learn....

Now, when I finally got around to making my first options trades, I did so with the typical trepidation of someone who had learned the academic material first. For my first-ever spread trade, I placed my order and then created a little spreadsheet to calculate the risk and reward of my trade. I was horrified to find that my maximum reward for this trade was precisely ZERO! I immediately cancelled the order (which hadn't yet been filled) and concluded that if *I* could make that kind of mistake then perhaps a few others could be doing just that same thing...without even knowing it! Hence was born the *OptionEasy* software application.

Chapter 1 is a step-by-step introduction into the world of options. It's important that you follow the examples of the *Risk Profile Charts* and understand these simple diagrams. The Risk Profile Chart is remarkably straightforward but is undoubtedly the cornerstone to your entire understanding of options. Even intermediates should pay attention to this part of the book. You'll find yourself understanding far more than you thought was possible, so I challenge you to go through this section, even if it only takes you a few minutes.

Chapter 2 takes us into the marketplace. A common question I get asked is,

"If I buy a stock option at $2.50, why do I have to pay $250.00 for it?" The answer to this question is easy but needs to be understood. We also take you through some real-life examples to get you acclimatized to trading.

Chapter 3 is about *Fundamental Analysis*. This is what the "analysts" work on. In other words, the health of the company, its assets, liabilities, turnover, cash flow, profits, and so on. In the long term, markets always revert to the fundamental health of individual companies; however, as we've so recently witnessed (not for the first time), in the short term it can be all about hype in either direction and human behavior *en masse*. How else can you explain PE ratios in excess of 100 times projected net earnings? People will say, "Well, did you look at the growth rate of that company?" Yes, I did, and very few companies can sustain that kind of absurd valuation for long simply because not many organizations can continue to grow at absurd levels for very long. At the end of the chapter is a list of *news events* and *Fundamental Analysis* headings that you need to be aware of if you're a long-term trader.

Chapter 4 runs through some basic and well-known concepts of *Technical Analysis* and chart reading. This book is not intended to be an authority on charting, so it is left as brief as possible; however, you do need to be able to appreciate the rudiments of Technical Analysis so you can readily apply the appropriate strategy to the prevailing trading conditions. Entire books are dedicated to single areas of Technical Analysis, so, while this chapter is a useful summary, please undertake to do more work in this area. I stick to a couple of Technical Analysis techniques for my trading, and it suits both my personality and psychology to do it that way. Numbers don't daunt me, so I take a more mathematical and numerical approach to my Technical Analysis. My approach doesn't suit everyone, but it's clean and clear.

Chapters 5, 7, 8, and 9 take us through some simple options spread strategies and how to do them correctly and with minimal risk. It's important to always follow the rules. By all means make up your own if you like, but always stick to the rules you adopt. And if the rules you invent or adopt are bad ones, then change them or stick to the ones here. They're designed to be easy to understand and to keep you out of serious trouble!

In Chapter 6 we discuss the "Greeks." These are simply "sensitivities" to various factors affecting the pricing of options. From your point of view as traders, these sensitivities have consequences for your trading. We show you what the Greeks are, what their consequences are, and how to prepare for or ensure against them.

Chapter 10 is about trading psychology...you'll find as you gain experience that many lessons in trading life generally are ones where it's the intensity of the *experience* that is the greatest teacher. How many of us have let profits slide by because we fell in love with a stock and wouldn't sell it before it reached $XXX.00? And for some reason it never quite got to $XXX.00 and we still never sold...even when we'd been in massive profit! I have tried most of the strategies contained within the *OptionEasy* software application—we try not to tell people what to do, but to give you an informed choice. You can have real choice only when you are armed with the tools to make that choice. It's our job here to arm you with those tools, via our teachings, our applications, and our experience.

Over the course of my trading career so far, I have been fortunate to experience incredible highs and some pretty awful lows too! Luckily the lows entailed me giving a portion of profits back to the market (as opposed to my being wiped out), and the highs happened before the lows! As a result of all this, I have developed practical concepts on how we can stick to our trading discipline whatever our rules may be. My job here is to take you through my experiences and make it as painful for you as it was for me. For example, my worst ever trading day was the day that I finally implemented the rule on stops. And that was it. I would never fail to implement stops again because the experience was so intense. Alas, I had given back over 50% of my gains to learn this invaluable lesson, but at least my returns were still in the 100s of percent at that stage! And it felt wonderful to apply one of the golden rules of trading at such an intensely bad time.

Chapter 11 is where we bundle everything together and create coherent sample *trading plans*, so you're armed to get out there and put everything into practice. This book is not about theory; it's about being armed in a *practical* sense. We don't spend time on strategies that sound great but can only be used by the professionals in reality. We concentrate on what you can do in the real world, accepting both our opportunities and the minor limitations we have in being private investors and traders.

Finally, Chapter 12 runs through some of the implications of the introduction of Stock Futures and the impact that it might have for stock and options traders.

We aim to make this an enjoyable experience for you as you find yourself learning dynamically and interactively as you go through the examples and illustrations. Trading stocks and options is fun but it's also a serious business. Some of the most successful traders I know stick to just one or two strategies. With *OptionEasy* we want to give you the choice of whatever strategy suits your trading style and individual psychology.

Enjoy the reading, enjoy the learning, and enjoy the fact that this is only a stepping stone for you on your journey to gain as much knowledge as you possibly can in this arena. The issue is not that there's not enough education in the trading world—there's actually too much. But where's the wheat and where's the chaff? The challenge is for you to find not only what suits you, but also to distinguish between the evangelical types who tell you how rich you're going to become with their "amazing new proprietary techniques" while you actually line *their* pockets and the serious educators out there who are honest enough to tell you that it's actually up to you. This isn't supposed to be an easy game. You can do it, but don't be fooled into thinking that it's going to take one book or one seminar. This has to become a hobby for you, one that you'll enjoy and one that's a continuing challenge. The truest thing I know about trading is that the learning never stops. It's incessant and compelling. It's best to avoid people promising you ludicrous returns per month and "guaranteed" results with no effort on your part. If it looks too good to be true, *it usually is*! Having said that, you can make trading and investing an unusually predictable and successful vocation by your own efforts, enthusiasm, and discipline.

chapter 1

Introduction to Options

Why is it that options are so misconceived as a minefield of danger and risk? How can we make sense of this and look at options as tools to limit our risks, maximize our returns, and SEE WHAT WE'RE DOING at the same time? This is the essence of *OptionEasy* and this book—how to make seemingly complex things simple.

Options are becoming more and more popular each day. Far from being confined solely to the institutions and professional money managers, options trading is now a worldwide phenomenon for "retail" traders of all walks of life. The concept of options is still, however, treated with fear and trepidation in some quarters. When I first embarked upon serious trading, one of my friends warned me profusely about what I was getting into. I calmly pointed out that I wasn't a gambler and that I would be perfectly safe and successful. And so can you.

Criteria for Successful Investing

- patience
- perseverance
- knowledge
- honesty
- pre-planning
- discipline

Patience

Learning that you can make a lot of money on the markets is one of the most exciting moments you can experience in your professional life. A whole new world of possibilities opens up before you as you begin to imagine your dream house, car, boat, and vacations with your family. I've seen people get so excited after just one little seminar that they actually started trading right there and then. Not smart! Give yourself some time to get used to the idea. And never start trading on an emotional wave of any kind whatsoever. You need to be switched on, alert and calm. Many workshops give you the emotional high but without the substance of real experience (and sometimes many other things, like knowledge!).

Think about it this way. Would you consider yourself able to do brain surgery after just one conference? Well, in a different context the same applies to trading, and even more so for options trading (although the same principles apply). Give yourself time to learn. By reading this book, you are doing just that, giving yourself a learning opportunity. By now, you're probably used to trading stocks or futures in the markets. So now is the next step. And just as you had to get comfortable with trading stocks or futures at first, you also now have to get comfortable with trading options.

> **I've seen people get so excited after just one little seminar that they actually started trading there and then. Not smart!**

Furthermore, when you are comfortable enough to trade, you need to have an abundance of patience to do the trading itself. We've all had the experience of jumping into an investment too early even when we weren't quite convinced it was the right thing to do. Be patient, take a deep breath if you have to, and stick to your plan of action.

Finally, patience also involves selecting a trading strategy where time works in your favor and where your downside is covered. Be patient in your attitude to acquiring wealth. The more patient you are in this way, the better off you will be. This doesn't mean sitting back and doing nothing—that's apathy, not patience! Give yourself time to learn, gain experience and then start to apply consistently time and time again so that you begin a process of making money and building wealth.

Consistent with the art of patience is your embracing the concept of *compounding*. If you can make just 1% per week, this would mean more than 67% in just one year, a record of which any fund manager would be envious. The following table illustrates the power of compounding if you start with just $10,000 in your account:

Weekly Return %	Monthly Return %	1 year	2 years	3 years	3-year return %
1%	4%	$16,777	$28,146	$47,220	472%
2%	8.24%	$28,003	$78,418	$219,597	2,196%
3%	12.55%	$46,509	$216,307	$1,006,021	10,060%
4%	16.99%	$76,866	$590,836	$4,541,517	45,415%
5%	21.55%	$126,428	$1,598,406	$20,208,201	202,083%

This table is simply here to convince you about the need to be patient. Allow your returns to accumulate, and let the magic of compounding do its work for you. We're not suggesting these as consistent, realistic growth targets for you, but it helps to see where you'd be in three years even if you were succeeding with modest returns.

Perseverance

Keep going for it! If there's one thing I've learned in life, it's that if you believe in something you have to keep at it until you reach your goal. And once you've reached your goal, then set another target.

Having embarked on the mission of becoming a successful trader (whether full-time or part-time), you must stick to it. Anyone can do it. Even those who don't think they can. Babies don't give up trying to walk or talk after a few unsuccessful attempts, do they? Well, follow their example and now you're here, stick to it and prepare yourself to be rewarded richly from this process of learning.

To be practical, give yourself attainable targets to reach in a realistic time frame. So by next week you'll be fully familiar with the four main options risk profiles. You may be able to do it tonight. Keep on setting the attainable targets (do make them a slight challenge, though!) and in this way you'll be able to keep up the momentum of learning and gaining experience. You'll also start to build up your confidence as you go along, reassuring yourself of your ability to understand anything you put your mind to. This book will help you in building your confidence because it's a practical book and it's easy to follow and understand. So keep going and enjoy the process of accumulating. . ..

Knowledge

Having established the need for patience for both acquiring the knowledge and for trading itself, let's remember that knowledge is attainable now with such ease and speed that it is eminently achievable in a reasonably quick time. Tools exist now to simulate the trading experience, and there are myriad publications and web sites designed to help you build up your knowledge database.

The best knowledge you will ever get is experience. It's all very well to say, "trade mechanically," but very few people do. Why? Because we're human beings and have emotions and feelings. It's true to say that they are best left away from the trading environment, but we have to learn how to do that first. It's no good just saying, "Do it!" Moreover, why can't we use our feelings and emotions to our advantage? Well, we can, and that's what we discuss in Chapter 10 on trading psychology.

Remember that learning is *experience*-based. We can all remember the most extreme of our teachers at school, right? You can recall the funniest, the scariest, the prettiest and the ugliest, but I'll bet you have a problem remembering anything about the teachers who were somewhere in the middle—those who barely made an experiential impact on you in years of being in the same classroom!

The same applies to trading. A lot of the learning involved in trading is experience-based. In fact, the most pertinent form of learning about trading is experience-based. It's through the extreme experiences that you find more out about yourself in good times and bad. Most brilliant traders have had terrible experiences but, crucially, have stepped back up to the plate and *applied* what they had learned. Just like me. I made a lot of money very fast, thought I was "the don" (tut-tut!) and then gave some of it back again! Believe me, then I didn't feel too good at all, but did I learn! And more importantly, did I apply those lessons? . . .you bet I did!

So, remember, learning is based on experience, so allow yourself to get experience, which is what this book and our workshops are all about—building experience. As you continually acquire experience, apply it consistently, continually, and carefully.

Honesty

You must be honest with yourself if you're to develop into a decent trader or investor. A company has not made you make or lose money, so part of being honest is to cut out the emotions of trading. Ultimately, your decisions are down to YOU! No matter what you were taught, even if it was by someone who had no right to teach, you're the one who's in control, and when you look in the mirror, make sure you're being true to yourself. I've always found that blaming other people never really helps, and in trading you'll save yourself a lot of time if you can apply this lesson fast. Blaming the stock or the teacher or tipster only wastes energy and stops you asking what more you can do to improve your technique, your knowledge, and your performance. We'll cover more of this in Chapter 10.

Pre-Planning

You *must* pre-plan each and every trade. By this you must know your:

● maximum *risk*.

● maximum *reward*.

● breakeven points.

You also must plan

● your entry point.

● your exit point whether it's to. . .

    ● take profit or

    ● stop losses.

With options trading, I tend to base any loss cut on the basis of the underlying asset. In most cases the underlying asset will be more liquid than the options chain, so it makes it easier to make your loss-cutting decision based on the price of the stock, future, or whatever the underlying asset is.

This pre-planning stage also embraces the choice of the underlying asset itself, the strategy you're using, and using fundamental and technical analysis to assist you in the decision-making process. The most important thing, though, is to make a good plan and then stick to it by using massive. . ..

Discipline—the Key to Success

When you have had the patience to acquire the knowledge and apply the principles above, it's imperative not to waste it all. You must be disciplined and apply that discipline rigorously each and every time.

This means that:

● you do your pre-planning every time.

● you use your (and others') experience.

● you do not deviate from your stated sensible plan.

In this way you are taking the first steps to becoming more mechanical. Discipline is the single most important part of trading. In other words, it is *money management*, and without money management, even the most sophisticated of trading systems will not work.

By sticking rigorously to sensible money-management principles, you will ensure that your losses are minimized and your profits are allowed to run.

By sticking rigorously to sensible money-management principles, you will ensure that you will avoid suicidal risk profiles. I'm often amazed at so-called experts teaching options strategies that have terrible risk profile curves. So let's have a look at a risk profile and why it is so important to your success as an options trader. . .

Risk Profile Charts

Do you know what buying an asset such as a stock or a future looks like? To find out, we need to learn how to draw a *Risk Profile Chart*. This is the cornerstone on which we build far more complex strategies, so it's important to understand this right now.

Example 1.1

Consider a stock XYZ Inc. You buy the stock for $25.

1 The X-axis is the stock price, with the price rising as the line moves right.

2 The Y-axis is your profit for the trade.

3 The 45° diagonal line is your risk profile for the trade. As the price of the stock (or underlying asset) rises, so does your profit in this example. So when the asset price rises to $50, you make $25 of profit:

Current price	–	Buy price	=	Profit (loss)
$50	–	$25	=	+$25
$10	–	$25	=	($15)

Chart 1.1 ● Buying an asset risk profile.

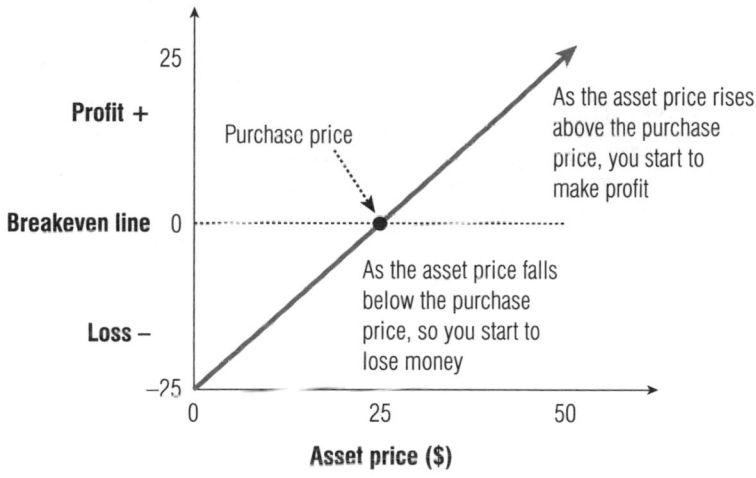

Profit +

Purchase price

As the asset price rises above the purchase price, you start to make profit

Breakeven line

As the asset price falls below the purchase price, so you start to lose money

Loss –

Asset price ($)

Steps to Creating a Risk Profile Chart

Step 1 ● Y-axis for profit/loss position

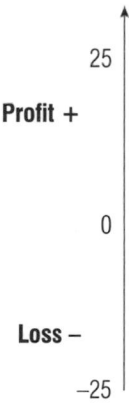

Profit +

Loss –

Step 2 ● X-axis for underlying asset price range

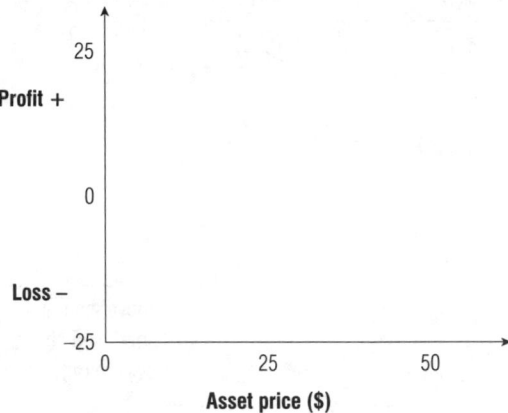

Step 3 ● Breakeven line

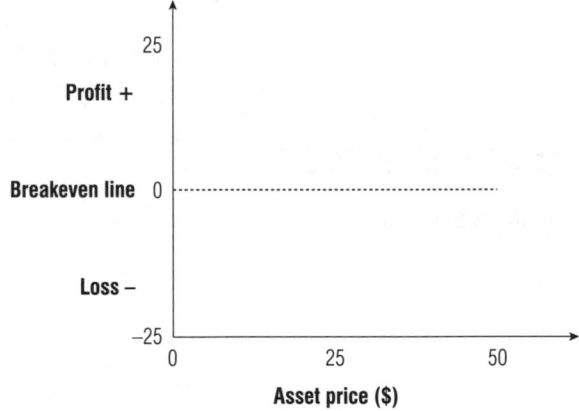

Step 4 ● Risk profile line

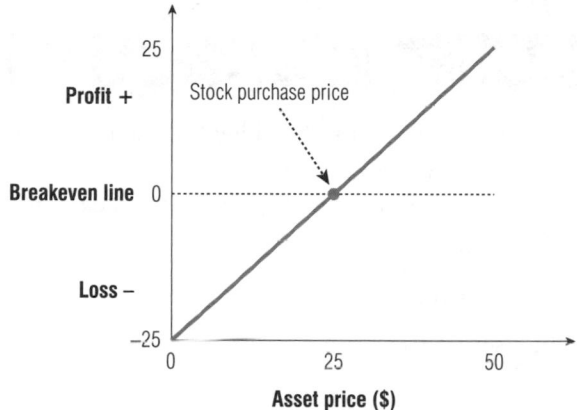

Now that you know what buying an asset looks like, we can move straight onto what *shorting* an asset looks like. Shorting simply means selling something that you don't already own. Shorting is an accepted concept in some stock markets such as the USA, but is not currently allowed in some other stock markets such as the UK.

Remember that when you short you can lose an unlimited amount as the asset price rises, and your maximum profit is the shorted price. To make maximum profit from a short stock position, the asset would have to fall to zero.

Chart 1.2 ● Shorting an asset risk profile.

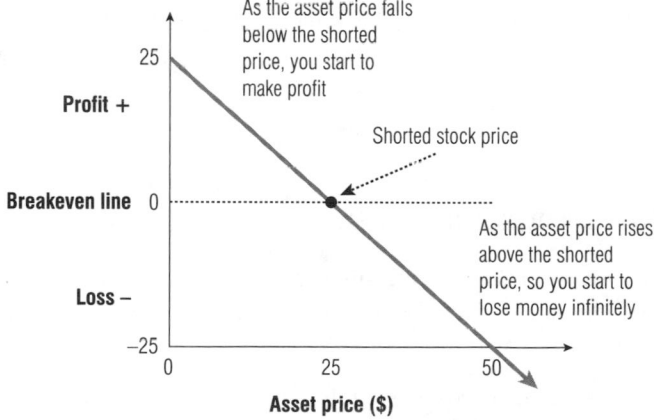

So now that you know how to draw the most basic risk charts, let's talk about options. . .

The Definition of an Option

An *option* is defined as the "right, not the obligation, to buy (or sell) an asset at a fixed price before a predetermined date."

Let's have a look at that definition and see if we can pick out the component parts:

● the right, not the obligation

● to buy or sell an asset

● at a fixed price

● before a predetermined date

These component parts have important consequences on the valuation of an option. Remember that the option itself has a value, which we will look at after we finish with the definitions.

Before we go ahead and look at the ways in which options are valued, let's consider the words, "*right, not the obligation.*"

The Right, Not the Obligation

Buying Gives You the Right

● Buying an option (call or put) conveys the *right*, not the obligation, to buy (call) or sell (put) an underlying instrument (for example, a share).

● When you buy an option, you are NOT obligated to buy or sell the underlying instrument—you simply have the right to do so at the fixed (exercise or strike) price.

● Your risk when you buy an option is simply the price you paid for it.

Selling (Naked) Imposes the Obligation

● Selling an option (call or put) *obliges* you to buy from (with sold puts) or deliver (with sold calls) to the option buyer if he or she exercises the option.

● Selling options naked (for example, when you have not bought a position in the underlying instrument or an option to hedge against it) will give you an unlimited risk profile.

Combined with the fact that you are *obliged* to do something, this is generally NOT a preferable position in which to put yourself. Only advanced traders should ever contemplate selling naked options, and even then they should have a protective strategy in mind to cover the downside (see Figure 1.1).

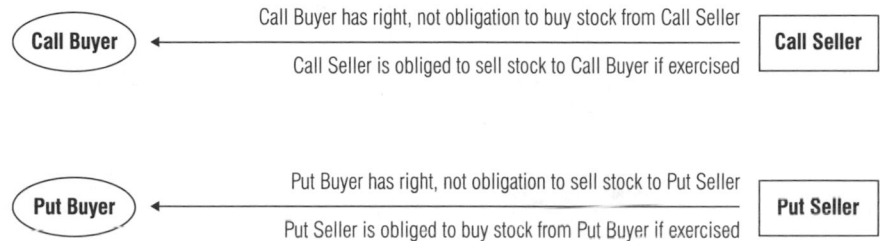

Figure 1.1

Now let's consider the words, *"to buy or sell an asset."*

Types of Option—Calls and Puts

A *call* is an option to BUY.
A *put* is an option to SELL.

Therefore,

- A call option is the right, not the obligation, to BUY an asset at a fixed price before a predetermined date.

- A put option is the right, not the obligation, to SELL an asset at a fixed price before a predetermined date.

> ### *Memory Tip*
>
> *Call Is to Buy*—think of calling UP a friend on the phone.
>
> *The reason it is named a call is because when you buy a call, you can "call" the underlying asset away from the person who sold the option to you.*
>
> *Put Is to Sell*—think of putting your pen DOWN on the table and walking away.
>
> *The reason it is named a put is because when you buy a put, you can "put" the underlying asset to the person who sold the option to you.*

Types of Calls and Puts

Options can be either American-style or European-style.

- *American*-style options allow the option buyer to exercise the option at any time before the expiration date.

- *European*-style options do *not* allow the option buyer to exercise the option before the expiration date.

Most traded options are American-style, and all US equity options are American-style.

American-style options are slightly more valuable than European-style options because of their added flexibility. It is logical that being able to exercise before expiration must be more valuable than not being able to.

As a rule, stock options are generally American style. Futures options are generally European style.

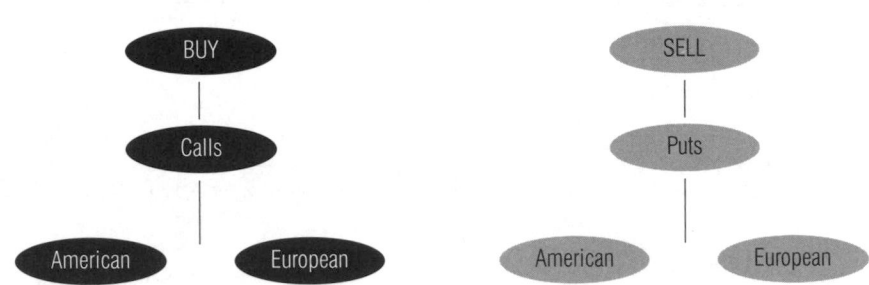

Diagram 1.1 ● American and European -style options.

Now we need to look at the words, "*at a fixed price.*"

Exercise (or Strike) Price

The *Exercise (Strike) Price* is the fixed price at which the option can be exercised.

So if you buy a call option that has a strike price of $50, then you have bought yourself the option to buy the asset at a price of $50.

However, in the real world you will only want to exercise your right to buy that asset at $50 if the underlying asset is actually worth MORE than $50 in the market. Otherwise there would be no point. It would mean buying the asset for $50 when it's only actually worth, say, $40 in the marketplace. No one would do that because they could buy it for $40 in the market.

This leads us to the words, "*before a predetermined date.*"

Expiration Date

This is the date before which the option can be exercised.

At expiration, the call option's own value is only worth the price of the asset less the exercise price, and at expiration, the put option's own value is only worth the exercise price less the price of the asset. (For US equity options, the expiration dates fall on the Saturday after the third Friday of every month.)

This leads us onto the topics of *Intrinsic Value* and *Time Value*.

The Valuation of Options

As we said before, options themselves have a value. Remember that options are totally separate entities to the underlying assets from which they are derived (hence the term, derivative). But in themselves they do have a value, which can be split into two parts: **Intrinsic Value** and **Time Value**.

In general:

- *Intrinsic Value* is that part of the option's value that is *In the Money (ITM)*.

- *Time Value* is the remainder of the option's value. *Out of the Money (OTM)* options will have no Intrinsic Value, and their price will solely be based on Time Value. Time Value is another way of saying hope value. This hope is based on the amount of time left until expiration and the price of the underlying asset.

- A call is *ITM* when the underlying asset price is greater than the strike price.

- A call is *OTM* when the underlying asset price is less than the strike price.

- A call is *At the Money (ATM)* when the underlying asset price is the same as the strike price.

Put options work the opposite way:

- A put is *ITM* when the underlying asset price is less than the strike price.

- A put is *OTM* when the underlying asset price is greater than the strike price.

- A put is *ATM* when the underlying asset price is the same as the strike price.

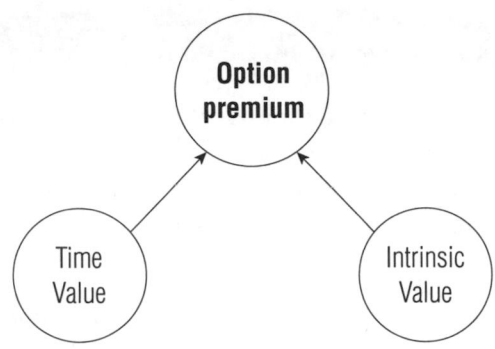

Diagram 1.2 ● Intrinsic Value and Time Value.

Why Trade Options?

The main reason for trading options is that for a smaller amount of money you can control a large amount of stock, particularly with call options. Call options are always cheaper than the underlying asset and put options usually are. Options are generally more volatile than their underlying instruments, therefore investors get "more bang for their buck" or more action. Clearly this can lead to danger, but as you'll see, it also can lead to more safety and security. You'll also see that it can mean much greater flexibility in your trading and even give you the ability to make profit when you don't know the direction in which the stock will move.

> Options are generally more volatile than their underlying instruments, therefore investors get "more bang for their buck" or more action.

Those investors with portfolios can set up protective measures in the event of a market downturn. It is also quite possible to set up a position whereby you can only make profit. Perhaps not a hugely exciting profit in triple digits, but a certain profit nevertheless. Options make this type of scenario possible, and we will cover that particular strategy in Chapter 5, "Two Popular Strategies and How to Improve Them."

In short, options give the investor added flexibility, potentially much greater gains for a given movement in the stock price, and protection against risk. On the flip side, used in the wrong way, options can lead people to serious losses. You will be learning safe strategies only and the simple rules governing those types of trade.

Intrinsic and Time Value for Calls

Example 1.2 **Where There is Intrinsic Value**

Call Intrinsic Value			Call Time Value	
Stock price	$56.00		Stock price	$56.00
Call premium	$7.33		Call premium	$7.33
Exercise Price	$50		Exercise Price	$50
Time till expiration	2 months		Time till expiration	2 months
Intrinsic Value	$56 - $50 = **$6.00**		Time Value	$7.33 - $6.00 = **$1.33**

Notice how: (Intrinsic Value + Time Value) = the option price

Formulas for Intrinsic and Time Values for calls:

● Call Intrinsic Value = stock price–exercise price

● Call Time Value = call premium–call Intrinsic Value

The minimum Intrinsic Value is zero.

Example 1.3 **Where There is no Intrinsic Value**

Call Intrinsic Value			Call Time Value	
Stock price	$48.00		Stock price	$48.00
Call premium	$0.75		Call premium	$0.75
Exercise Price	$50		Exercise Price	$50
Time till expiration	2 months		Time till expiration	2 months
Intrinsic Value	$48 – $50 = **$0.00**		Time Value	$0.75 – $0.00 = **$0.75**

Intrinsic and Time Value for Puts

Example 1.4 Where There is Intrinsic Value

Put Intrinsic Value		Put Time Value	
Stock price	$77.00	Stock price	$77.00
Put premium	$5.58	Put premium	$5.58
Exercise Price	$80	Exercise Price	$80
Time till expiration	4 months	Time till expiration	4 months
Intrinsic Value	$80 – $77.00 = **$3.00**	Time Value	$5.58 – $3.00 = **$2.58**

Notice how: (Intrinsic Value + Time Value) = the option price

Formulas for Intrinsic and Time Values for puts:

- Put Intrinsic Value = exercise price–stock price
- Put Time Value = put premium (or value)–put Intrinsic Value

The minimum Intrinsic Value is zero.

Example 1.5 Where There is no Intrinsic Value

Put Intrinsic Value		Put Time Value	
Stock price	$85.00	Stock price	$85.00
Put premium	$1.67	Put premium	$1.67
Exercise Price	$80	Exercise Price	$80
Time till expiration	4 months	Time till expiration	4 months
Intrinsic Value	$80 – $85.00 = **$0.00**	Time Value	$1.67 – $0.00 = **$1.67**

The Seven Factors that Influence an Option's Premium

There are seven factors that affect the pricing of an option. Again, we look to the definition of an option to give us the clues. An option is defined as the:

- right, not the obligation
- to buy or sell
- an asset
- at a fixed price
- before a predetermined date.

Now let's take the seven factors:

Quote from definition	Comment
"buy or sell"	The *type of option* (call or put) will affect the option price.
"underlying asset"	The *underlying asset* and its *own price* will affect the option price.
"at a fixed price"	The exercise price or strike price will affect the option price.
"before a predetermined date"	The *Expiration Date* and *Time Value* will affect the option price.

There are three other major influences on option pricing, which we will discuss later in further detail.

Factor	Comment
VOLATILITY	Worthy of a book in itself. Volatility is a crucial and major influence in the pricing of options. Understanding volatility gives the options trader the ability to select specific trades most profitably. The most advanced traders will always use volatility to their advantage.
Risk-free rate of interest	This is the short-term rate of government money. It is known as risk free owing to the perceived covenant strength of (developed world economy) governments.
Dividends payable	This applies to any asset that offers an income "reward" for owners of the underlying asset. For stock options, this will be the dividend payable.

Quick Summary

Option prices are affected by the type of option (call or put):

1. the price of the underlying asset

2. the exercise price (or strike price) of the option

3. the expiration date

4. volatility—Implied and Historical (see Chapter 6, "An Introduction to the Greeks")

5. risk-free interest rate

6. dividends and stock splits

Risk Profile Charts for Call Options

Now that you know what makes up the valuation of an option, let's look at the risk profile of a call option.

We already know that a call option is the right to *buy* an asset. Logically, this suggests that the call option risk profile direction will be similar to that of buying the asset itself. So let's have a look at an example:

Chart 1.3 ● Long Call option risk profile.

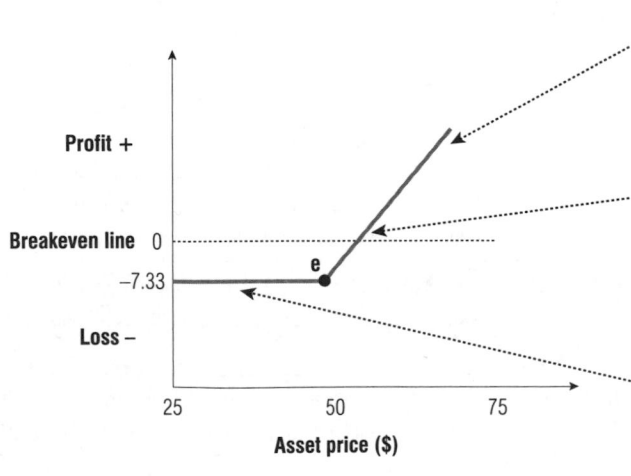

As stock price rises over $50, the buyer of the call begins to move into profit.

However, you also have to recover the price of the call you paid for (here $7.33) so your **breakeven point** *is $57.33.*

While the stock price remains less than $50, the *maximum loss on the trade is capped to the premium paid, i.e. $7.33.*

Look back to Example 1.2 where you buy a call option:

Stock price	$56.00
Call premium	$7.33
Exercise price	$50
Time till expiration	2 months

Remember that. . .

Buying Gives You the Right

● *Buying a call option gives you the right, not the obligation, to buy an underlying instrument (that is, a share).*

● *When you buy a call option, you are not obligated to buy the underlying instrument—you simply have the right to do so at the fixed (exercise or strike) price.*

● *Your risk, when you buy an option, is simply the price you paid for it.*

● *Your reward is potentially unlimited.*

For every call that you buy, there is someone else on the other side of the trade. The seller of an option is called an *option writer*. Logic and common sense tell us that the option seller's risk profile must be different from that of the option buyer.

So, staying with calls, let's see the option writer's risk profile perspective:

Chart 1.4 ● Short Call option risk profile.

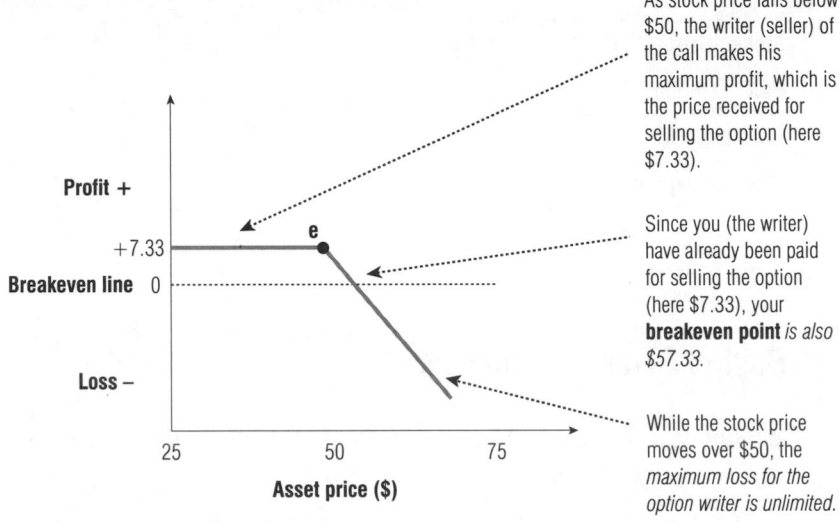

As stock price falls below $50, the writer (seller) of the call makes his maximum profit, which is the price received for selling the option (here $7.33).

Since you (the writer) have already been paid for selling the option (here $7.33), your **breakeven point** *is also $57.33.*

While the stock price moves over $50, the *maximum loss for the option writer is unlimited.*

Still taking Example 1.2 of the following call option:

Stock price	$56.00
Call premium	$7.33
Exercise price	$50
Time till expiration	2 months

Remember that we already discussed the implications of selling an option—here's a reminder:

Selling (Naked) Imposes the Obligation

● *Selling a call option obliges you to deliver the underlying asset to the option buyer.*

● *Selling options naked (for example, when you have not bought a position in the underlying instrument or an option to hedge against it) will give you an unlimited risk profile. The continuous downward line is generally not a good sign because it means unlimited potential risk.*

● *Combined with the fact that you are obliged to do something, this is generally not a preferable position in which to put yourself.*

Risk Profile Charts for Put Options

Now that you know what long and short calls look like, let's look at the risk profile of a put option.

We already know that a put option is the right to *sell* an asset. Logically, this suggests that the put option risk profile direction will be the opposite to that of calls or buying the asset itself. So let's have a look at an example:

Chart 1.5 ● Long put option risk profile.

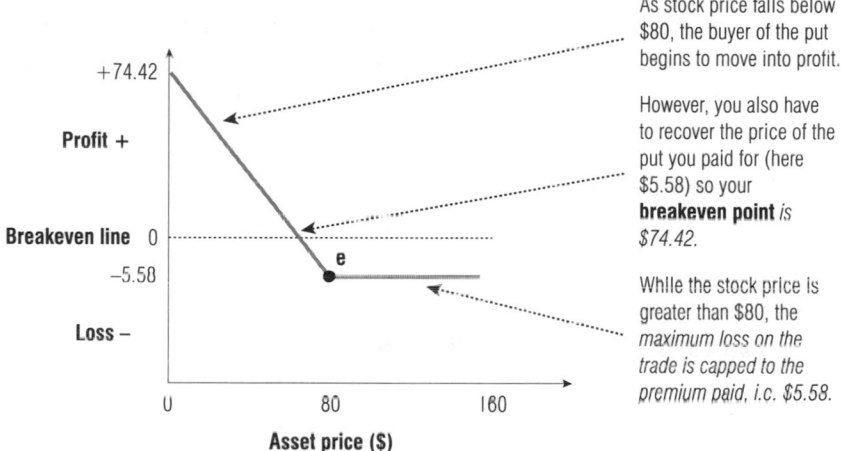

As stock price falls below $80, the buyer of the put begins to move into profit.

However, you also have to recover the price of the put you paid for (here $5.58) so your **breakeven point** *is $74.42.*

While the stock price is greater than $80, the *maximum loss on the trade is capped to the premium paid, i.c. $5.58.*

Look back to Example 1.4 where you buy a put option as follows:

Stock price	$77.00
Put premium	$5.58
Exercise price	$80
Time till expiration	4 months

Remember that. . .

Buying Gives You the Right

- *Buying a put option gives you the right, not the obligation, to sell an underlying instrument (that is, a share).*
- *When you buy a put option, you are not obligated to sell the underlying instrument—you simply have the right to do so at the fixed (exercise or strike) price.*
- *Your risk, when you buy an option, is simply the price you paid for it.*
- *Your reward is potentially unlimited until the stock falls to zero. With long puts your reward is unlimited to the downside, for example, the exercise price less the price you paid for the put itself. In this example that is: $80 − $5.58 = $74.42.*

For every put you buy, there is someone else on the other side of the trade. The seller of a put option will have a different risk profile to that of the put option buyer.

Chart 1.6 ● Short put option risk profile.

Still taking Example 1.4 of the following put option:

Stock price	$77.00
Put premium	$5.58
Exercise price	$80
Time till expiration	4 months

Remember that we already discussed the implications of selling an option—here's another reminder for puts:

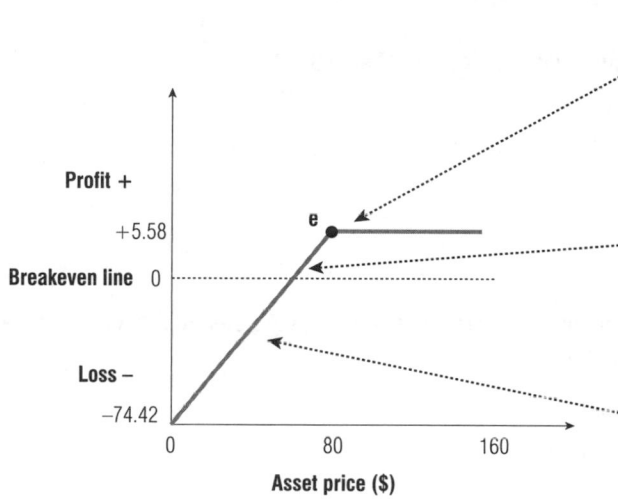

As the stock price rises to $80, the writer (seller) of the put makes his maximum profit, which is the price received for selling the option (here $5.58).

Since you (the writer) have already been paid for selling the option (here $5.58), your **breakeven point** *is also $74.42.*

While the stock price falls under the breakeven point, the *maximum loss for the option writer is unlimited down to $74.42, i.e. $80 – $5.58.*

Selling (Naked) Imposes the Obligation

- *Selling a put option obliges you to buy the underlying asset from the option buyer. Remember, when you sell a put, you have sold the right to sell to the person who bought that put.*

- *Selling options naked (for example, when you have not bought a position in the underlying instrument or an option to hedge against it) will give you an unlimited risk profile. The continuous downward line is generally not a good sign because it means unlimited potential risk.*

- *Combined with the fact that you are obliged to do something, this is generally not a preferable position in which to put yourself.*

If any of that was slightly confusing to you, here are some simple ways to remember:

Memory Tips for Long and Short Calls and Puts

Step 1 ● Remember your basic math at school:

+ +	=	+
+ -	=	-
- +	=	-
- -	=	+

Step 2 ● Think buying something as a + and selling something as a –, therefore:

Buying a call would be a **+ +**

Selling a call would be a **– +**

Buying a put would be a **+ –**

Selling a put would be a **– –**

Step 3 ● Remember your risk profiles:

Where you end up with a **+** risk profile, the diagonal line will be upward from left to right.

Where you end up with a **-** risk profile, the diagonal line will be downward from left to right.

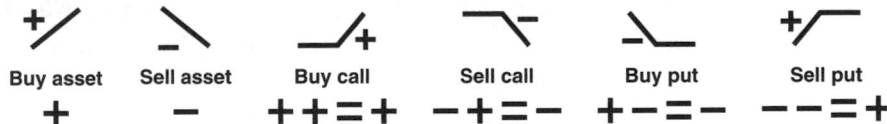

Buy asset	Sell asset	Buy call	Sell call	Buy put	Sell put
+	**–**	**+ + = +**	**– + = –**	**+ – = –**	**– – = +**

These are the four charts you need to remember. Even if you just remember the long call option risk profile, you should now be able to construct the other three basic option positions. When you are comfortable with these and the logic behind them, you'll be ready to look at spreads and combinations with ease.

The Four Basic Risk Profiles for Options

The four basic options risk profiles

Imagine the dotted lines are mirrors and see how each strategy is the opposite of the one on the other side of the mirror.

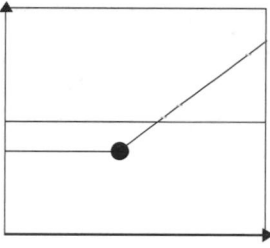 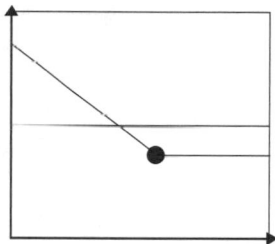

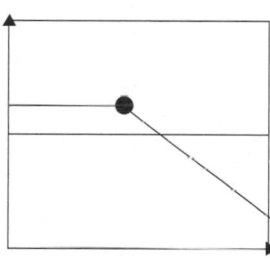 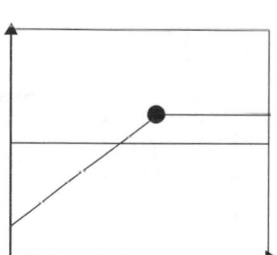

This page is duplicated overleaf.

The four basic options risk profiles

Imagine the dotted lines are mirrors and see how each strategy is the opposite of the one on the other side of the mirror.

Buying a call

- belief that stock will rise (bullish outlook)
- risk limited to premium paid
- unlimited maximum reward

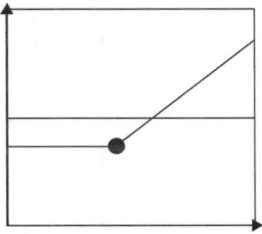

Buying a put

- belief that stock will fall (bearish outlook)
- risk limited to premium paid
- unlimited maximum reward up to the strike price
- less the premium paid

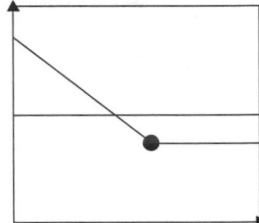

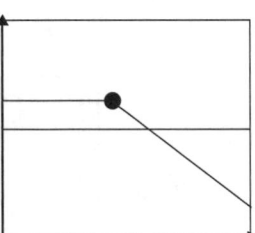

Writing a call

- belief that stock will fall (bearish outlook)
- maximum reward limited to premium received
- risk potentially unlimited (as stock price rises)
- can be combined with another position to limit the risk

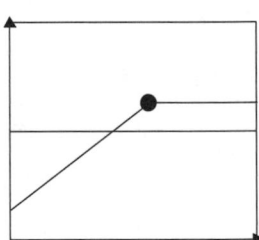

Writing a put

- belief that stock will rise (bullish outlook)
- maximum risk is the strike price less the premium received. We can think of this as either being "unlimited" until the stock reaches zero, or "limited" to the [strike price – premium] formula.
- maximum reward limited to the premium received
- can be combined with another position to limit the risk

Chapter 1 Major Learning Points

Remember the six major prerequisites:

- patience
- perseverance
- knowledge
- honesty
- pre-planning
- discipline

Start to build a plan. The plan should encompass the following:

1. **What stocks or other assets should I be considering for successful trading?**

2. **What direction do I feel comfortable trading in (up or down)? Could I consider trading put options if a stock or the market is falling?**

3. Have I checked the news items for the particular asset I am trading? Are quarterly or other results out soon? Is there a major announcement from the government out soon? Could these announcements affect my trade? Can I use them to enhance my position, or shall I wait until the announcements are made?

4. Do I want to check whether this company makes money and other Fundamental Analysis?

5. Have I checked the graphs and done any Technical Analysis? Am I missing something obvious like a basic Double Top or Triple Top chart pattern?

6. What strategy and risk profile do I feel comfortable with trading?

7. For each trade, what is my entry point, exit point, and time of exit?

8. Do I know my Risk, Reward, and Break-even Points?

9. What price am I looking for to execute my trade?

10. Where do I take my profits, and where is my STOP LOSS?

We'll review this list as we go along every chapter. So far, the **main questions** you should be able to start to consider are **those in bold**. By the end of the book, you'll be able to answer all of them and begin to build your own plan.

You have now learned what the essential risk profiles look like and what they mean to you in terms of maximum risk and reward.

Profile	Description	Risk	Reward	Breakeven
⟋	**Buy asset**	Purchase price	Unlimited	Purchase price
⟍	**Sell asset**	Unlimited	Short sale price	Short sale price
⟋	**Buy call**	Call premium	Unlimited	Strike Price plus call premium paid
⟍	**Sell call**	Unlimited	Limited to the call premium received	Strike Price plus call premium paid
⟍	**Buy put**	Put premium	Strike Price less put premium paid	Strike Price less put premium paid
⟋	**Sell put**	Strike Price less put premium received	Limited to the put premium received	Strike Price less put premium paid

We can now progress to Chapter 2, "Into the Marketplace," where we start to explore the reality of trading options with real numbers.

chapter 2

Into the Marketplace

How to Read Option Prices

The main components of an on-screen options price are

- the underlying instrument
- the expiration date of the option
- the exercise (strike) price of the option
- the bid/ask of the option price
- the volume of the particular option on that day
- the Open Interest of the specific option

Example 2.1 A Call Option Chain

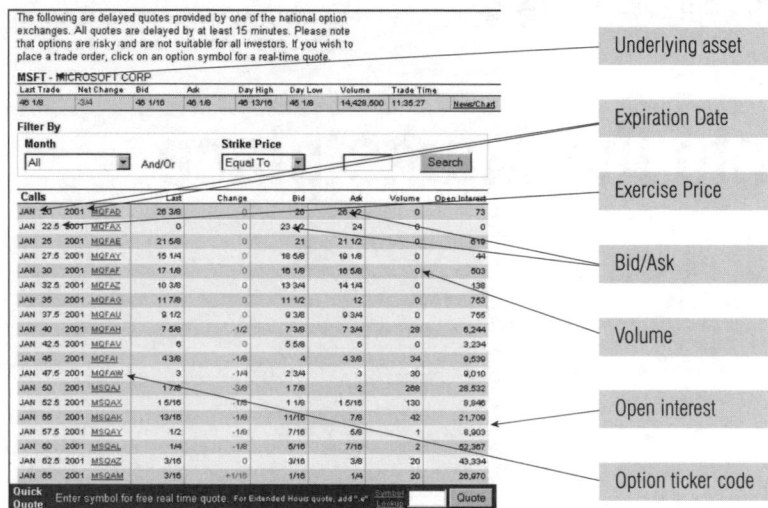

As you can see, here is part of a call option chain for Microsoft Corp (MSFT). There are hundreds of individual options for Microsoft, spanning a number of exercise prices and different expiration dates. Each option has a strike price and an expiration date. For each option there will be a different bid/ask price quote, volume, and open interest.

Definitions from the option chain page are as follows:

Last	The last price transacted (here delayed by 15 minutes).
Change	Change in option price since yesterday's close.
Bid	The highest price at which the floor trader is willing to bid (to buy). This is the price at which you will sell if you place a "Market Order." The floor trader makes his profit from the spread.
Ask	The lowest price at which the floor trader is willing to ask (to sell). This is the price at which you will buy if you place a "Market Order."
Volume	The amount of contracts traded during the day so far.
Open interest	The number of contracts being held currently in the market.

Remember that the stock itself has figures for all of the above except for the Open interest, which is specific to options.

Example 2.2 **A Put Option Chain**

The same headings as previously listed apply here.

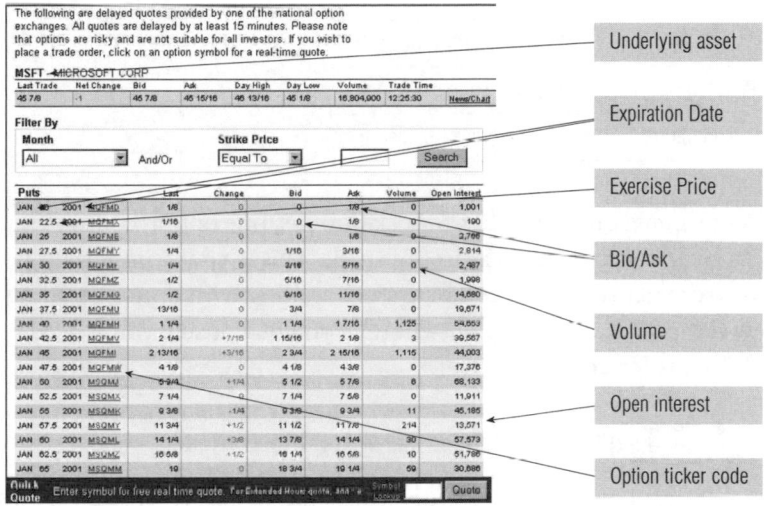

Option Contracts

Stock options are traded in contracts, not as individual derivative units. Each contract will represent a certain number of units of the underlying asset. This number is different for different types of assets worldwide. US stock option contracts represent 100 shares of the underlying stock, and UK stock option contracts represent 1,000 shares of the underlying stock.

Therefore, when you see a US equity call option price of, say, $1.45, you will have to pay $1.45 × 100 for just one contract. One contract is the minimum amount you can trade, and for US equity options, one contract represents 100 individual shares. In other words, by paying $145.00 you now have the right to buy 100 shares of the stock.

The following table outlines the amount of underlying securities that represent one contract for all sorts of different markets where options are traded on an exchange.

Underlying asset	Units per options contract
US equities	100 shares
UK equities	1,000 shares
S&P futures	1 future—worth $250 each
Gold futures	1 future—worth $100 each
Crude oil futures	1 future worth $1,000 each

So continuing our theme of US stock options, one option contract represents the right over 100 individual shares of stock. This is vitally important when considering spread orders that combine stock trading with options trading to create a new risk profile. For every one contract you buy or sell, you'll need to be trading 100 shares for complete cover.

Example 2.3 A Covered Call (or Buy Write) Illustration

This example is purely to demonstrate that one contract is "covered" by 100 shares of stock (for US stock options). The Covered Call strategy is used by traders who are looking to lower their cost of buying shares by capturing call option premium on, say, a monthly basis.

Steps to trading a Covered Call/Buy Write:

1   Buy the stock.

2   Sell calls one or two strikes Out of the Money (OTM) (for example, calls with strike prices one or two strikes higher than the stock—the aim here is to capture a decent amount of premium, so we don't sell calls too far OTM because they'd hardly be worth it).

Buy stock   +   Sell call   =   Covered Call

If you are looking to sell **five** contracts of MSFT $50 calls at $1.88 (where the MSFT share price is $46.88), you will receive a premium for selling the calls (before commissions) of $940. But you will need to buy **500** MSFT shares to be "covered." This will be at a cost of 500 times the MSFT share price.

So your net cost of doing this trade will be

Description	Calculation	Cost
Sell 5 Microsoft call option contracts	5 × $1.88 × 100	$940
Buy 500 Microsoft shares at $46.88	500 × $46.88	($23,440)
		($22,500)

We will discuss the relative merits of Covered Calls in Chapter 5, "Two Popular Strategies and How to Improve Them," and go through a real example in more depth. Personally I am not over-keen on this type of risk profile for a lot of investors because the diagonal line keeps going down without stopping. For now, just keep in mind that when you combine stocks with stock options, you need to remember that one option contract represents rights over 100 shares of a US stock.

Option Exchanges

There are many (options) exchanges around the world now. The USA is undoubtedly the hub of the options trading world with more than ten major exchanges. Options volumes are increasing almost every month now, particularly stock options, as more and more retail (non-professional) traders become interested. The major US option exchanges are as follows:

Option exchange	Description
American Stock Exchange (AMEX)	• Stocks • Options on individual stocks • Stock indices
Chicago Board of Trade (CBOT)	• Futures • Options on futures for agricultural goods, precious metals, stock indices and debt instruments
Chicago Board Options Exchange (CBOE)	• Options on individual stocks • Options on stock indices • Options on Treasury securities
Chicago Mercantile Exchange	• Futures • Options on futures for agricultural goods, stock indices, debt instruments and currencies

New York Stock Exchange (NYSE)	• Stocks • Options on individual stocks • Stock index
Pacific Stock Exchange (PSE)	• Options on individual stocks • Stock index
Philadelphia Stock Exchange (PHLX)	• Stocks • Futures • Options on individual stocks • Currencies • Stock indices

Option Expiration Dates

Every option has an expiration date, which is usually specified as a month. US equity, index, and Treasury/interest-rate options expire on the Saturday following the third Friday in the expiration month. Trading in the options ceases on the Friday, but the owner can exercise the options on the final Saturday.

Exercise Prices

Generally in the USA, option strike prices start at $5 and then go in $2.50 increments; once they hit $25, they go in $5 increments; and at $200, they go in $10 increments. Anomalies occur where there have been stock splits and company mergers.

Option Ticker Symbols

In the real world, you'll rarely have to understand precisely how an option symbol is constructed. However, it's useful to have a reference, just in case you're feeling curious.

Individual options have ticker symbols just like individual stocks do. The symbol identifies the underlying stock, the expiration month, the strike price, and the type of option.

A series of letters identify the option. They appear in the order of root, expiration month, and strike price. The letter that is used for expiration month is also used to identify whether the option is a call or a put.

The first letter or group of letters (up to three) identify the underlying stock and is called the *root*. It doesn't have to be the same as the stock symbol. Microsoft has the stock symbol of MSFT. But because that's more than three letters, a root symbol is devised by the standardizing authority and a group of three letters is used. MSQ is the primary root for Microsoft options. There can be others under certain conditions, but for now let's keep it simple. The root for Microsoft is MSQ.

The next-to-last letter in an option symbol indicates the expiration month. If the option is a call, the first half of the alphabet is used. If the option is a put, the second half of the alphabet is used. The following table illustrates the codes.

	Jan	Feb	Mar	Apr	May	Jun	Jul	Aug	Sep	Oct	Nov	Dec
Calls	A	B	C	D	E	F	G	H	I	J	K	L
Puts	M	N	O	P	Q	R	S	T	U	V	W	X

The last letter of the option symbol indicates the strike price. Again there are codes to decipher the strike price.

A	B	C	D	E	F	G	H	I	J	K	L	M
5	10	15	20	25	30	35	40	45	50	55	60	65
105	110	115	120	125	130	135	140	145	150	155	160	165
205	210	215	220	225	230	235	240	245	250	255	260	265
305	310	315	320	325	330	335	340	345	350	355	360	365

N	O	P	Q	R	S	T	U	V	W	X	Y	Z
70	75	80	85	90	95	100	7.5	12.5	17.5	22.5	27.5	32.5
170	175	180	185	190	195	200	37.5	42.5	47.5	52.5	57.5	62.5
270	275	280	285	290	295	300	67.5	72.5	77.5	82.5	87.5	92.5
370	375	380	385	390	395	400	97.5	102.5	107.5	112.5	117.5	122.5

By using all this information, we can decipher the option symbol MSQAF:

● The MSQ is the root identifying Microsoft, the "A" is for the month of January, and it also lets us know that the option is a call option.

● The last letter "F" tells us the option is for the $30 strike price.

Don't worry about remembering or memorizing all the codes. They are readily available and easily obtained when you need them.

For another example, let's examine the option symbol PGDL:

● The last letter tells us the strike. You need to have an idea of where a stock trades to know the strike. For instance, the letter "B" could be for the strike price of 10, 110, 210, 310, and so on. In this case the letter "L" is for the strike price of $60.00.

● The letter "D" is for the month of April and indicates a call.

● The letter "PG" is the root symbol for the stock of Procter & Gamble as well as being the stock symbol.

Margin

Margin is defined as the amount of liquid funds required on deposit to maintain the viability of the trade. A margin account is effectively the mechanism by which you can borrow funds from your broker account but you are required to cover your potential risk liability with liquid funds in your account. This is particularly relevant to those traders who sell short, sell naked, or trade net credit spreads.

When you buy shares, you either pay in cash or use a margin account (effectively borrowing funds from your brokerage) for around 50% of the share purchase price. The *maintenance margin* is set to ensure that the balance in the margin account never becomes negative. This has in the past been set at around 25% of the value of the shares, although it does vary.

A margin account is effectively the mechanism by which you can borrow funds from your broker account, but you are required to cover your potential risk liability with liquid funds in your account.

When you buy call or put options, you must pay the purchase price in full. You cannot buy options on margin because options themselves already contain significant leverage, and buying options on margin would raise the leverage to unacceptable levels.

Selling (writing) options naked means that there are no covering trades to hedge the risk of the naked sale. Remember the risk profiles of selling calls and puts and how the diagonal lines continue uninterrupted on the downside? It is this uninterrupted downside that needs to be protected. Therefore, when you sell naked call or put options, you are required to maintain funds in a margin account. This is to ensure that the option writer does not default on his or her obligation if the option buyer (who has the right…) exercises his or her right. Again, the size of margin can vary.

When you sell short, sell naked, or trade a net credit spread, while money is deposited into your account by the trade itself, there is still (in most cases) a contingent liability risk, which must be covered by sufficient funds in your account.

These funds can either be represented in cash or marginable securities. A *marginable security* is defined as an asset deemed by the brokerage to be secure enough to stand as collateral against your risk on the trade. A blue chip stock such as MSFT may well be considered a marginable security, while low-priced stocks (under $10) with little trading history, low trading volumes, and high volatility may not be considered as acceptable collateral.

Remember that in many cases of selling short and selling naked, your potential risk liability may be unlimited (or at least substantial). Using *OptionEasy* to determine your risk profile will help you to identify those situations where your risk potential is unacceptably high, depending on your own personal appetite for risk.

Example 2.4a Buying Stock

Profile	Description	Risk	Reward	Breakeven
	Buy asset	Purchase price	Unlimited	Purchase price

XYZ Inc. has a stock price of $48.00 per share. You buy 300 shares and use margin to fund 50% of the total purchase price.

Stock Price	×	No. of shares	=	Total Purchase Price
$48.00	×	300	=	$14,400

Using 50% margin to fund your cost of acquisition you will therefore need to pay $7,200 in cash for the trade.

| $14,400 | × | 50% | = | $7,200 |

Example 2.4b **Shorting Stock**

Profile	Description	Risk	Reward	Breakeven
＼	Sell asset	Unlimited	Short sale price	Short sale price

Let's flip Example 2.4a, so instead now we're selling the stock short. We will assume the same price information for the stock we are selling. The stock price is still $48.00.

Stock Price	×	No. of shares	=	Total Short Proceeds
$48.00	×	300	=	$14,400

However, in this example we require margin to cover our potential liabilities. The margin is calculated as follows:

100% of the amount of short sale proceeds in addition to the cash raised by the short sale

$14,400	+	$14,400 (short sale proceeds)	=	$28,800

Example 2.4c **Buying Calls**

Profile	Description	Risk	Reward	Breakeven
／	Buy call	Call premium price	Unlimited	Strike price plus call premium Paid

Continuing with XYZ Inc., let's assume that the call options have a premium of $6.00 for the strike price of $50, and we are buying four contracts.

Option Premium × Units per contract × No. of contracts = Total Purchase Price
$6.00   × 100   × 4   = $2,400

Because you are not allowed to purchase options with margin, there is nothing else to work out here.

Example 2.4d Writing Naked Calls

Profile	Description	Risk	Reward	Breakeven
⟍	Sell call	Unlimited	Limited to the call premium received	Strike price plus call premium paid

Let's flip Example 2.4c, so instead now we're selling calls (naked). We will assume the same price information for the call options we are selling. The calls have a premium of $6.00 for the strike price of $50, and we are selling four contracts. The stock price is still $48.00.

Because we're now selling options, we are required to show sufficient funds in our account to cover the risk of being exercised.

The initial margin cover we need to show is the *greater of the following*:

a. 100% of the option sale proceeds + 20%* of the underlying share price − any amount by which the option is out of the money (OTM)

$6.00 × 4 × 100   + 20% × $48.00 × 4 × 100   − $2.00 × 4 × 100
$2,400   + $3,840   − $800 − $5,440

b. 100% of the option sale proceeds + 10%* of the underlying share price

$6.00 × 4 × 100   + 10% × $48.00 × 4 × 100
$2,400   + $1,920   = $4,320

* Note that the percentage figures quoted may not be those used by your broker account. These are simply examples to illustrate how margin works in principle.

You can use the option sale proceeds of $2,400 to set off against the initial margin requirement. This means that:

	Margin requirement	Sale proceeds	Additional funds required
a.	$5,440	$2,400	$3,040
b.	$4,320	$2,400	$1,920

Because we have to take the greater amount, the initial margin requirement is $5,440 in calculation (a), and we therefore need a further $3,040 in liquid funds in our account to facilitate this trade.

Example 2.4e Buying Puts

Profile	Description	Risk	Reward	Breakeven
	Buy put	Put premium price	Strike price less put premium paid	Strike price less put premium paid

Continuing with XYZ Inc., let's assume that the put options have a premium of $7.50 for the strike price of $50, and we are buying four contracts.

$$\text{Option Premium} \times \text{Units per contract} \times \text{No. of contracts} = \text{Total Purchase Price}$$
$$\$7.50 \times 100 \times 4 = \$3,000$$

Because you are not allowed to purchase options with margin, there is nothing else to work out here.

Example 2.4f Writing Naked Puts

Profile	Description	Risk	Reward	Breakeven
	Sell put	Strike price less put premium received	Limited to the put premium received	Strike price less put premium paid

Let's flip Example 2.4e, so instead now we're selling puts (naked). We will assume the same price information for the put options we are selling. The puts have a premium of $7.50 for the strike price of $50, and we are selling four contracts. The stock price is still $48.00.

Because we're now selling options, we are required to show sufficient funds in our account to cover the risk of being exercised.

The initial margin cover we need to show is the greater of the following:

a. 100% of the option sale proceeds   **+**   20%* of the underlying share price   **–**   any amount by which the option is out of the money (OTM)

$7.50 × 4 × 100   **+**   20% × $48.00 × 4 × 100   **–** $0 × 4 × 100 *(remember this is a put and here the put is actually In the Money (ITM)*

$3,000   **+** $3,840   **–** $0 = $6,840

b. 100% of the option sale proceeds   **+**   10%* of the underlying share price

$7.50 × 4 × 100   **+**   10% × $48.00 × 4 × 100
$3,000   **+** $1,920   **=** $4,920

* Note that the percentage figures quoted may not be those used by your broker account. These are simply examples to illustrate how margin works in principle.

You can use the option sale proceeds of $3,000 to set off against the initial margin requirement. This means that:

Margin requirement	Sale proceeds	Additional funds required
a. $6,840	$3,000	$3,840
b. $4,920	$3,000	$1,920

Because we have to take the greater amount, the initial margin requirement is $6,840 in calculation (a), and we therefore need a further $3,840 in liquid funds in our account to facilitate this trade.

Placing Your Trade Order

Trades can be placed either online or offline, depending on your broker account.

Use *OptionEasy's Strategy Guides* to assist you in placing your spread orders over the telephone quickly, efficiently, and accurately. By knowing what to say and how to say it clearly, concisely, and correctly, you will help save both your time and the broker's time, as well as ensure that there are no misunderstandings.

Make sure you fill in the right figures and have them in writing before picking up the phone to place your order. Then simply read out the order to the broker with your limit order prices. Always prepare what you're going to say beforehand. This will help both you and your broker who, in any case, is required to read back to you the order you have just placed.

Because options prices are not always "clean," it is preferable to place limit orders, particularly on spreads.

Because options prices are not always "clean" it is preferable to place limit orders, particularly on spreads. This will ensure that you will be filled at your specified price or not at all. By using *OptionEasy*'s Limit Order facility, you will be able to overwrite the market prices to base your calculations on your preferred limit order on all types of trade and still have a view on your limit order risk profile.

Types of Order in the Market

Market Order

This is where you authorize your broker to buy or sell stock or options at the best price in the market.

Limit Order

This is where you:

● only buy if share falls to a certain price or lower; or

● only sell if share rises to certain price or higher.

Limits are recommended with options, particularly for spreads and combination trades. The reason for this is that the bid/ask spread prices can fluctuate dramatically and often not in your favor, so it's better to specify your prices.

Stop Loss/Sell Stop (Defensive)

This is where you:

- Sell if stock falls below a certain price (sell stop is placed below the current price).

You can increase the stop loss if the share rises.

Buy Stops

This is where you will only buy once the stock has reached or exceeded a certain price. This is like the opposite of a limit order where you look to buy a stock when it has fallen to a certain price. A Buy Stop is appropriate where you expect a stock to rise beyond a resistance level or bounce up from a support level.

- *Buy Stop with limit*

Only buy when stock is between two prices.

- *Buy Stop with limit and Stop Loss*

Buy between two prices and sell if below another price.

Time Limits with Trade Orders

Good Till Cancelled (GTC)

This is where the order is valid unless and until you cancel it or until it is filled. For example, a limit order GTC means you authorize your broker to buy the stock at a particular price or lower, today or any time in the future where the stock is selling at that particular amount, until you have bought the requisite number of shares.

Be careful with GTC orders because these orders generally do not go to the top of the list of floor traders' priorities.

Day Only

The order will be cancelled if it is not filled by the end of the day. This is a good ploy because it encourages the floor traders to deal. If they don't by the end of the day, then they won't get their commission, so there is an incentive for floor traders to put this type of trade nearer to the top of their list.

Week Only

The order will be cancelled if it is not filled by the end of the week.

Fill or Kill

The order of maximum priority. If it isn't filled immediately, the order is cancelled. A fill or kill order is bound to capture the attention of the floor trader, but if it's a limit order, then you need to make it realistic!

All or None

Either the entire order is filled or none of it. This is not generally a good idea given that many trades aren't filled all at once anyway because there has to be a buyer or seller on the other side, and most of the time they won't be specifically dealing in the same lot sizes as your order. So if you want to be sure to get filled, don't go for all or none!

Always Have a STOP in Mind Whenever You Make a Trade

This is covered in Chapter 10, "Trading and Investing Psychology," and in Chapter 11, "Putting It All Together—A Call to Action." It is imperative that you know where you will exit a position, whether it is a profitable situation or otherwise. Some people don't like to actually place stops with their brokers. Fair enough, but you must have one in your mind at the very least, and once there, you must act on it if the stop has been breached. Also, you must always have in your mind when you are likely to want to take profits and you must act on that too if and when the situation occurs. You can set a *mental stop*, where the market makers cannot see what you are doing and artificially manipulate the price to take advantage of you. If you set a mental stop, write it down and be honest enough to stick to it, however much it may hurt!

> It is imperative that you know where you will exit a position, whether it is a profitable situation or otherwise.

Where you place your stops is up to you, but in general with stocks you can place them quite tight (within 10%) and with plain call or put options, perhaps a little looser. I recommend that when trading options, you base your stops on the stock price, not the option prices UNLESS you are doing combination option spreads (where you have more than one leg to a trade) or unless you are day trading options (not recommended) with Level II type screens.

Whipsaws

A *whipsaw* occurs when a price changes direction twice or more in very quick succession; in intraday trading terms, this can literally happen in a few ticks.

While I do advocate the use of stops to limit your losses, you should be aware of the dangers of whipsaws and how you can get "stopped out" thereby surrendering what might have turned out to be a winning position. For example, if you buy a stock for $51.00 and put in a tight stop at $50.00, the stock may initially rise, then within a few ticks or five minute bars, it may break down through $50.00 before resuming its uptrend. The problem is that you've been stopped out when the price broke down through $50.00 even though the price may later recover to, say, $55.00. This type of action is particularly relevant to intraday traders and options intraday traders. Personally I don't recommend intraday trading options unless you are very experienced and have the fastest online connection speeds and brokerage account facilities to execute trades in a few seconds maximum. Speed is a vital prerequisite if you are trading options intraday so don't let anyone tell you otherwise.

You should be aware of the dangers of whipsaws and how you can get "stopped out," thereby surrendering what might have been a winning position.

Trading Tips

Remember, the most important things you need to know about any trade you ever do are

- your maximum *risk* on the trade;
- your maximum *reward* on the trade; and
- your *breakeven* point(s).

OptionEasy's Analyzer gives you these crucial figures in both nominal and actual formats for 64 different strategies.

In addition, you also should know in advance:

- the maximum loss you will accept and when to get out of a loss-making trade and
- when to take your profits.

These are crucial money management criteria, which you must preset in your own mind (and preferably on paper) before you commit to any trade. There are wide parameters concerning money management techniques, and much depends on your own appetite and respect for risk. Just keep in mind that it is generally a good thing to cut your losses short and to let your profits run. We will discuss trading psychology in greater depth in Chapter 10.

Leverage and Gearing

The words "leverage" and "gearing" are used frequently in the financial world. In terms of a company's financial structure, it means the ratio of borrowings over assets. The higher a company's gearing, the higher its return on equity will be, but also the greater risk to the company because if fixed and variable costs are not exceeded by turnover, then the company's creditors may be able to foreclose the company by calling in the loans.

The words have a similar but not identical meaning in the options world. Options have high leverage because a small percentage move in the underlying asset can mean a very high percentage move from the corresponding options.

How Does Leverage with Options Work?—A Worked Example

Example 2.5 Leverage with Options

ABCD Company has a stock price of $20.00. You decide to buy a call option with an exercise price (e) of $25.00. The call option costs you $1.00. Remember an option has two parts to its value:

● Time Value

● Intrinsic Value

In this example, until the stock price of ABCD rises beyond $25, there will be no Intrinsic Value because the exercise price is $25.00. So even if ABCD stock rises up to $25, there is no Intrinsic Value until it goes above $25.00. *For this example, let's assume that there is no change to the Time Value element.* So if ABCD stock price now rises to $30, what is the Intrinsic Value of the option?

Answer: $30 - $25 = $5.00.

Therefore, in most cases the value of the call option must be *at least* $5.00.

Conclusion:

ABCD stock price has risen from $20 to $30 - this is an increase of 50%. The option price has risen from $1 to $5 - this is an increase of **400%**. Now *that's* leverage!

But remember that leverage works the other way too, and this is why we encourage you to trade in certain ways, to protect you in the event of things going the other way.

If ABCD stock price moves back down to $20 from $30, this is a decrease of 33%.

The option price may move from $5 back down to $1—a far larger percentage decrease. It is these potential decreases that we need to be protected from.

A Brief Introduction to Delta (Hedge Ratio)

What you have seen in Example 2.5 is the phenomenon of *Delta*. Delta is measured as the change in option price divided by the change in the underlying asset price.

Delta = $\dfrac{\text{change in option price}}{\text{change in underlying asset price}}$

As you just witnessed, when a call option becomes In the Money (ITM), the Delta increases. So the higher the Delta, the faster the option price is moving as compared with the stock price. However, buying Out of the Money (OTM) options is not the answer either because by doing that you reduce your chances of success because the change in option price (compared with the stock price) is much slower, therefore it is more difficult to make profit; besides which, the probability of the option expiring ITM is that much lower as well.

When we discuss basic strategies later on, we will uncover how you can protect yourself against Delta by using combination or "spread trades." These spread trades are intended to reduce your risk exposure to Delta by bringing the Delta value close to zero, so that you are not exposed to such wild swings on the downside, while also keeping your probability of success high. This is known as *Delta Neutral Trading*.

Even at this stage it's important for you to understand that Delta Neutral does not mean you have no risk. Delta Neutral trading is sometimes talked about as some sort of nirvana. This is not the case, although it should be pointed out that it can significantly reduce risk in certain scenarios and with particular strategies—but is mainly useful for the professionals only.

Chapter 2 Major Learning Points

In this chapter you have learned:

- how to read options prices on your screen.

- how options contracts work and that with stocks, a contract represents more than one share.

- how options expiration dates and exercise prices work.

- margin—its benefits, risks, and characteristics.

- the different types of trade orders in the market.

- leverage with options.

- a brief understanding of Delta.

Before we go on to explore some options strategies, it's important that we cover some basic concepts of *Fundamental* and *Technical Analysis* so that you can begin to understand how to spot possible stocks (targets) for the strategies you're going to learn to apply later in this book.

The Basics of Fundamental Analysis

Fundamental Analysis is the study of individual companies and how they are performing in terms of:

● revenues,

● profits,

● assets, and

● borrowings.

In simple terms, most of the key financial ratios that you will see are manipulations of these four items. We'll have a look at the main ratios and their significance later in this chapter.

Why do we need to know about Fundamental Analysis? Because the company's share price is ultimately the market's reflection of how valuable that company is. If a company is making profits and these profits are growing year after year, with borrowings contained to low levels and revenues also growing, then this is an ideal company to invest in, provided we expect the company to continue growing at such levels.

Remember that stock prices are primarily driven by expectations. Expectations are fuelled by current sentiment. Sentiment is influenced primarily by news and past history. News, on the corporate level, involves the company's financial results and its plans for the future. From a wider perspective, news involves the economy at large both nationally and internationally.

Diagram 3.1 ● Fundamental influences on stock prices.

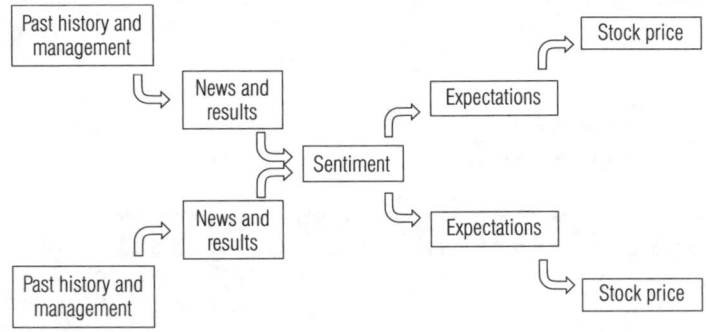

Past History and Management

What does the company do? How has it performed in the past, and what is the track record of its management team? Is this company in an industry or sector that has a prosperous future where its goods and services are going to be in demand for the foreseeable future? Does the incumbent management have a track record of consistently increasing earnings and shareholder value in this or other companies?

Many investors make their investment decisions based solely on the quality and track record of management. For example, Microsoft's earnings record up to the beginning of 2001 was nigh on impeccable, constantly exceeding expectations quarter after quarter and constantly growing. And until 2000, its stock price did the same.

News and Results

News concerns the world at large, the wider economy, the sector of the stock, and the company itself.

An example of news that might affect the markets and stock prices is if oil prices rise wildly and the knock-on effects this could have. These effects might include higher transportation costs, leading to higher production prices, leading to higher inflation, and then higher interest rates, all of which would impact many companies negatively as their own cost bases rise, therefore impacting on their margins and overall profitability. The specter of inflation and the use of higher interest rates to combat it is a problem for many stocks in general. When sentiment is worried about the increasing risk of higher inflation, the markets will generally become more uncertain, volatile, and might fall.

The specter of inflation and the use of higher interest rates to combat it is a problem for many stocks in general.

With Microsoft a persistent news story has been the anti-trust lawsuit, following allegations of the company exploiting an unfair monopoly. Whatever happens, every time the story develops, the latest news item will have an impact on the stock price and the volume of shares traded as a result of that news (or the expectation of its consequences). Many investors are now unconcerned about a possible break-up of Microsoft because they feel that scenario is already factored into the current stock price.

Earnings results reflect the financial performance of the individual company and in the USA, are published quarterly (UK half yearly). Again, the most important numbers you are looking to pinpoint are those reflecting the company's earnings and *Earnings per Share*.

Sentiment and Expectations

Is it true to suggest that the markets are driven by emotions? Well, certainly greed and fear do make a significant contribution to prices in any market context. How can it be that a company with little history and no earnings whatsoever can be valued in the billions of dollars? Does that company have proprietory technology that will change the world as we know it? Does the company have such a convincing marketing and growth strategy that investors are purely valuing the company based on expected gross revenues?

Whatever the case, market sentiment doesn't necessarily work in a logical way, and sometimes it's difficult to understand how a company like Coca-Cola or McDonald's can get panned when delivering consistently good results when others who don't earn a dime are being hailed as the new saviors of the markets! It is this sentiment that drives expectations of the company's future performance. And as we know from our everyday lives, sentiment can turn on a dime!

Expectations come in numerous forms, both in terms of the company's results but also in terms of the analysts' recommendations on the company's share price. It's astounding how wildly inaccurate analysts' recommendations can be, and yet they all get away with it. Of course, no one can be right all the time, but sometimes they're nowhere near. So be careful when it comes to analysts' recommendations and remember that analysts work for firms who ultimately want to do business with the companies on whom they report. This is why you rarely see a "Sell" recommendation on a stock, even if it's an obvious screaming sell! They don't want to be seen as being too insulting, just in case a business opportunity arises in the future.

Continuing with the Microsoft theme, suddenly in 2000 Microsoft's share price hit the buffers for three major reasons: first that the market as a whole, particularly the technology sector, got a significant revaluation or correction (downward) and second because of continued uncertainty regarding the anti-trust issues. Uncertainty is never good for the markets. The third reason was because of growing negative sentiment about the company's ability to continue its phenomenal growth. With computer box-makers suffering because of declining growth in sales, surely Microsoft would inevitably suffer as a knock-on effect given that a major part of its revenue has been sourced from Windows being pre-installed in new PCs. In basic terms, all these factors led to a decline in investor sentiment leading to performance expectations falling and hence the share price falling too. But notice how it didn't have anything to do with serious doubts over Microsoft's management, and certainly no one I've ever spoken to has ever questioned the capabilities of those who run one of the world's most successful companies in history.

Hopefully you're beginning to see how you can chain events in such a way that you can ask yourself who or what might be affected if such and such is happening in other sectors or other parts of the same or other sectors. Common sense plays a considerable part in determining your overall success in the markets. Common sense overrides greed and fear and compels you to make smart decisions, such as not putting all your eggs into one basket, such as asking yourself insightful questions that mean you're beginning to think laterally, such as avoiding options strategies that expose you to unlimited risk, such as selecting options strategies that limit your risk while bringing down your breakeven points and enhancing your maximum reward and likelihood of success.

A word of caution: Be careful about listening to gurus' recommendations. Instructors are always under pressure to give recommendations and watch lists out to their students. It can become a rod for the instructor's back because if just *one* recommendation goes wrong (even temporarily), the student can become disillusioned. No one gets it right all the time, and in most cases it's how you *manage* your winners and losers that counts, not how many good or bad ones you pick. We'll talk more about money management in Chapter 10, "Trading and Investing Psychology."

The Wider Economy

Before delving into an individual company's fundamentals, we need to take a brief look at some basic economics. Those of you who have previously been scared of economics, don't be here! In the overall scheme of things, we're just talking common sense here, and a good place to start is with the country at large and the wider economic climate. This is called taking a "top-down approach." It means we are looking at the broader picture—in other words, how is the general economy performing? Are any storm clouds looming? This is a sensible approach and your success will depend on keeping your senses alive and alert to what is going on around you anyway. It really doesn't take much; just keep up to date with the news, and you will have enough background knowledge to get a feel. And from here you can start to chain events into likely scenarios developing later on.

Remember, this is not an economics book, but there are some key figures that have major significance in each economy wherever you live in the world. Those in the following table are specific to the USA; however, they'll have equivalents in every Western economy.

Statistic	Meaning and Significance	Look for
Gross Domestic Product (GDP)	The broadest measure of economic activity, GDP measures the output of products and services located within a country irrespective of whether their owners live there or abroad. GDP is a measure of the economy's performance within its own territory. This is why a foreign company building a factory within a host country is seen as good news for the host country. The obvious knock-on effect will include increased employment within that host country. When GDP is positive, the economy is growing; when GDP is negative, the economy is shrinking.	1% to 5% consistent growth per annum. In a mature economy this range is healthy. Obviously, if GDP is negative, the economy is shrinking, thereby diminishing the wealth of the country. A recession is contentiously defined as two successive quarters of negative GDP.
Gross National Product (GNP)	Not as widely followed as GDP, GNP includes goods and services produced abroad by the domestically owned organizations. Hence, net property income from abroad must be added to GDP to obtain the GNP.	Same as above, but it's fine to simply use the GDP figures.

Statistic	Meaning and Significance	Look for
Inflation	Inflation is the measure of price changes within the economy. Inflation is the measure of how much each unit of currency is diminishing in its buying power. So if inflation is 10% per annum, then in one year's time, $1.00 will buy you 10% less than it does today, meaning you'll need $1.10 to buy the equivalent products in a year's time. Inflation is seen as damaging to an economy, and it has obvious implications on an economy's currency. All other things being equal, a high-inflation economy's currency will fall in value. Logically this has to be the case because if you go to a high-inflation economy where prices are rising all the time, you don't want to pay as much for that currency, hence the currency value will fall as a result of a lack of demand for it. A word of caution however: Governments and central banks will manipulate interest rates and money supply within the economy in order to influence inflation.	0.5% to 4% per annum is historically a healthy figure since inflation became a major issue for economies in the 1960s. At this time, however, we have enjoyed historically low inflation over the last five years, under 3%. Look for the trend to remain steady with no significant increases.
Interest rates	Set by the central banks or governments in each economy as the borrowing rate of the central bank. In a "monetary economy" interest rates are used by economic managers to control inflation and keep it low. High interest rates mean higher borrowing charges for companies and individuals, particularly mortgage holders, which in turn means less money for buying goods and services, which in turn reduces demand for goods and services, which in turn increases supply for those goods and services, which in turn reduces prices, thereby reducing inflation. The trick is to keep inflation and interest rates stable while also managing a steadily growing economy.	Look for low and declining interest rates. Historically in the USA and UK, between 4% and 7% has been low in the last 30 years, although, like inflation, the immediate trend of the last five years has been to the low side.

Statistic	Meaning and Significance	Look for
Unemployment	In the last few years unemployment has dropped to its pre-1980s levels when maturing economies, such as the USA and UK, were undergoing massive restructuring away from the manufacturing, labor-intensive sector toward the service sectors. This was typically a long and painful process for many developed economies as technology swept through old manufacturing processes, abolishing the need for massive workforces. With union powers constricted during the 1980s by more conservative governments, unemployment soared until such time that the services and technology sectors were able to swallow up those people who were made redundant.	Low and declining. Somewhere between 3% and 8%, although note that recent levels are returning to levels not seen since the early to mid-1970s.

**Economic events
to watch out for:**

- FOMC meetings.
- Earnings results from blue chip companies and stock market 'bellwethers' (for example, Microsoft, IBM, Intel). The health of these types of companies will help to shape the health of the rest of the market.
- Employment figures every first Friday of the month.
- PPI/CPI/Leading Economic Indicators (LEI).

- Interest rates and monetary policy decisions made.
- The general health of the economy and how individual companies are performing.

- Interest rates on the decline.
- Rising profits and confident projections from management.

Economic Indicators to Watch (USA Only)

CPI: Consumer Price Index

The CPI is the most widely cited inflation indicator and is used as a measure of the price levels of goods and services purchased by consumers. The CPI is seen as the best measure of the underlying inflation rate in the US economy.

The figures are released at 8:30 a.m. EST around the thirteenth of every month, reporting with respect to the prior month (details can be found at (http://stats.bls.gov/news.release/cpi.toc.htm).

The Employment Report

Made up of two separate surveys, the Household Survey (60,000 households) and the Establishment Survey (375,000 businesses), the Employment Report produces the unemployment rate figures.

The Employment Report figures are released at 8:30 a.m. EST on the first Friday of every month, reporting with respect to the prior month (details can be found at http:///stats.bls.gov/news.release/empsit.toc.htm).

Gross Domestic Product (GDP)

The broad components of GDP (described in the previous section) are consumption, investment, net exports, government acquisitions, and inventories.

GDP figures are released at 8:30 a.m. EST on the third or fourth week of the first month of the new quarter with respect to the prior quarter's activity. Subsequent revisions are made in the second and third months of the quarter (more details can be found at http://bea.doc.gov/dn1.htm).

Housing Starts and Building Permits

Housing Starts are a measure of the number of residential units on which construction has begun each month. A start is defined as the beginning of excavation of the foundation for the building and is comprised primarily of residential housing. Housing Starts are led by Building Permits (which allow the excavations to subsequently happen), but permits are not required in all regions of the USA; therefore, the Starts figure is more telling. The Housing Starts figures are notoriously volatile, being affected as they are by extreme weather and natural disasters.

The figures are released at 8:30 a.m. EST around the sixteenth of the month, with respect to the previous month's data (more details can be found at www.census.gov/ftp/pub/indicator/www/housing.html).

National Association of Purchasing Managers (NAPM)

The NAPM report is a national survey of purchasing managers and is calculated by way of a weighted average of items including new orders, production, employment, inventories, delivery times, prices, and export and import orders. NAPM only covers the manufacturing sector, but is seen as a leading indicator for other economic releases.

The figures are released at 10 a.m. EST on the first business day of each month with respect to the prior month's data (more details can be found at www.napm.org/public/rob/lastrob1.html).

Producer Price Index (PPI)

The PPI is another measure of inflation. It measures the prices of goods at the wholesale level.

The figures are released at 8:30 a.m. EST around the eleventh of each month, with respect to the prior month's data (more details are available at http://stats.bls.gov/news.release/ppi.toc.htm).

Retail Sales

This is a measure of the total receipts of retail stores. Often analyzed excluding figures for automobiles, food and gasoline, it's the changes from month to month here that we're looking for to identify shifts in consumer demand. Retail sales figures exclude spending on services, which nowadays makes up over half of total consumption. Total personal consumption figures are normally available around two weeks after the Retail Sales figures are published.

Retail Sales figures are published at 8:30 a.m. EST around the thirteenth of each month (more details can be found at www.census.gov/svsd/www/advtable/html).

The Economic Calendar

Sun	Mon	Tues	Weds	Thurs	Fri	Sat
1	2 NAPM	3	4	5	6 Employment Rate	7
8	9	10	11 PPI	12	13 Retail Sales CPI	14
15	16 Housing Starts Building Permits	17	18	19	20 Expiring equity, index and Treasury/ interest-rate options cease trading	21 Expiring equity, index and Treasury/ interest-rate options expiration date*
22	23	24 Consumer Confidence FOMC	25	26 FOMC Minutes	27 New Home Sales GDP	28
29	30 Employment Cost Index	31 PMI				

*Equity LEAPs expire in January. Index LEAPs expire in December or January. Interest-rate LEAPs expire in December.

For a complete view of the economic calendar, go to http://biz.yahoo.com/c/e.html.

Expiring equity, index and Treasury/interest-rate options typically cease trading on the third Friday of every month and officially expire on that Saturday.

Each option has its own ticker code, made up from the underlying asset, the strike price and the expiration date. The expiration months are allocated a code as follows:

	Jan	Feb	Mar	Apr	May	Jun	Jul	Aug	Sep	Oct	Nov	Dec
Calls	A	B	C	D	E	F	G	H	I	J	K	L
Puts	M	N	O	P	Q	R	S	T	U	V	W	X

Futures contracts typically close during the third week of each quarter. Each quarter is a three-month period, and the year starts on January 1st. The expiration quarter symbols are as follows:

March	June	September	December
H	M	U	Z

Bonds

T-bills (government) and bonds (corporations) are known as "fixed-income" securities because the amount of income they generate each year is "fixed" or set as a "coupon" when the T-bill or bond is issued. No matter what happens or who holds the T-bill or bond, it will generate exactly the same amount of money each year. This coupon is effectively an obligatory interest payment made by the issuer.

Bonds are issued by corporations that need to raise money. Corporate bonds will normally carry higher interest rates than T-bills or government bonds because there is a higher risk that the company could go bankrupt and default on the bond. Both government bonds and corporate bonds can be traded in the open market, and when we see CNBC or Bloomberg TV referring to the *Bond Markets*, this is what we mean. The 30-year bond is generally seen as the "cost of doing business"

Bond Basics

- We already understand that bonds are DEBT instruments, requiring the issuer (borrower) to pay a fixed interest payment (coupon) with respect to the amount raised by the issue of the bond.

- Bonds are issued at *par value*. Par value is the amount that you (the lender) will receive back from the borrower at the end of the term when the bond matures (that is, when the borrower has to pay back the loan).

- The coupon rate is the amount of interest the bondholder will receive (per annum) expressed as a percentage of the par value of the bond. For example, if a $100 million bond is issued with a coupon rate of 8%, the owners of the bond will collectively receive $8 million per annum from the bond-issuing company.

- At maturity, say, September 2002, the bond-issuing company (borrower) will have to redeem (pay back) the principal amount of the loan, in the above example, $100 million.

- The bigger and safer the corporation, the lower the coupon rate will be.

For example, GE will typically pay a lower coupon rate than Joe Schmo's because GE is rated by Moody's as a AAA covenant, unlikely to default on the loan; whereas, Joe Schmo's is only rated at, say, a C!

Bond Markets

Bonds are traded on the markets. What we want to know is how bonds relate to the equity markets.

● If our bond is issued at par for $100 million, let's assume for simplicity that each unit of that bond can be bought for $100. This means that the bond has 1 million units of itself being traded on the open market.

● We already know that 8% is payable on that bond, with respect to its par value of $100 million in total, or $100 per unit. Therefore, if we buy one unit, we know that we will receive a coupon of $8 per unit per annum.

● Bonds go up and down in price on the open market. So while par value may be $100 per unit, in a strong market the bond may trade at greater than $100, and in a weak market the bond may trade at less than $100. Whatever the bond is trading at, the same coupon of $8 per annum is payable. What this means is that as the values of bonds fluctuate on the open market, so do the yields on those bonds. The following table illustrates this.

	Weak market	Strong market
Bond issued at par value	$100	
Coupon rate (per annum)	8%	
Coupon payment (p.a.)	$8.00	
Bond trading value	$90	$110
Bond yield	8.9%	7.3%

See how the lower bond price (in the weak market column) translates directly into a higher yield and how the higher bond price (in the strong market) translates directly into a lower yield. Remember that the coupon payable remains at $8 per annum. What has changed is the price the market is prepared to pay for that bond that was originally issued with a par value of $100. Here, it's easy to see that if you pay $90 to get $8 in interest payments, your yield is higher than if you had to pay $110 to get $8 in interest payments.

Generally Speaking

Rules of thumb:

- When the bond market is strong, bond prices are higher, bond yields are lower, and the stock market is stronger.

- When the bond market is weak, bond prices are lower, bond yields are higher, and the stock market is weaker.

- Where bond yields are greater than around 6.75%, the stock market may suffer because yields are that much better in bonds.

- Where bond yields are less than 3.5%, the stock market may become stronger because bond yields are too low for an acceptable return.

Remember, everything doesn't work all the time—these are very rough and ready rules of thumb.

Supply and Demand

In economics, virtually everything ultimately boils down to supply and demand. Prices are a result of supply and demand. Many economic indicators are there to guide us so we can make a likely assessment of supply and demand in the overall economy. When you look at any sort of economic indicator, the trail you want to follow is the one that asks what effect there'll be on supply and demand.

For example, if unemployment is rising, how will this affect the economy? Well, with fewer people at work and companies cutting back on their workforce, it's likely that those people will have less money to spend. Those who are still working might not feel so secure in their jobs, so they will be more inclined to beef up their savings and cut back on spending. The result could be that demand for various goods and services like leisure and consumer goods (such as furniture) will decrease, meaning less revenue and less profit for companies in the consumer goods, leisure, and retailing sectors. What do you imagine would happen to stocks in those sectors? Of course, they'd be inclined to go down just merely at the whiff of a slowdown because more traders will sell the stocks in anticipation of inferior results in the future.

The Basic Rule of Supply and Demand

- *When demand outstrips supply, prices go up.* This can occur either because demand becomes rampant or supply becomes restricted or bottlenecked. If there is a bad harvest of oranges, then orange prices are bound to go up even if demand only remains static—because the equilibrium will have been shifted.

● *When demand drops relative to supply, prices go down.* Rarely do winter sales at the department stores include the most popular items of clothing! You usually just get those items which fall into the category of "inventory to clear" to make way for the newer trendier ranges. Again, it's the classic case of demand declining for the old stuff so the retailers sell it off cheaply, and that's why the best bargains can be found at the very end of the sales. Unfortunately those bargains are often the most hideous garments, and you have to be an odd shape to fit into them since only the extreme sizes are left. Still, the lessons of demand and supply are all around us!

● *When the relationship between demand and supply is steady, prices will be more or less steady.* This is one of the reasons why up to the end of 2000, the US economy has not suffered major inflation during the boom cycle. Supply managed to keep pace with the immense demand, say, for processing chips and other key computer components. The Chairman of the Federal Reserve, Alan Greenspan was constantly referring to this phenomenon during his many speeches during 2000. And while many people had misgivings over his tough stance with regard to interest rates, history shows that he was both prudent in this stance and observant of the basic laws of supply and demand in the US economy. It's easy to forget now that slack monetary policy in various Western economies in the late 1980s led to soaring demand, inflation, and then recession in the early 1990s.

Nasdaq Level II traders can see the laws of supply and demand on their screens as they trade. Do you think being able to interpret a Level II screen would help you intra-day trade a stock? You bet it would—because not only would you be able to see how many buyers and sellers there are at the various price levels, but you'd also get to see WHO they are too! Nasdaq Level II trading is a serious business and one that is worthwhile for any of you who is serious about trading in general.

Take care in your interpretation of "rules" in the marketplace. Many myths are created and can be proliferated and even accepted by the masses even when they are simple to disprove. A popular myth is that the real estate market performs well with high inflation or is a good hedge against inflation. This simply is not the case. A more in-depth study into the real facts shows conclusively that the statement is a dangerous myth, yet it's widely believed to be true. It's not within the scope of this book to give a complete explanation of how and why, but it is worth noting that during the higher inflationary periods of the early 1980s and early 1990s, real estate values suffered drastically while the stock markets in the USA and UK did not suffer nearly as badly. Not my idea of a good hedge. The fact is that there were many other factors involved that can be simply explained. But the point is that sweeping generalizations are myriad in the financial markets, and many of them are misleading and dangerous.

Avoid Forecasting—Learn to Recognize What's Happening

Many people will try to see what they want to see and not necessarily what is actually going on. Don't fall into that trap. Pay attention to what is going on, be aware of indicators that suggest things may change, but do not get into forecasting. The greatest investor of them all, Warren Buffett, has a wonderful saying, *"Forecasting tells you much about the forecaster and nothing about the future!"*

If the year 2000 told you anything, it should have told you that there is no such thing as a "new economy." If you still believe in a so-called new economy and new fancy ways of valuing companies, please read the book, *Extraordinary Popular Delusions and the Madness of Crowds* (Mackay, 1980), and you'll see that hype has existed long before our current new economy, all the previous new economies before that and will continue to exist well into future new economies! Ultimately, company values will depend on their financial performance in the long term. Sure, there are wild short-term swings and great opportunities in the short term. Sure, there were some amazing opportunities during the early part of 2000. I participated in a couple of rockets myself. But eventually when the market woke up to its senses, guess what happened to the stock prices of those false pretenders? Collapsed right back down to more sensible levels, in fact, a number of them had a sensible level of a few cents, and that's where they went back to, having been over $100 at one point![*]

> **Hype has existed long before our current new economy, all the previous new economies before that and will continue to exist well into future new economies!**

---

[*]Some commentators refer to the modern approach of valuing intangible assets within more service-orientated companies as a phenomenon of the new economy. In this context, the term "new economy" is valid since in the past, companies with a balance sheet bias toward intangible assets were often undervalued. This was in part due to a lack of consistency and understanding of how to standardize the valuation of those intangible assets.

The markets are certainly affected by events in the wider economy, such as those listed here and others, such as oil prices (a major influence on inflation) and government announcements, which can lead to short-term panic buying, selling, or both! Be aware of these news items and their impact on short-term volatility swings. Markets in general have major personality disorders, and one of our jobs is to make sense of it and stick to our principles, whatever they may be. In *The Intelligent Investor* (1973), Benjamin Graham, one of the legendary investors and inspiration of Warren Buffett, refers to "Mr. Market" being your business partner who gives you prices at which he'll buy and sell your stocks. Being something of a "manic depressive" Mr. Market often has wild mood swings and will change his mind on prices in just a matter of seconds. The point is that it doesn't affect the Intrinsic Value of the stock, and it shouldn't sway your opinion of it either if you are a long-term investor. Short-term traders simply don't care about intrinsic values of shares and will pay far more attention to the Technical Analysis Indicators (Chapter 4, "The Basics of Technical Analysis"). And for that type of trading, that outlook is fine. Ultimately you'll have to decide for yourself what kind of trading or investing you're most suited to.

Market Direction

If you get nothing else out of this book, do get this: Learn to recognize which prevailing direction (if any) the market is moving in, but never try to predict it. Anticipation and recognition are different from making a prediction. There are now several useful tools and software products to help you recognize the prevailing market direction. In the next chapter, we discuss Technical Analysis, which will assist you in finding chart patterns and indicators to help you determine market trends and movements.[1] A simple rule is to buy the safest stocks and long-term bullish options strategies when the market is going up and to sell the worst stocks (ones that don't make money and don't look likely to) when the market is going down. Why fight the tide? It simply doesn't make sense, so don't do it. You can sleep a lot better at night as a result, and you don't even have to bother to try to forecast anything if you're going by fundamentals in this way.

---

[1] Chapter 4 is specifically designed to simply enhance your awareness of *Technical Analysis*. It does not go into such depth as to discuss preferred settings or preferred indicators.

Corporate Fundamentals

When we invest in a company, we invest in its potential to make more products, more profits, to continue to grow, and add value to the price of each individual share.

A share of stock represents one unit of ownership in that company. All shares of that stock in circulation, multiplied by its value per share (share price) make up the market's estimate of the value of that company—that is, the *market capitalization*.

The more profits a company makes and the faster those profits are growing and are projected to grow, the higher the company's value IN THE LONGER TERM at least. History tells us that consistent growth in sales and earnings lead to a higher stock price in the longer term...and vice versa.

Earnings (per share) Growth—The Driver for Higher Stock Prices

This is what the market looks for in great companies. Not just earnings (profits), but earnings that are growing quarter on quarter, year on year. If you're looking for the best companies, then you can simply base your search criteria on this. However, there is one word of caution. Ensure that the overall earnings growth is reflected in the *earnings per share (EPS)*. After all, you are looking to buy and sell shares, not the entire company. The significance of this is that companies can change their share structures as a result of takeovers, mergers, large acquisitions and scrip (bonus) issues. This can lead to a dilution in shares, that is, there could be more shares in circulation, meaning that if increased profits have to be divided by an increased number of shares, the profit per share may not increase that much or at all, even if the company has increased its profit overall.

> Ensure that the overall earnings growth is reflected in the earnings per share (EPS). After all, you are looking to buy and sell shares, not the entire company.

Remember, all you own are the shares, and each share is a unit of ownership. If there are suddenly more units of ownership, then your own single unit of ownership declines as a percentage of total ownership in the company if the overall earnings or value remain constant.

Example 3.1 Impact of Share Dilution (Rights Issue Example)

Takeoverco Inc. has 10 million shares outstanding. Each share is priced at $50.00. Last year's profits were $25 million. You buy 1,000 shares of Takeoverco Inc. at $50.00 per share.

- The market capitalization (market value) of Takeoverco Inc. is: $50 × 10 million = $500 million.

- The current value of your holding in Takeoverco Inc. is therefore: $50 × 1,000 = $50,000.

- The percentage ownership stake you have in the company is 1,000/10,000,000 = 0.01%.

- Earnings per share (EPS) is $25 million divided by 10 million shares = $2.50 per share.

- The price/earnings ratio (PE ratio) is the price of the stock divided by the EPS. Therefore the PE ratio = $50/$2.50 = 20 times.

- The PE ratio represents the number of years the company will have to make the same amount of profits in order to equal the current share price. The higher the PE ratio, the higher the stock is rated by investors.

Takeoverco Inc. wants to buy a smaller company called Targetco Inc. To do this, it needs to raise $100 million. To raise the $100 million, Takeoverco will issue 2.5 million shares at a discounted price of $40.00 per share. (*Rights issues are usually made at a discount to current value; however, we have simplified and exaggerated the numbers here for illustration purposes.*)

There are now 12.5 million shares outstanding in Takeoverco. You still have 1,000 shares (assuming you don't take up your pre-emption rights). The newly merged company posts results of $30 million in profits. Let's assume that the PE ratio is still the same at 20 times. This means that the overall company value (market capitalization) is now $30 million × 20 = $600 million.

- So now the share price of Takeoverco is $600 million/12.5 million = $48.00.

- The current value of your holding is now $48.00 × 1,000 = $48,000. This is 4% below your entry price of $50.00.

- The percentage ownership stake you have in the company is now 1,000/12,500,000 = 0.008%, which is 25% less than you had before.

This isn't great news so far! Your percentage ownership in the company has been reduced, as has the value of your shares, even though the company's market value has increased. So, let's look at Earnings per Share:

Post-merger earnings are $30 million, and we divide this by the number of new shares outstanding (12.5 million).

EPS = $30 million/12.5 million = $2.40

When you originally bought the shares, you bought them with an EPS of $2.50. Even though the company is now making more profits overall, the company has actually decreased shareholder value because in making that extra $5 million profit, it has diluted existing shareholders by a greater degree, and therefore EPS has declined.

The next few paragraphs outline the full implications of a rights issue. If you want to skip it, proceed to the heading below entitled, "Key Financial Terms."

We didn't include the fact that in a rights issue, the stockholder would either be able to pay for new shares at the discounted rate of $40.00 per share or would have received a payment instead.

Even if you did take up your rights, this would have been the scenario:
You owned 0.01% of the company's shares, thereby entitling you to rights over 0.01% of the new shares.

0.01% × 2,500,000 = 250

You can buy 250 new shares at $40.00, so you would spend another $10,000 on top of the original $50,000.

Your average cost of entry is now: $60,000/1,250 = $48.00.

Your shares are worth $48.00 each now. So you have made no loss, although the EPS is lower. Remember they are worth $48.00 because the company value in the market is $600 million, and there are 12.5 million shares post merger.

If you'd taken cash instead of taking up your rights then, provided that the share price on the share issue date is greater than the issue price ($40.00), you'd receive a cash payment. The cash payment is based on the following calculation:

(Issue date share price − Issue price) × (Number of shares you own at the record date)

So, if the share price on the issue date is at or below $40.00, you'll receive no payment at all, and you'd suffer from the dilution effect as outlined previously.

Let's assume the markets have been a little unsteady and the share price has fallen to, say, only $42.00 on the issue date, then you would receive the following:

● **Calculation to evaluate the ex-rights price**
Remember, this is a 1 for 4 rights issue

$$\frac{\text{(Issue date share price x No. of shares you already own)} + \text{(Issue price x No. of new shares)}}{\text{Combined no. of shares}} = \text{Ex rights price of share}$$

$$\frac{(\$42.00 \times 4) + (\$40.00 \times 1)}{5} = \$41.60$$

- **Calculation to evaluate the value per right that you own**
  $42.00 – $41.60 = $0.40

- **Calculation to evaluate the expected payment for not taking up your rights in the rights issue**

$0.40 × 1,000 (shares you owned originally) = $400.

So if you didn't take up your rights and the share price on issue date was $42.00, you would receive a check for $400. Hardly enough to compensate for the loss in shareholder value you are suffering in this scenario where the share price has fallen.

This example is a little extreme and is included to demonstrate the significance of Earnings per Share, as opposed to straight earnings. You must be aware of how companies can raise their money for acquisitions so that you can fairly assess whether they are going to enhance shareholder value. When assessing the growth of a company, you must look at the growth in EPS.

Key Financial Terms

Term	Description and Definition	Comments and Significance
Balance Sheet	The statement of the company's assets and liabilities at a given "snapshot" in time. It is prepared with the Income Statement and Cash Flow Statement.	This is the part of the company's quarterly, half yearly, and annual results that shows you the company's health in terms of assets and liabilities. The company may have increased profits, but has it achieved this by increasing its financial leverage (i.e. more borrowings), and are these borrowings at a healthy level?
Cash Flow	This is net earnings before depreciation, amortization, and non-cash charges. Cash Flow is calculated by adding depreciation to net earnings and subtracting preference share dividends. Cash Flow is one of the ultimate ways of determining the health of a company.	A profitable company can still go bust. Why? Because it isn't generating enough cash. Young companies often have negative cash flows. Just look at a selection of Internet companies for examples. Many of these companies aren't even profitable and will never be, let alone their ability to generate cash. Remember that a company needs CASH to pay its bills. If it cannot pay its bills, it will go bust. Cash Flow is an extremely important figure, but as with all of these figures, don't just look at it in isolation.

Term	Description and Definition	Comments and Significance
		You need to check it with some of the other figures. For example, a new start-up with negative cash flow may look very unhealthy on the surface. But you might find that it has millions tucked away in cash and cash equivalents. Many of the Internet start-ups have survived in this way up to now, even in spite of their weak business models. It was only a matter of time for many of them!
Cash Flow Statement	Shows the cash position of the company.	Remember we distinguished between profitability and liquidity. Cash Flow is influenced not only by revenues and expenses, but also by the company's operating, investment, and financing decisions.
Current Assets	These are assets that can be easily converted to cash within 12 months. Current Assets include cash, marketable securities, debtors, (accounts receivable) and inventory (stocks, UK translation).	Current Assets are another measure of the immediate health of a company. A healthy sign is where Current Assets exceed Current Liabilities, since this demonstrates the company's ability to pay its bills.
Current Liabilities	These are obligations that must be paid by the company within 12 months. These include short-term creditors (Accounts Payable), short-term debt, principal and interest on long-term debt.	
Deferred Taxes	Deferred Taxes arise when a company makes provision for future (deferred) tax liabilities. Such provision is necessary because of timing differences between accounting profits and taxable profits. An example of a timing difference includes losses carried forward, in which case these would be stated as a deferred tax asset.	
Depreciation	An accounting term and non-cash charge imposed on companies to reflect the reduction in value of their fixed assets (that is, properties, computer	Depreciation is purely an accounting phenomenon. Assets are depreciated every year according to the Depreciation policy of the individual company. The

Term	Description and Definition	Comments and Significance
	equipment, plant, and machinery) in a designated fashion.	problem is that Depreciation is subtracted from profits, so a company that relies heavily on investment into Fixed Assets (with the exception of real estate assets, which may be reassessed to market value) can suffer diminution of profits because of high Depreciation charges. This is why it is important to look at the Cash Flow.
Dividends	The cash payment made by the company per ordinary share periodically during the year. In the UK this is often twice per annum, and in the USA each quarter.	Dividends constitute the element of profit that the company does not reinvest back into itself. Dividends can be considered a reward to the ordinary shareholders for the risk they take in holding common stock. Shareholders will pay income tax with respect to their dividend income.
Earnings per Share (EPS)	Total earnings divided by the number of outstanding common shares (issued ordinary share capital).	As mentioned earlier, from a shareholder's perspective, this is more important than the overall earnings figure.
EBITDA (or Operating Cash Flow)	Earnings before interest, taxes, depreciation, and amortization.	EBITDA is calculated by subtracting cost of sales and operating expenses from revenues. It can be a useful indicator in highlighting Cash Flow for companies with large investment projects where depreciation and amortization have dented the earnings figures.
Free Cash Flow	This is cash not required for operations or for reinvestment. Free cash flow is calculated by subtracting capital expenditure (capex) from cash flow. Capex includes investment in new plant and machinery, property, and equipment.	Free Cash Flow can be used to pay dividends, pay off debt, or buy back stock. In some cases it can be used for a takeover war chest, although many fund managers have misgivings over this and would rather that Free Cash Flow be utilized for dividends or stock repurchases.
Income Statement (Profit and Loss Account)	This is the company's Earnings or Profits Statement within its quarterly, half yearly, and annual reports.	This is the earnings report analysts and investors pay most attention to when evaluating the attractiveness of the stock.

Term	Description and Definition	Comments and Significance
Interest Cover	Measures the company's ability to pay its interest charges on its debt. Calculated by dividing net earnings before interest and taxes by the interest expense on all long-term debt.	Look for high Interest Cover since this will demonstrate that the company will be able to easily cover its interest payments. Failure to pay its debt-interest obligations could result in the company's creditors calling in their loans and winding up the company.
Inventory (Stocks, UK translation)	The value of the company's raw materials, work in progress, and finished goods.	Inventory cannot really be judged in isolation. You really need to compare current figures with those of the past to see if any trends are forming. High inventory could suggest that goods are not being sold fast enough. Low inventory could either indicate faster sales growth or production difficulties.
Long-term Liabilities	Debt that is expected to be repaid after 12 months from the last balance sheet date.	Long-term debt can include simple bank debt, mortgages, or bonds.
Market Capitalization (market value)	The value of the company, as determined by the market at any given moment in time. This fluctuates with the price of the stock.	Market cap is calculated as follows: No. of Shares x Share Price
Minority Interest	The part of a subsidiary company's shareholders' funds that is not owned by the parent company. This is usually shown as a separate item on the consolidated balance sheet.	
Net Earnings (Net Profit)	The company's revenues less all expenses including depreciation, taxes, and amortization.	"Earnings" is principally an accounting figure because of the non-cash inclusions within its calculation. This is why we also rely on EBITDA.
Net EPS	Net earnings divided by the number of shares of common stock. The number of shares is adjusted to reflect the conversion into equity of all securities which potentially can be converted, hence dilute the shareholding.	Net EPS increases the number of shares to reflect the possibility of share dilution (described earlier) as contained within the company's capital structure. Therefore, all employee company stock options are assumed to be fully converted into equity, as are any convertible loans, bonds, and so on.

Term	Description and Definition	Comments and Significance
Ordinary Shares/Common Stock	These are the shares that make up the market value of the company. These shares typically have equal voting rights and are the main source of equity finance for corporations. These are the shares that you see traded on the NYSE or Nasdaq or LSE. Some companies pay a dividend with respect to each ordinary share.	The number of ordinary shares multiplied by the value per share equals the market capitalization of the company. Ordinary shareholders are at the bottom of the pecking order if the company folds. Ordinary shares carry with them more risk, but also more potential reward.
Preference Shares	These shares are issued by corporations for cash, and have preferential rights over ordinary shares. This means that in the event of the company liquidating, the preference shareholders will be in front of ordinary shareholders in the pecking order.	Preference shares are redeemable by the company at par either at the holder's or company's option. The company issues them and pays a fixed rate of return on them until redemption. The return is lower than for ordinary shareholders as is the risk. Preference shares act far more like bonds or debt instruments and as such many people believe they should be considered as debt, not equity.
Revenues (Turnover)	Includes all net sales and turnover of the company, which form part of the main operations of the company.	Revenues do not include dividends paid to the company, interest payments due to the company or any non-operating income.
Share Price	The value of each individual share of a company, as determined by the market at any given moment in time.	
Share Split	This is where a company decides to increase the number of shares in order to enhance the liquidity of the shares for its investors. The net effect is that investors will end up with more shares, although the share price will obviously be revalued downward to take this into account. All in all, the net effect is theoretically zero difference, but the market generally takes a positive view on stock splits, and often the shares will increase in value prior to the actual split date.	Typically, share splits are a sign of confidence by the company. A share split is often interpreted as reward for investors, and in a bull market it is commonplace to see the shares rise in price from the date of the announcement up to the point of the split itself.

Term	Description and Definition	Comments and Significance
Shareholders' Equity (Shareholders' Funds)	This is the balanced figure on the balance sheet, signifying the Book Value of the company for the ordinary shareholders (common stock holders).	Used in calculating the gearing ratio, this will be the same as the figure for Net Assets.
Net Assets	This is the company's total assets less its total liabilities, also known as book value.	This figure should be positive! Shareholders' Equity represents the shareholders' ownership of the company in terms of its Book Value.
Shares Outstanding (Issued Share Capital)	These are the shares that are currently owned by investors.	A company may have more shares than those that are already owned, and these form part of the company's authorized share capital. Only issued shares (outstanding shares) form part of the company's market value, and it is only the outstanding shares that we use in calculating the key financial ratios.
Total Assets	Total Assets include all short-term (current) assets (that is, cash, debtors, readily convertible securities) and fixed assets (property, plant and machinery, and investments).	Needs to be compared against itself over previous years and against liabilities for a meaningful insight to be made.
Total Liabilities	Include all short-term (current) liabilities (short-term creditors, overdrafts) and long-term debt and deferred taxes.	Needs to be compared against itself over previous years and against assets for a meaningful insight to be made.
Total Return	The stock price change plus dividends over a period of time.	Obviously we want this to be high. We would compare this figure against the market and against the stock's past performance.

Key Financial Figures and Ratios

If you really like to invest based on fundamental analysis, I would recommend you try out software applications, such as *Vector Vest* or *ValueLine*, which provide not only all the fundamental analysis for you, but also include automated searches and filters for the Fundamental Analysis of stocks. Let's have a look at the most important figures you'll see when analyzing a company and what the best search criteria are.

Figure	Calculation	Comments and Significance
Beta	Beta measures the relationship of a stock's returns relative to the market in general (S&P 500 in the USA). With par set at one, anything at a Beta of 1 indicates that the stock will move in the same direction as the market and at the same rate. If a stock has a Beta of 1.2, it will move in the same direction as the market but where the market moves by, say 10%, the stock will move by 12% (10% plus another 2%) in the same direction. If a stock has a negative Beta, this means that it moves in the opposite direction to the market. −1 indicates that the stock will move at the same speed as the market but in the opposite direction.	If you want to trade the market as it goes up and down, then Beta is a useful figure for you. If the market is rising, pick top quality stocks with a high positive Beta. If the market is falling, you can sell short the worst stocks with a high Beta. Beta is a useful addition to any search criteria once you are comfortable with the prevailing direction of the market.
Current Ratio	$$\frac{\text{Current Assets}}{\text{Creditors due within 12 Months}}$$	The Current Ratio is a measure of the company's liquidity, and its ability to pay its immediate debts. Again, you want this figure to be high. A figure below one would indicate that the company doesn't have the liquid funds to pay its obligations. Look for some safety margin in this area.
Dividend Cover	$$\frac{\text{Earnings per Share}}{\text{Net Dividend per Share}}$$	As with Interest Cover, if you're interested in dividends, then look for companies with sufficient dividend cover, to ensure that the dividends will continue. There is often a trade-off between dividend yield and dividend cover. Obviously where there is high dividend cover (and therefore a safer dividend), the dividend yield may be lower because the PE ratio (hence share price) may be higher, thus lowering the dividend yield.

Figure	Calculation	Comments and significance
Dividend Yield	$$\frac{\text{Dividend per Share}}{\text{Price per Share}}$$	Many US stocks pay low or no dividends. In the UK, many investors hold stocks purely for the dividends. Look for consistency in the company's dividend policy and for dividends to rise steadily over time. Companies with wildly fluctuating (up and down) dividends year after year are those that suggest poor management.
Earnings per Share (EPS)	$$\frac{\text{Net Earnings}}{\text{Number of Ordinary Shares}}$$	
Estimated EPS Growth	This is the average estimate of EPS growth for the indicated period, as derived from all polled estimates from Wall Street or City analysts.	The thing to watch out for here is if actual results exceed beyond or lag behind analysts' expectations. Look for companies that consistently exceed analysts' expectations—Microsoft did this consistently up until 2000.
Financial Gearing or Leverage	(Interest Bearing Loans + Preference Shares/Ordinary Shareholders' Funds) Interest bearing loans will include all long and short-term debt obligations including bonds, notes payable, mortgages, and lease obligations. "Ordinary shareholders" funds' effectively shows the funds provided to the company by its common stockholders. The Shareholders' Funds figure comes from the balance sheet. This figure will incorporate common equity, long-term debt, deferred taxes, and minority interests. The ratio indicates how much financial leverage or gearing the company has.	This is a juggling act for the company. Generally you don't want to see it gearing too high, and it really does depend on the sector and type of business the company operates within. Sectors differ as to commonly acceptable gearing ratios. Beware of companies whose gearing is significantly higher than their competitors. High gearing generally means higher risk because if the company defaults on a loan, it could spell disaster if the creditor calls it in.
Forward P/E	$$\frac{\text{Latest Closing Price of the Stock}}{\text{Latest EPS Estimates as derived from all polled estimates from Wall Street or City analysts}}$$	This is based on a prediction of earnings.

Figure	Calculation	Comments and Significance
Interest Cover	$$\frac{\text{Profit Before Interest and Taxes}}{\text{Interest Payable}}$$	Highlights the company's ability to pay its interest obligations. The higher the figure, the safer the company is. I would look for at least three times interest cover.
Net Assets per Share (Book Value per Share)	$$\frac{\text{Ordinary Shareholders Funds}}{\text{Number of Ordinary Outstanding Shares}}$$	Shows the Book Value per share. If the share price is lower than the book value per share, either the stock is a complete dud, or it is undervalued.
Payout Ratio	$$\frac{\text{Dividend}}{\text{EPS}}$$	The payout ratio is a useful way of looking at how much a company is reinvesting in itself. High-growth companies tend not to pay dividends because they are constantly reinvesting for future growth. Mature companies, such as Phillip Morris, will pay a dividend, but you need to make sure that they are also reinvesting adequately. Property companies and REITs (Real Estate Investment Trusts in the USA) tend to pay higher dividends than most; REITs are compelled to pay out a high percentage of their net revenues as dividends or face punitive tax measures.
PEG Ratio	$$\frac{\text{Forward PE}}{\text{Projected EPS Growth Rate}}$$	A popular ratio made famous by the Beardstown Ladies Investment Club. The PEG Ratio is often used to spot undervalued or overvalued stocks. If a company has high growth prospects but a PEG Ratio of less than one, then this company could be thought of as being undervalued. A PEG Ratio of less than one means that the forward multiplier (PE ratio) is less than the projected growth of the company. Many investors look for PEGs of less than one in the search for undervalued or good value stocks.

Figure	Calculation	Comments and significance
Price/Book Value	$$\frac{\text{Stock's Latest Closing Price}}{\text{Book Value per Share}}$$	If a stock price is less than the Book Value per share, the stock is described as being at a "discount to Net Asset Value." Either this can mean that the company is undervalued (because the company could be liquidated for more than its market capitalization), or it can mean that the company is in really bad shape, hence its poor rating and stock price.
Price/Cash Flow	$$\frac{\text{Stock's Latest Closing Price}}{\substack{\text{Cash Flow per Share for Latest} \\ \text{Year's Results}}}$$	All figures incorporating elements of cash flow are useful for investors. Look to see that the company is generating cash consistently over time. If there is a sudden change, check the news to see if the company has a major investment drive going on or some changes in its investment strategy that may have affected its cash flow.
Price/Sales	$$\frac{\text{Stock's Latest Closing Price}}{\text{Revenue per Share}}$$	Useful for cross-comparing companies that have made earnings with those that haven't.
Price Earnings (P/E) Ratio	$$\frac{\text{Stock Price}}{\text{Earnings per Share}}$$ The same end figure can be reached by the following calculation: $$\frac{\text{Market Capitalization}}{\text{Net Earnings}}$$	Signifying the market's rating of the company, the PE ratio is a multiplier of the company's earnings to evaluate its value in the marketplace. As with all these figures and ratios, you shouldn't look at the PE ratio in isolation. Instead, compare it with past price data on the stock and with the stock's competitors within its industry sector. A low PE ratio signifies a low rating by the market; this can either mean the stock is fundamentally weak or that it is undervalued. A high PE ratio can either mean the company is fundamentally strong or that the company is overvalued. To assess what is the reality, analysts look at other facts, figures, and ratios as well.

Figure	Calculation	Comments and Significance
Quick Ratio (Liquid Ratio)	$$\frac{\text{Current Assets-Inventory}}{\text{Creditors due within 12 Months}}$$	A more examining test of a company's liquidity, the Quick Ratio facilitates easier comparison between companies because they might take on different valuation approaches for inventories.
Return on Assets (ROA)	$$\frac{\text{Latest full year's Net Income}}{\text{Total Assets}}$$	The percentage rate of return on all the company's assets.
(Return on Capital Employed (ROCE))		Unlike ROE (return on equity), ROA does not net off the company's liabilities and is a measure of how effectively a company is investing its money.
Return on Equity (ROE)	$$\frac{\text{Latest full year's Net Income}}{\text{Shareholders Funds (Equity)}}$$	ROE is a measure of how effectively a company is using its investors' money.
Five-year EPS Growth Rate	The five-year annualized growth rate of Earnings per Share.	Good for measuring EPS growth over a period of time. This figure takes into account management's track record of adding to shareholder value and, as such, is a useful pointer to the future. Use in conjunction with five-year sales growth to ensure that the growth in EPS is attributable to increasing revenues, and not simply management using corporate and accounting policies and financing techniques to bolster EPS. Such techniques may be totally legitimate and useful, but a company's long-term performance will be partially based on its ability to produce quality products and services of which it can continue to sell more. An example of a method used to enhance shareholder value includes share buybacks where the company buys back some of the shares, which reduces the float and therefore increases EPS because there are fewer shares now to divide into the Earnings figure.

Figure	Calculation	Comments and Significance
		Similarly, a company might be able to enhance EPS by cutting down its expenses and making mass redundancies. Efficiency is to be applauded, but you must ask the question: how is it improving sales revenue in the longer term?
Five-year Sales Growth	The five-year annualized growth rate of Sales or Revenues.	This figure demonstrates that the company has a compelling product or set of products and services that are being bought by its customers in increasing amounts. Sales growth can occur as a result of increasing sales units and/or increased unit prices. Think about the markets to which the company already sells its products and services and whether it can expand into new markets, both geographically and in terms of business sector.

Search Criteria and Screening Filters for Fundamentals

So how can you put this all together to execute a simple-to-use filter to find good stocks to buy (or buy calls or use bullish options strategies) or bad stocks to sell short (or buy puts or use bearish options strategies)?

Here are some examples of useful filters—you can alter the figures if the searches aren't picking up enough stocks or if they're picking up too many:

Criteria		Value	Comments
Five-year Sales growth	>=	20%	Our rationale here is to find low risk stocks that have high sales and earnings growth rates. Notice how the filter refers to EPS as opposed to earnings. This ensures that any stock dilutions are accounted for and that we are purely concentrating on shareholder value.
Five-year EPS growth	>=	20%	
Projected EPS growth	>=	20%	
Debt as a % of Capital	<=	33%	

Criteria		Value	Comments
Five-year EPS growth	>=	10%	Here, our aim is to pick out high market value stocks that combine safety (low gearing) with solid past growth and increasing future growth prospects. With sales of over $6 billion p.a., we're really looking at market leaders on a global basis, so this filter is likely to catch the worldwide industry leaders.
Projected EPS growth	>=	12%	
Past 12 months' Sales Revenue	>=	$6 billion	
Market Capitalization	>=	$10 billion	
Debt as a % of Capital	<=	50%	

Criteria		Value	Comments
Five-year EPS growth	>=	10%	A slightly riskier strategy, here we're looking for the likely future high fliers, although we have stipulated a five-year EPS growth rate. We've made no specifications for financial gearing or for the particular size of company, so this filter may uncover some hidden gems.
Projected EPS growth	>=	20%	

Here we're looking for undervalued stocks which haven't yet been detected by the wider market.

Criteria		Value	Comments
EPS growth	>=	15%	...preferably for the last 5 – 7 years.
Sales growth	>=	15%	...preferably for the last 5 – 7 years.
ROE	>=	15%	...for the last 5 years
Free Cash Flow			...growing every quarter for the last 5 years *
Market Capitalization			...around Book Value
PE Ratio	<	30	
Current EPS			...around 10% of current stock price

* We specify that Free Cash Flow has been growing every quarter for the last 5 years to ensure we're targeting stocks that are growing because of continuing operations, not from asset disposals.

Criteria		Value	Comments
Dividend Yield	>=	4.50%	Here, we're looking for high-dividend-paying stocks. This probably means we're looking at mature companies that have been around for some time and have parts of their business that are "cash cows," requiring little reinvestment to sustain sales. Notice that we haven't included growth in our criteria.
Dividend Payout	<	70%	
Debt as a % of capital	<	50%	

Remember, you can add the Beta criteria to these filters.

Common Sense and Being Alert

Some Examples

● Do you ever notice that a particular retailer's trucks are prolific on the roads, suggesting that the masses are ordering goods from them?

● Have you noticed a new product in everyone's homes? Like those massive digital clocks with temperature gauges and thermometers? Who makes those? Look on the back, find out who makes them, and then find out if the company is listed on the stock market or whether it is a subsidiary of another company which is listed on the stock market.

- What toys are in vogue with your kids? What are the latest crazes? Who makes those toys? Who has the marketing and distribution rights on those toys?

The common sense approach is one endorsed by the greatest investors such as Warren Buffett and Peter Lynch. Nowadays there's no excuse for not being able to find things out. The Internet has enabled each of us to become a modern day Sherlock Holmes when it comes to tracking down information. Research isn't half the pain it was only five years ago; you can simply plug in any criteria to a search engine and sure enough, a whole collection of answers will pop out in seconds.

Statistics show that 50% of a stock's movement is attributable to the overall market direction and 30% to its sector direction.

There is no substitute for common sense, and this applies to your trading as well as your alertness for selecting stocks. If you have a reliable indicator that tells you that the market is going down, does it make good sense to start picking stocks to buy? Well, some would argue that a good stock is a good stock is a good stock. This is partially true, but it's still not massively smart to buy into a sector that is in the midst of tumbling—the old expression of catching a falling knife springs to mind. For our purposes, don't try to be too clever. Wait for the sector to have fallen, and then join in the fun! Remember, you really don't want to get into predicting or forecasting. But you do want to be able to recognize which way the prevailing direction is and when it's changing. Many software products now have their own indicators that give a reasonably accurate measure of overall market direction.

Statistics show that 50% of a stock's movement is attributable to the overall market direction, and 30% of a stock's movement is attributable to its sector direction. Is it no wonder, therefore, that you greatly improve your odds of success if you can find a tool that shows you the overall market direction?

Ultimately we can all be right, even those doomsday merchants forever predicting Armageddon for all of us. However, it's timing that determines our profitability in the markets. We know that one way of improving our timing is to use indicators to show us the prevailing direction of the markets. The other way of improving our timing is to use Technical Analysis, the art of interpreting price charts....

Chapter 3 Major Learning Points

In this chapter you have learned:

- the key drivers of stock prices in the marketplace, including:
  - management's track record,
  - news and results,
  - market sentiment, and
  - market expectations.
- the key economic drivers including supply and demand.
- the key elements of corporate fundamentals.
- the key financial terms and their significance.
- the key financial ratios and their interpretations.
- how to set up simple but powerful screening filters to narrow down your search for great stocks to long or short.
- that common sense is vital for both your general awareness of opportunities but also for your trading itself.

Remember that there is a world of difference between investing and trading.

Fundamental Analysis is more relevant to *investors* because it involves taking a longer term approach to finding value in a company. Investors do not mind taking a longer-term approach because when they find a company they consider to be undervalued, they're happy to wait until it fulfills its price potential as reflected in the stock.

Traders, on the other hand, don't care about long-term values, and so Fundamentals are irrelevant to them. Traders are looking to take advantage of pricing patterns, short or medium term, and are much more sensitive to price swings because their time horizons are so much shorter. I would personally advocate some basic Technical Analysis techniques to investors as well as traders because there's nothing like making an investment for the right reasons but messing up the timing! You don't need to be a Technical Analysis guru to identify the obvious signs, so we're now going to identify them so that if you're more of an investor-type, you can confidently take a glance at the charts to make sure you're not making a bad mistake.

You are now ready to explore some basic Technical Analysis techniques that will enable you to improve your timing into and out of the markets before choosing from a myriad of powerful yet responsible options trading strategies....

chapter 4

The Basics of Technical Analysis

What is Technical Analysis? Essentially, it is chart reading. More specifically, it is the science (or art) of recognizing chart patterns and interpreting them to make buying and selling timing decisions and implementing a trading plan. Technical Analysis can help you not only make your decisions but make them more precisely, make them more disciplined, and can help you in managing your money more effectively.

Technical Analysis comes in two forms: Price Patterns and Indicators.

Many Technical Analysis protagonists believe that everything you need to know about a security can be seen by looking at the charts.

Technical Analysis comes in two forms:

- *Price Patterns*—these are simply visible patterns of what is happening to the price of the security.

- *Indicators*—these are mathematical algorithms that take all aspects of the price movement, including volume, and are put together to form all kinds of ratios and analysis by which future price movement may be guesstimated.

Three Ways to View Price Patterns

Price Patterns are simply the patterns of a security's price movements for a known timescale. There are three main ways of viewing price action for any period of time:

1. Simple line graphs

2. Bar graphs

3. Japanese Candlesticks

Chart 4.1.1 ● Simple daily line chart of NASDAQ (July 2000–January 2001).

TC2000®.com. Courtesy of Worden Brothers Inc.

In itself, this chart is fairly meaningless, although you can clearly see that the price has halved within just four months from the beginning of September 2000 to the beginning of January 2001. Just by looking at this simple chart, we can already see one of the most common chart patterns screaming out at us, indicating the possibility of a market fall. We'll revisit this particular chart during the course of this chapter.

With simple line graphs, the line is charted at the average between the high and low for each period of time (here the line will cross at the mean between the high and low for each day, given this is a daily chart).

A more useful chart would be to see the daily prices represented in such a way where we can see the high, low, open, and close for each day.

Chart 4.1.2 ● **Simple daily open bar chart of NASDAQ (July 2000–January 2001).**

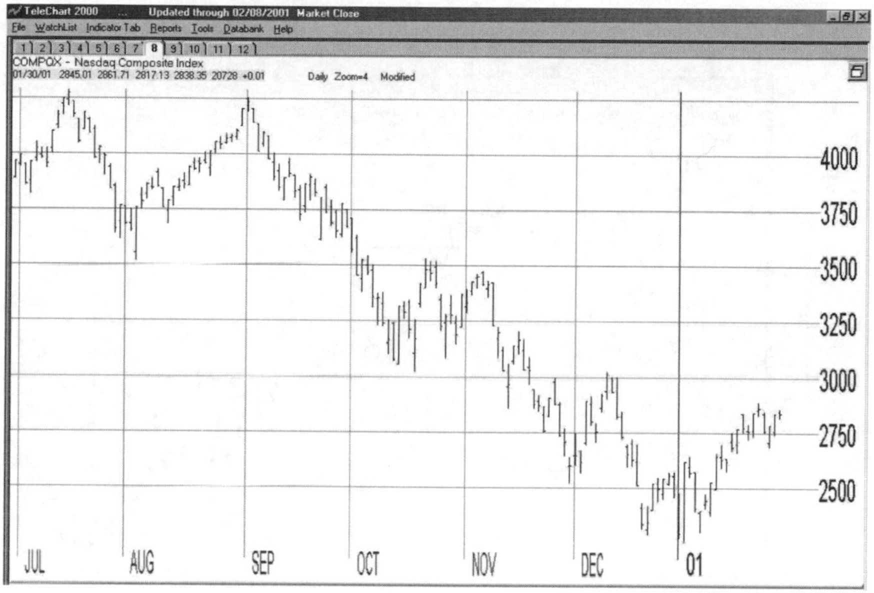

TC2000®.com. Courtesy of Worden Brothers Inc.

Notice how each period (a day in this instance) is represented by a vertical bar. Also notice how each bar has a small horizontal line to the left and one to the right. These lines signify the opening and closing prices for the NASDAQ for each day. The tops and bottoms of each vertical line represent the high and low prices reached on the particular day.

Diagram 4.1.1 ● **Simple open bar.**

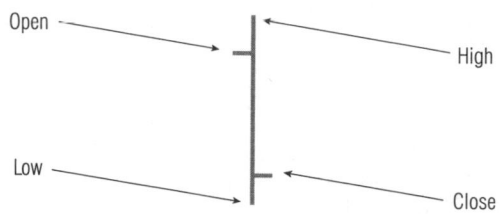

A clearer way of depicting price action for each period is by using Japanese candlesticks:

Chart 4.1.3 ● Japanese candlesticks chart of NASDAQ (July 2000–January 2001).

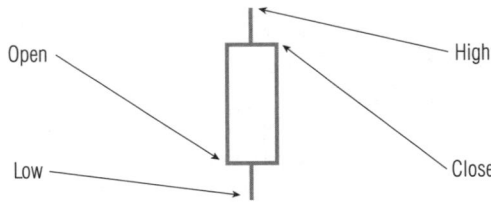

TC2000®.com. Courtesy of Worden Brothers Inc.

Here's how Japanese candlesticks work:

Diagram 4.1.2 ● Up candlestick.

- The up candlestick has a hollow body.
- The body represents the opening and the closing price of that period.
- With an up candlestick, obviously the closing price will be higher than the opening price.

Diagram 4.1.3 ● Down candlestick.

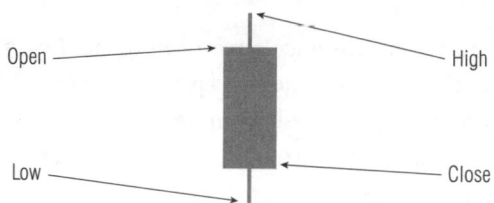

- The down candlestick has a filled body.
- The body represents the opening and the closing price of that period.
- With a down candlestick, obviously the closing price will be lower than the opening price.

Basic Chart Patterns

Here we are going to go through the standard chart patterns you need to become familiar with as you become a more accomplished trader. Some people take the view that Fundamental and Technical Analysis are mutually exclusive and incompatible. This is simply not the case. A far more balanced view is that while Fundamental Analysis is more reliable for the long-term health of a company, Technical Analysis can complement this and augment your shorter-term trading aspirations. You should get into the habit of looking at charts as well as doing your fast screenings for fundamentals.

There are two basic types of chart pattern, momentum (breakouts) where the security is gathering momentum and is likely to move further in that direction, and exhaustion (reversal) where we can see that the move is coming to an end. We outline some of the more instantly recognizable chart patterns for you now.

Support and Resistance

Most traders and investors use support and resistance. It is the simplest of patterns to understand and the easiest to identify just by glancing at the charts.

- Support is where the price finds a base off of which it bounces upward.

● Resistance is where the price finds a ceiling off of which it bounces downward.

Where clear lines of support and resistance have been formed by a stock price's activity, the psychology of these levels comes into play. Traders will become wary around the resistance level and sell, while becoming more enthusiastic when the stock hits support. If the stock breaks through these levels, then the pattern has changed and new rules come into play.

It is difficult to identify when support or resistance is going to hold or be breached, and we don't want to get into forecasting anyway. The best way to view support and resistance is to be prudent with your stops. Give yourself some leeway because the levels are rarely absolutely precise.

For example, if you bought a stock at its support level with the intention of selling it at its resistance level, at least allow it to test the resistance level before selling. If the stock breaks upward through the resistance level, you can let your profits run and can then make the resistance line your new support line. Often what happens is that when support and resistance lines are broken, they then form the opposite of what they were before, that is, Old support becomes New resistance and Old resistance becomes New support. This occurs as a result of pain being experienced by traders at these price regions, and people remember the pain they've experienced before. See Chart 4.2.2 for a perfect illustration of this.

Chart 4.1.4 ● Support and resistance (Fannie Mae January–June 1999).

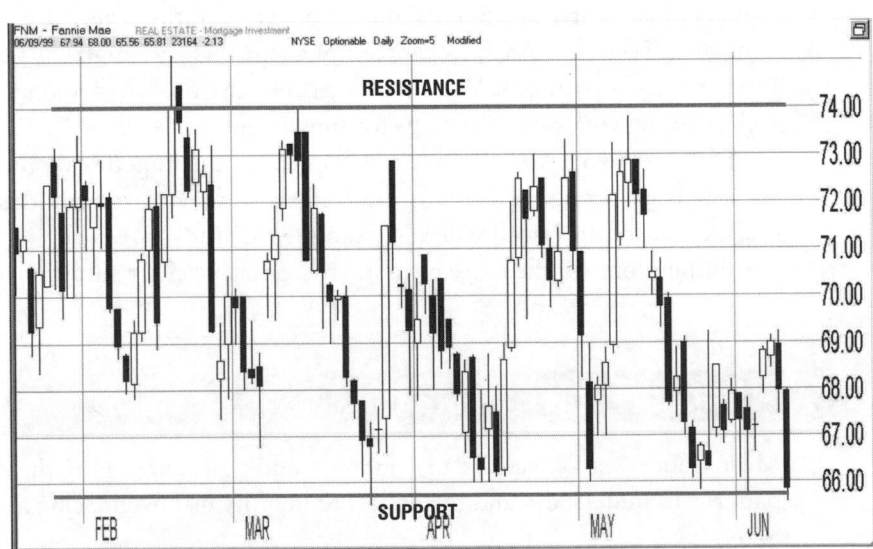

TC2000®.com. Courtesy of Worden Brothers Inc.

Chart 4.1.5 ● Support broken (Fannie Mae June 1999).

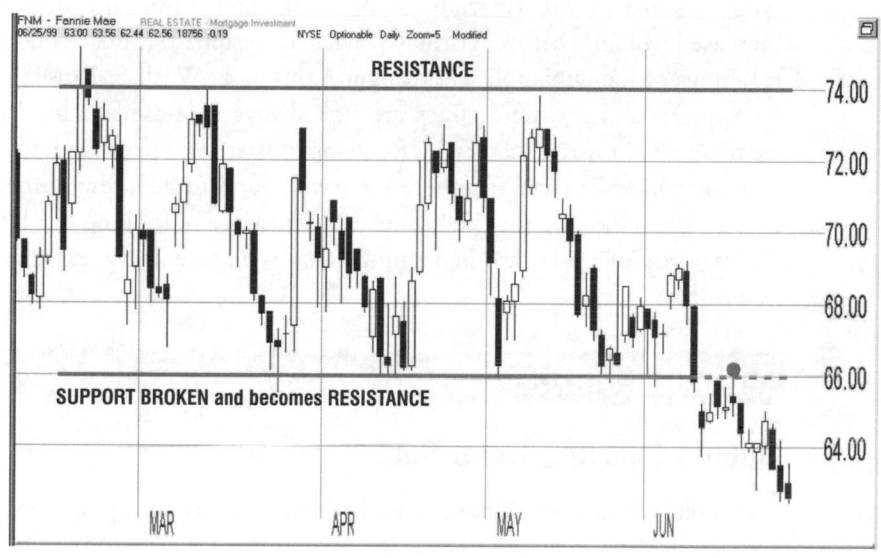

TC2000®.com. Courtesy of Worden Brothers Inc.

Fakes

Be aware that Technical Analysis is not what you'd call an exact science. In practical terms, this means don't get too hooked up on precision. You'll notice from the previous charts that the support and resistance lines are those that are best fitting the areas of support and resistance, and we're not talking about perfection here.

A Fake occurs where:

● the bottom is broken and then springs back up, or

● the top is broken and then falls back down.

Different stocks have different "personalities" and fake in different ways. As you get to know a few stocks intimately, you'll become accustomed to spotting how they fake, and you can then adjust your positions appropriately.

Fakes can occur where specialists and market makers identify extraordinary levels of interest around a support or resistance area and deliberately drive the price beyond that area to secure an advantageous position. For example, a stock is falling down to a known support level where there are lots of sell stop orders. Seeing this, the specialists work the price lower so that those stops are triggered. In the mayhem of all this automated selling action, the specialists are busy buying as much as they can, soon driving the stock price upward and securing a tidy profit for themselves. Here, support was broken, but only temporarily. This type of scenario will typically occur for a mad 30-minute time window of increased volume before normal service is resumed. Those who follow the teachings of Joe DiNapoli will recognize this as a "Wash & Rinse."

Support and resistance lines are not always supposed to be drawn at the extreme of the price bar tails. Remember that we're looking for a zone of support and resistance, and there's always bound to be a few outlier bars. The reason for us looking for the "zone" is because we're looking to identify where the majority of trades are happening. That won't be at the extreme outlier of one or two tails.

Double and Triple Tops and Bottoms

Double Tops and Triple Tops

A Double Top is where a high is reached twice before dropping down. In logical terms, the chart is telling us that the (stock) price did not have the strength to rise through a previous high. This is interpreted as weakness and imminent decline in the price is likely.

Let's take a look at our NASDAQ chart again because it's the Double Top with the peaks in mid-July and the end of August that is screaming at us as we look at the chart:

Chart 4.2.1 ● Double Top for NASDAQ (July–August 2000).

TC2000®.com. Courtesy of Worden Brothers Inc.

● Notice how the second peak is just slightly lower than the first peak—this is a strong sign of price weakness to follow, which, of course, is precisely what happened. This is a good time for puts or certainly a good time to start protecting yourself against big falls. And a 50% fall in four months is my idea of a big drop, particularly for an Index.

● If we go back in time just a few months, we can see another NASDAQ double top occurring in March 2000.

Chart 4.2.2 ● Double Top for NASDAQ (March 2000).

TC2000®.com. Courtesy of Worden Brothers Inc.

What Is a Trend?

● An *uptrend* can be defined as a series of higher lows, often in conjunction with (although not required) higher highs.

● A *downtrend* can be defined as a sequence of lower highs, often in conjunction with (although not required) lower lows.

Prices in general either follow a trend (up or down), or they simply move sideways. In our example the price has been trending up strongly until March 2000.

You'll notice that in between those peaks is a dip that bottoms at the drawn solid horizontal line. You can be sure that once this bottom has been breached downward after the second top, the price will continue to fall, which, of course, it did (by over 1,000 points in a single month).

You'll also notice that the double top occurs at the end of a significant trend that on this chart can be traced from the beginning of the sequence back in October 1999.

Chart 4.2.3 ● Double Top and trend break and reversal for NASDAQ (March 2000)*.

TC2000®.com. Courtesy of Worden Brothers Inc.
*Downs (1999).

The Rule for Double Tops

So now we have three criteria fulfilled:

(a) a Double Top

(b) an uptrend broken and reversal to the downside (end of March)

(c) the last significant bottom breached to the downside (end of March)

You can either:

● exit your long position when the trendline is broken or

● exit your long position when the bottom is breached.

Recap:

Diagram 4.2.1 ● Double Top with trend break and reversal.

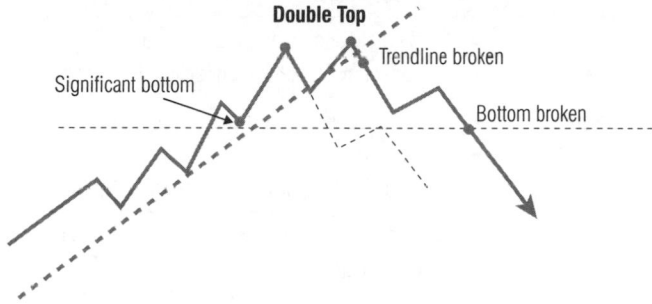

Diagram 4.2.2 ● Triple Top with trend break and reversal.

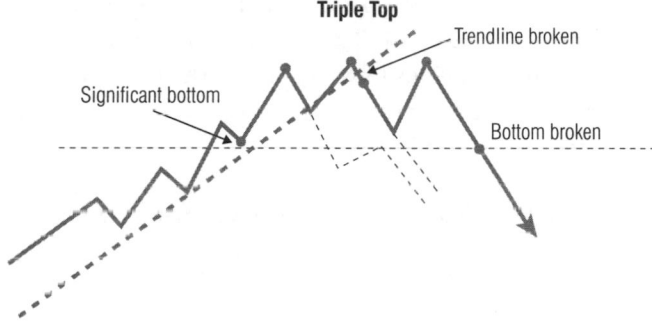

The rule for Triple Tops is the same as for Double Tops. Look for:

(a) a Triple Top,

(b) an up-trend broken and reversal to the downside (usually after the second top), or

(c) the last significant bottom breached to the downside.

You can either:

● exit your long position when the trendline is broken or

● exit your long position when the bottom is breached and enter into a short position.

Double Tops and Triple Tops Summary

What the patterns mean.	Weakness in the stock if it breaks down through the trendline after the second or third top.
What to do.	• Sell all holdings on breakdown through trendline. • Consider buying puts and/or selling the stock short.
How to identify the pattern.	• Two or three peaks (tops). • Broken upward trendline. • Reversal breaking down through latest significant bottom.
What is the cause?	• Lack of conviction in stock price appreciating beyond previous high.

Double Bottoms and Triple Bottoms

These work in the opposite way as Double Tops and Triple Tops.

In logical terms, the chart is telling us that the (stock) price wasn't weak enough to fall through a previous low. Furthermore, it has the strength to break upward through the previous peak. This is interpreted as strength, and imminent price appreciation is likely.

Diagram 4.2.3 ● Double Bottom with trend break and reversal.

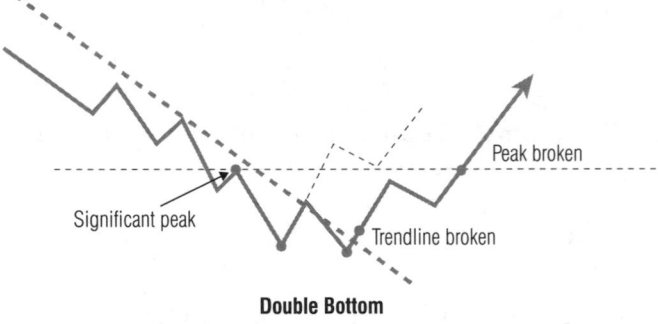

Significant peak

Peak broken

Trendline broken

Double Bottom

Diagram 4.2.4 ● Triple Bottom with trend break and reversal.

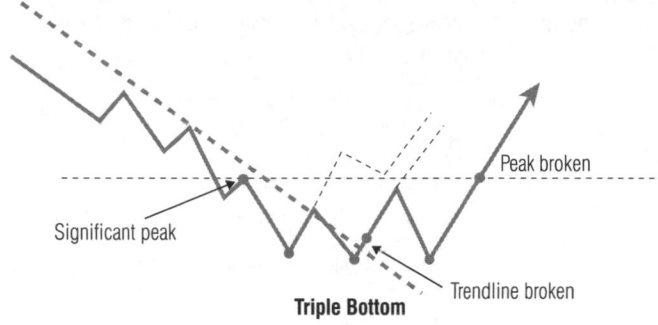

The Rule for Double Bottoms

(a) a Double Bottom

(b) a downtrend broken and reversal to the upside

(c) the last significant peak breached to the upside

You can either:

● enter your long position when the trendline is broken or

● enter your long position when the peak is breached.

The rule for Triple Bottoms is the same as for Double Bottoms. Look for:

(a) a Triple Bottom,

(b) a downtrend broken and reversal to the upside (usually after the second bottom), or

(c) the last significant peak breached to the upside.

You can either:

● enter your long position when the trendline is broken or

● enter your long position when the peak is breached.

Double Bottoms and Triple Bottoms Summary	
What the patterns mean.	Strength in the stock if it continues up through the trendline after the second or third top.
What to do.	• Consider entering into a bullish position by buying the stock or calls.
How to identify the pattern.	• Two or three bottoms. • Broken downward trendline. • Reversal breaking up through latest significant peak.
What is the cause?	• Conviction in stock price appreciating beyond previous highs.

Time Tip

Remember that the longer the time period the pattern takes, the stronger and more important the pattern becomes. A two-month Double Top (or Double Bottom) is a far more powerful indicator than a ten-minute Double Top (or Double Bottom).

Head and Shoulders

Diagram 4.3.1 ● Head and Shoulders.

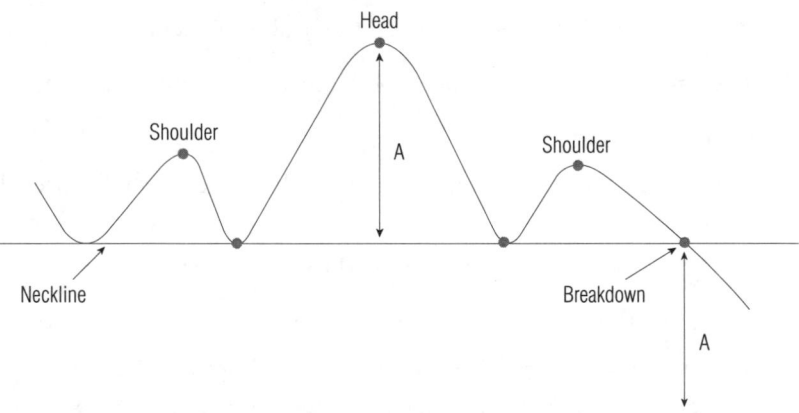

A Head and Shoulders pattern occurs when a peak (Head) is sandwiched between two lower peaks (Shoulders). In logical terms, the chart is telling us that the (stock) price did not have the strength to rise through either preceding highs. This is interpreted as weakness, and imminent decline in the price is likely by at least the amount of distance (A) between the neckline and the middle (Head) high.

Head and Shoulders Summary

What the pattern means.	Possible weakness in the stock if it breaks the support line (neckline).
What to do.	• Sell all holdings on breakdown and consider buying puts and/or selling the stock short.
How to identify the pattern.	From the neckline a pattern develops as shown here. First shoulder, head, second shoulder, followed by breakdown below the neckline.
What is the cause?	• A breakdown below the support line (neckline) of the stock.
	• One of the most reliable of the major reversal patterns.

Chart 4.3.1 ● Head and Shoulders for GM (March–August 1998).

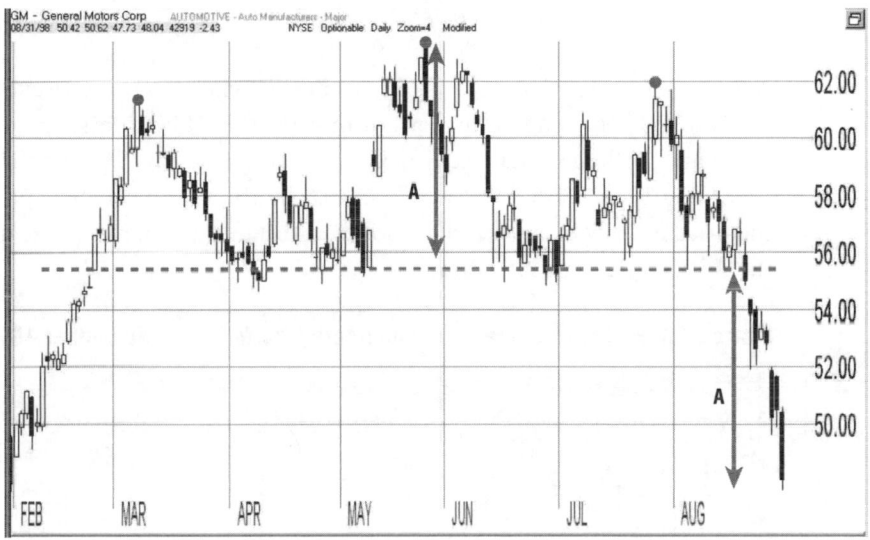

TC2000®.com. Courtesy of Worden Brothers Inc.

Reverse Head and Shoulders

Diagram 4.3.2 ● **Reverse Head and Shoulders.**

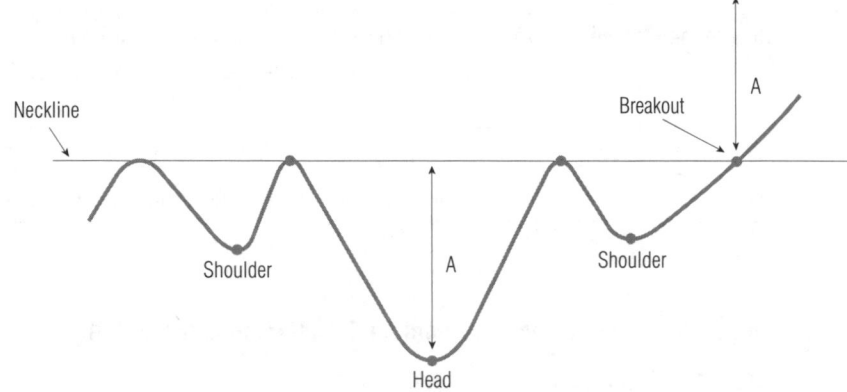

A Reverse Head and Shoulders pattern occurs when a bottom (Reverse Head) is sandwiched between two higher bottoms (Reverse Shoulders). In logical terms, the chart is telling us that the (stock) price has the strength to rise through either preceding lows. This is interpreted as strength, and imminent appreciation in the price is likely by at least the amount of distance (A) between the neckline and the middle (Reverse Head) high.

Chart 4.3.2 ● **Reverse Head and Shoulders for GM (June–November 1998).**

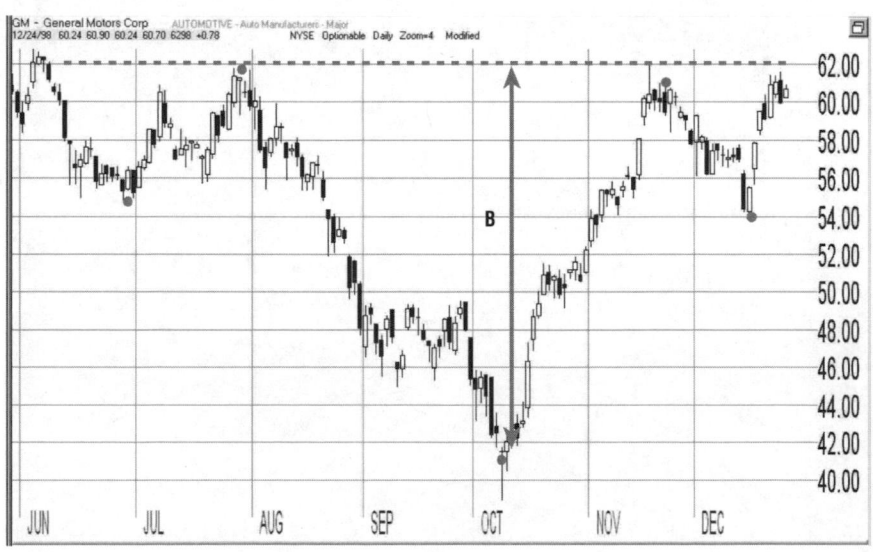

TC2000®.com. Courtesy of Worden Brothers Inc.

In this case, notice how the initial Head and Shoulders has turned into a Reverse Head and Shoulders. The next chart demonstrates the strength of the next upward move:

Chart 4.3.3 ● Reverse Head and Shoulders upward resolution for GM (November 1998).

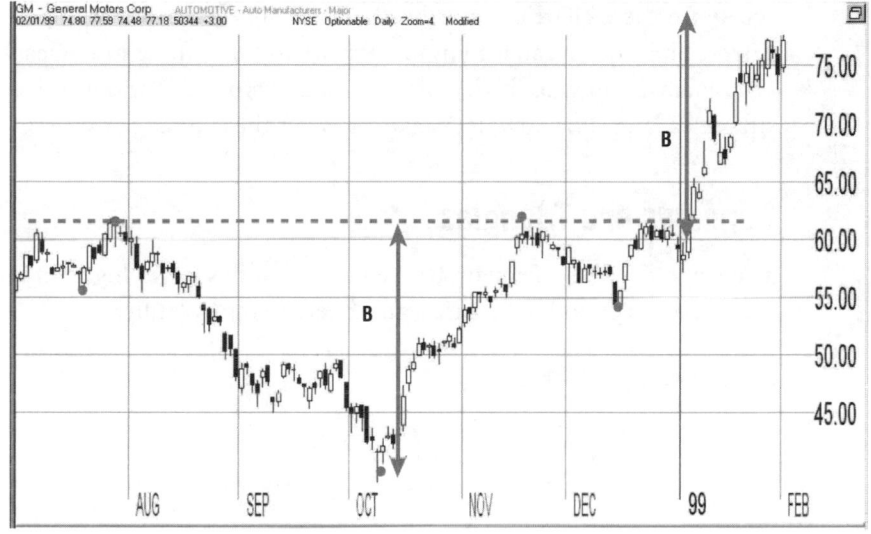

TC2000®.com. Courtesy of Worden Brothers Inc.

Reverse Head and Shoulders Summary

What the pattern means.	Possible strength in the stock if it breaks up through the resistance line (neckline).
What to do.	• Consider entering into a bullish position by buying the stock or calls.
How to identify the pattern.	From the neckline a pattern develops as shown here. First reverse shoulder, head, second shoulder, followed by breakout above the neckline.
What is the cause?	• A breakout above the support line (neckline) of the stock.
	• One of the most reliable of the major reversal patterns.

Consolidations—Pennants, Triangles, and Wedges

Consolidations occur where the individual price spreads are tight on each bar or candlestick, indicating that buyers and sellers are matching each other closely. This in itself is a sign of lower volatility. It's important for you as a trader to recognize these chart patterns because volatility has a direct impact on options prices. This in turn can lead us to uncover useful options strategies that can take advantage of low or high volatility and distorted options prices. More on strategies later. For now, let's take a look at these price patterns.

Pennants and Triangles

You can recognize a Pennant by the fact that it has lower highs and higher lows. These converge and are a sure sign of decreasing volatility.

Diagram 4.4.1 ● Pennant.

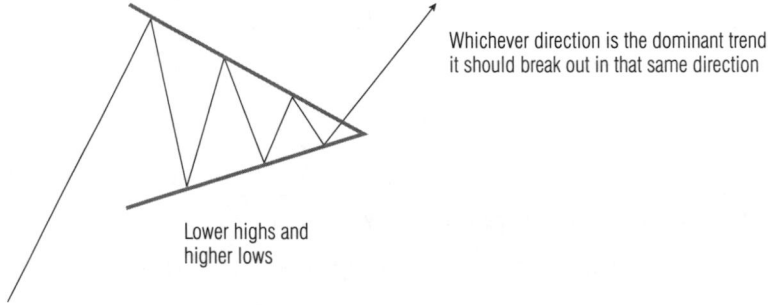

Whichever direction is the dominant trend, it should break out in that same direction

Lower highs and higher lows

● Pennants are good for identifying Straddle opportunities, which we'll talk about later.

Chart 4.4.1 ● Pennant for MNMD (May 1999).

TC2000®.com. Courtesy of Worden Brothers Inc.

Diagram 4.4.2 ● Triangle.

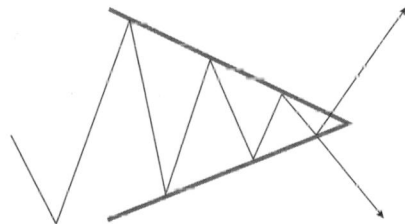

Triangles can resolve themselves either way, upward or downward. Again, they can be good for spotting good Straddle opportunities.

Diagram 4.4.3 ● Ascending and Descending Triangles.

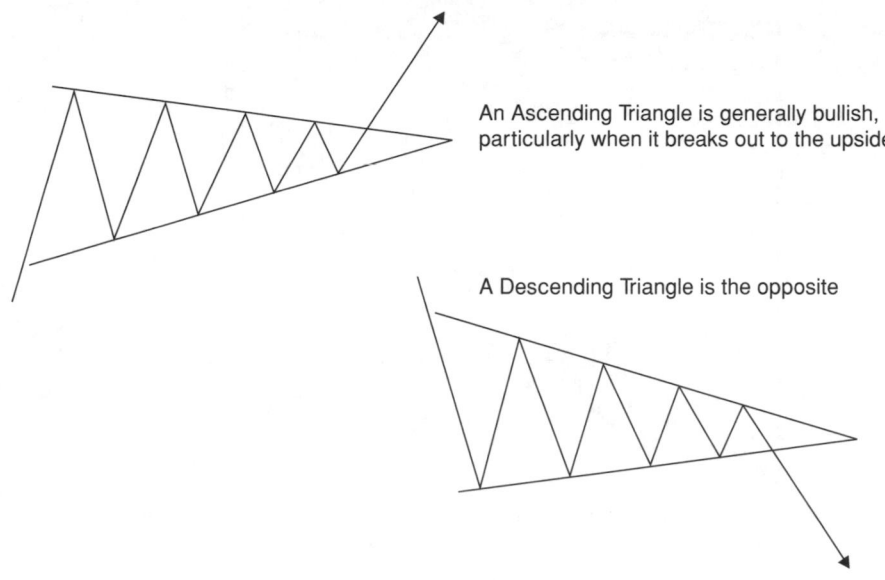

An Ascending Triangle is generally bullish, particularly when it breaks out to the upside

A Descending Triangle is the opposite

An Ascending Triangle can be looked on as a bullish signal. Notice that this pattern is characterized by multiple tops, which typically yield to the upside. The opposite typically occurs with a Descending Triangle, which typically yields to the downside.

Flags and Wedges

Diagram 4.4.4 ● Flag.

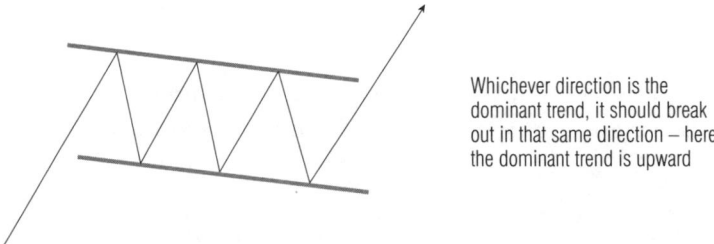

Whichever direction is the dominant trend, it should break out in that same direction – here the dominant trend is upward

A Flag occurs during a persistent and dominant trend and temporarily interrupts that trend before resuming it. The Flag itself consists of the price pattern rebounding off two parallel interim trendlines before breaking out in the direction of the dominant trend. Flags can be bullish (where the dominant trend is bullish) and bearish (where the dominant trend is bearish). Typically the flag will involve a gentle move in the opposite direction of the dominant trend before resuming. Often the flag will retrace to a Fibonacci retracement point (covered later in this chapter). As such, flags, in the context of trends, can provide traders with a dependable pattern around which we can form a reliable Trading Plan.

Chart 4.4.2 ● Bull Flags for SOL (May and June 1999).

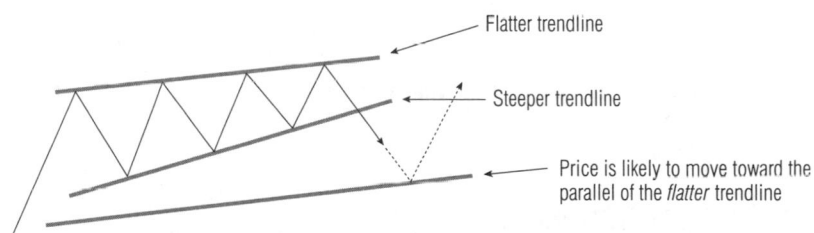

TC2000®.com. Courtesy of Worden Brothers Inc.

Diagram 4.4.5 ● Wedge.

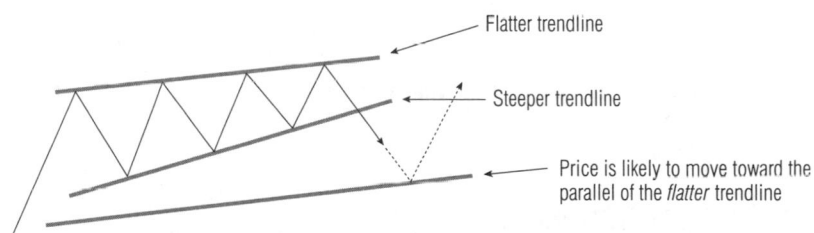

A Wedge differs from a Flag in that the interim trendlines converge as opposed to being parallel.

Where the price movement is trending between two non-parallel trendlines, the flatter line is the "stronger" line and the price is more likely to move toward the parallel of the flatter trendline and perhaps bounce off it to resume the trend.

To spot a Wedge, make a parallel line of the flatter line.

● *The flatter or shallower the line in a trendline pair is the STRONGER LINE. Here, the lower line parallel with the top line is the stronger line, and you should be aware that the stock price could fall to this level.*

● A *rising* Wedge is a temporary bearish sign (at least down to the shallow parallel trendline).

● A *falling* Wedge is a temporary bullish sign (at least up to the shallow parallel trendline).

Chart 4.4.3 ● **Wedge for ALTR (1999–2000).**

TC2000®.com. Courtesy of Worden Brothers Inc.

Notice how the price eventually came down to the flatter trendline, in fact breaking it.

Parallel Trendlines

Often when you draw a lower trendline, you can then draw a parallel upper trendline, which forms a channel through which the stock has been trending.

Diagram 4.4.6 ● Parallel trendlines.

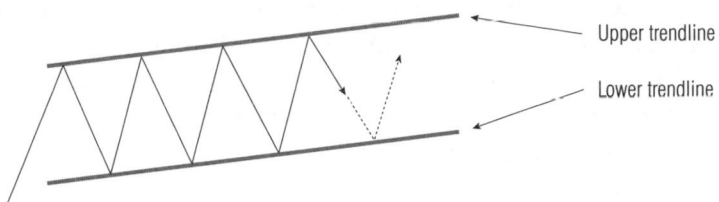

Obviously, the lower trendline is your target for buying, and the upper trendline is your target for selling or exiting. You must be strict with your stops in this scenario because if the price breaches the trendlines, it can signify the end of this pattern and leave you in a vulnerable position.

Chart 4.4.4 ● Parallel trendlines for ALTR (1999).

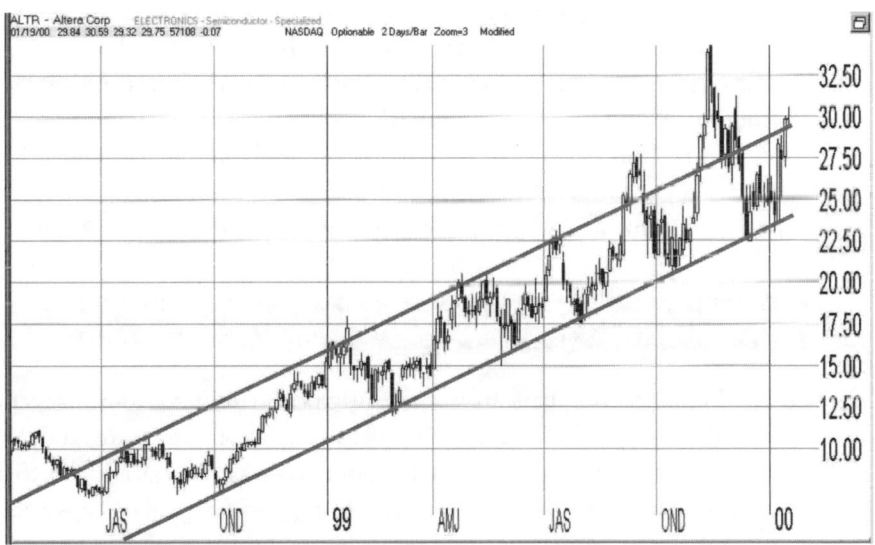

TC2000®.com. Courtesy of Worden Brothers Inc.

Notice in Chart 4.4.4 that the parallel trendlines are breached, yet the price consistently returns to the trend channel. Chart patterns do not have to be mutually exclusive. Charts 4.4.3 and 4.4.4 are of the same stock, and yet the charts, which have different timescales, show two distinct patterns at the same time.

When you find parallel trendlines in this way, you can identify price targets for trading various options strategies. With this one I personally traded a short-term "Bull Put spread" to take advantage of this particular chart pattern. We'll talk more about this strategy and how to use it in Chapter 7, "Bull Call Spreads and Bull Put Spreads."

For now it's clear to see where those price targets could be. On December 20, 1999, I identified $25 (or $50 as it was then, prior to a two for one stock split) as a potential low for the January 2000 expiration. I wasn't too fussed about the upper trendline given that I was trading a bullish strategy. All I was concerned about was that the stock wouldn't break down below $25 on the January 2000 expiration date.

The trendlines had been holding for more than one year, and there was no obvious sign of an imminent breach to the downside that might occur in January 2000. Where did I look to investigate the potential dangers? Well, I looked at the overall market including the NASDAQ, the Dow Jones Industrial Average, and the S&P 500, searched the news for potential events that might belie a change of sentiment and finally made a search of the company itself. In searching the company, I noticed that ALTR was publishing its quarterly earnings report just after the January 2000 options expiration, and I also noticed that ALTR had (at that time) a consistent habit of exceeding earnings expectations. (Please note that since March 2000, the market has changed significantly. Bull Put spreads are best employed in a consistently rising trending market.)

I ended up placing an extremely aggressive trade that yielded 74% in less than one month. Not the kind of trade that I would recommend, but it suited me at the time and was balanced against my portfolio at the time.

Fibonacci Retracements

The Fibonacci numbers are consistently powerful in various market conditions. The theory of the Fibonacci number sequence revolves around numbers that repeat themselves in nature. This sequence was used originally to explain the breeding cycles of rabbits. However, the numbers have a variety of other unlikely uses, for instance in interior design and trading.

Here's how the numbers work:

Each number in the sequence is the sum of the preceding two numbers. Beginning with 0, the sequence runs as follows:

0, 1, 1, 2, 3, 5, 8, 13, 21, 34, 55, 89…etc.

Eventually and with the larger numbers, one will divide into its successor 1.618 times. 1.618 is known as the "Golden Ratio" and, together with its reciprocal, 0.618, these two numbers are found over and over again in nature, in history, in science, and in many human activities. If you, like me, have an appreciation of numbers, then you'll enjoy a more in-depth study of the Golden Ratio.

For basic purposes, the numbers relate to each other in ratios of approximately 38.2% and 61.8%. The mid point between 38.2 and 61.8 is 50, so the key (rounded) ratios that we apply to trading are 38.2%, 50%, and 61.8%. Many price patterns seem to consistently adhere to these ratios in their individual movements (Dobson, 1984). The trick is to be able to spot when it's happening because when it is, often you can be confident that it will continue. Serious Fibonacci analysis involves a complex and layered approach. The more I learn about it, the more compelling it becomes, even to the point of altering some of my long-held philosophical beliefs—it's that powerful. I would strongly recommend some substantial, detailed study into this if you have the time and resources to dedicate to it. For the purposes of this chapter, however, we'll stick with the basics.

What Is a Retracement?

A *retracement* is where one of the following occurs:

(a) A price series reaches a top and then falls back before resuming the uptrend (we measure the amount of the retracement from the last significant bottom—see Diagram 4.5.1), or an up-trending price series reaches a top, falls back to make a bottom, and then resumes its uptrend only to falter at the retracement point and drop down, forming a new downtrend (see Diagram 4.5.3).

(b) A price series reaches a bottom and then rises before resuming the downtrend (we measure the amount of the retracement from the last significant top—see Diagram 4.5.2), or a down-trending price series reaches a bottom, rises up to make a top, and then resumes its downtrend only to change direction at the retracement point, start rising to form a new uptrend (see Diagram 4.5.4).

Where Fibonacci is relevant is that the amount of the retracement will often be one of those percentages, 38.2%, 50%, or 61.8%, the easiest to spot being 50%.

A word of caution—make sure that your charting software can draw the Fibonacci ratio lines automatically for you. This will not only save you time, but also on a price series the distances between highs and lows are often deceptive, so it's best to have a drawing tool you can place over the relevant highs and lows to be able to see what level of retracement has occurred. Remember that price series often have their own personalities, so if a particular stock consistently makes 50% retracements, it's likely that it could continue in the same way in the future. Please note also that Fibonacci retracements can apply to time, not just price. Many commentators ignore Fibonacci in terms of time. Let me assure you, this is a mistake. Fibonacci does apply to time as well.

Diagram 4.5.1 ● Fibonacci (downward) retracement with continuing upward trend.

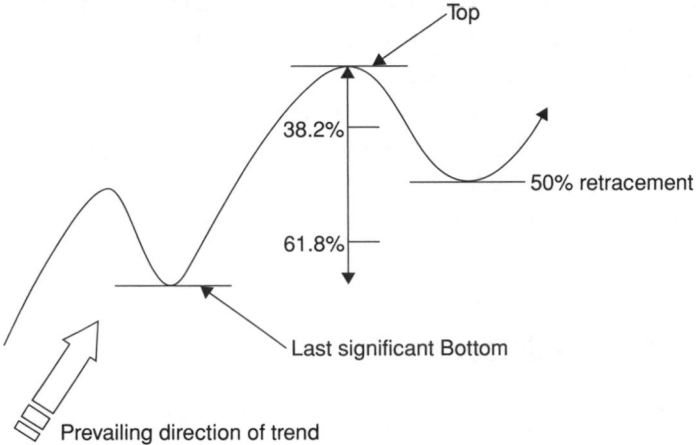

Diagram 4.5.2 ● Fibonacci (upward) retracement with continuing downward trend.

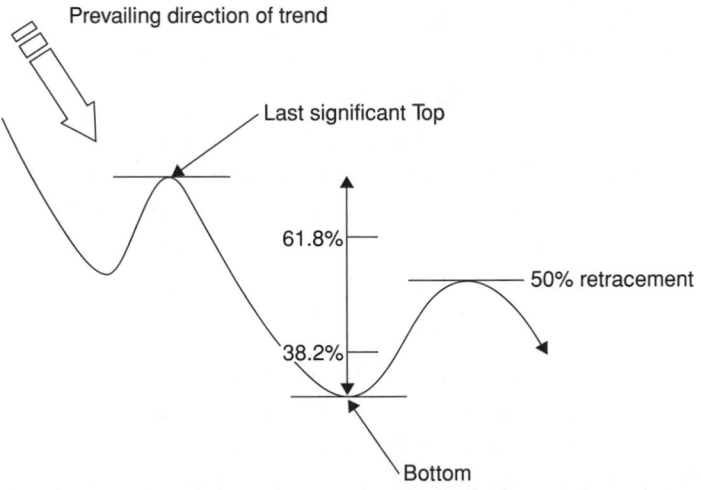

Diagram 4.5.3 ● Fibonacci retracement with change in trend direction.

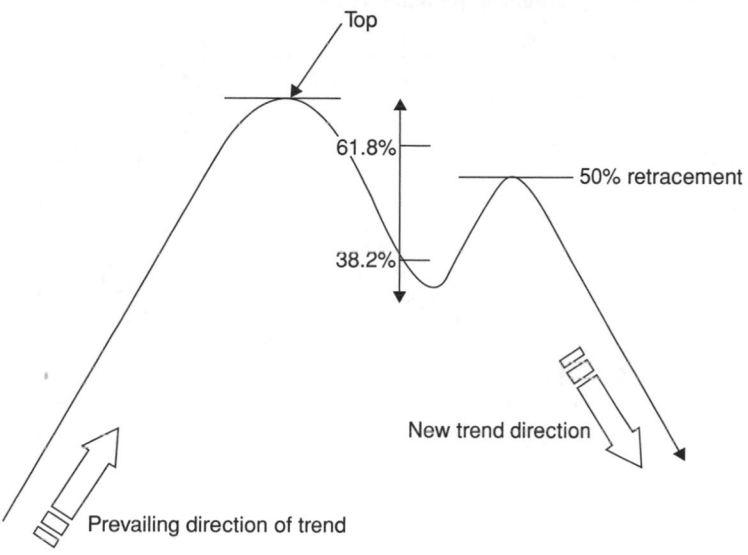

Diagram 4.5.4 ● Fibonacci retracement with change in trend direction.

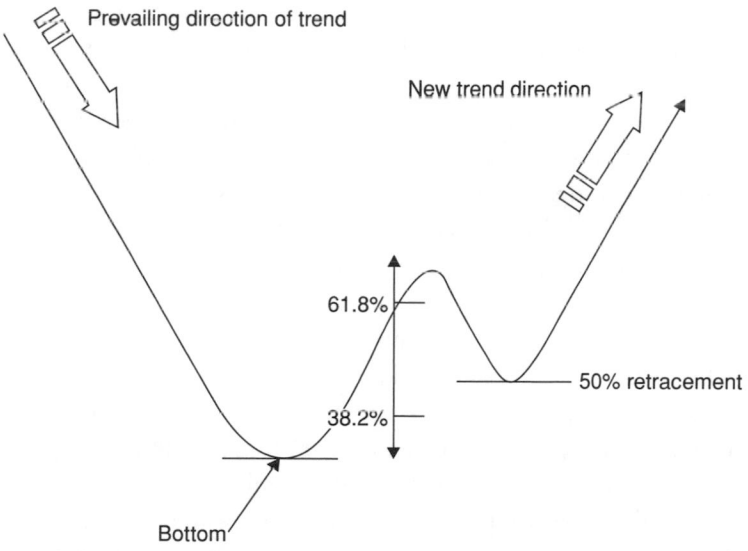

Chart 4.5.1 ● Fibonacci (downward) retracement for MNMD (October–November 1999).

TC2000®.com. Courtesy of Worden Brothers Inc.

In Chart 4.5.1 we can see that a 50% retracement has occurred, but this time the prevailing trend has stopped, and we can clearly identify a change in direction at point A, where the price pattern bounces off the 50% retracement line.

Many well-known traders use the Fibonacci numbers for their own trading. There are numerous ways of doing this. I have simply outlined the most basic. Further investigation into Fibonacci will be essential if you want to pursue your interest in it and trade consistently well with it. The examples given are illustrations of the most basic and common forms of Fibonacci retracements in action. You can get the best information on Fibonacci from www.themarket-matrix.co.uk. I strongly recommend an in-depth study of Fibonacci to anyone who really is serious about trading.

Please note that because this is a technique that uses targets to identify turning points, be sure to place your stops carefully. The markets are rarely precise when it comes to hitting predetermined targets. This means that some of you will prefer to place your exit stop just before it reaches the target. Remember, don't be greedy, so long as you're making a profit consistently—who cares anyway!

Elliott Wave

Elliott Wave is inextricably linked with the Fibonacci number sequence. The theory is that securities prices move in waves. These waves are coincidentally sequenced in the basic Fibonacci ratios. Let's go through each wave in turn:

The Basic Pattern

The basic premise is that there is an initial 5-wave impulse. This impulse itself has three impulses of its own (wave 1, 3, and 5) and two retracement waves (2 and 4).

Diagram 4.5.5 ● Basic Elliott Wave structure.

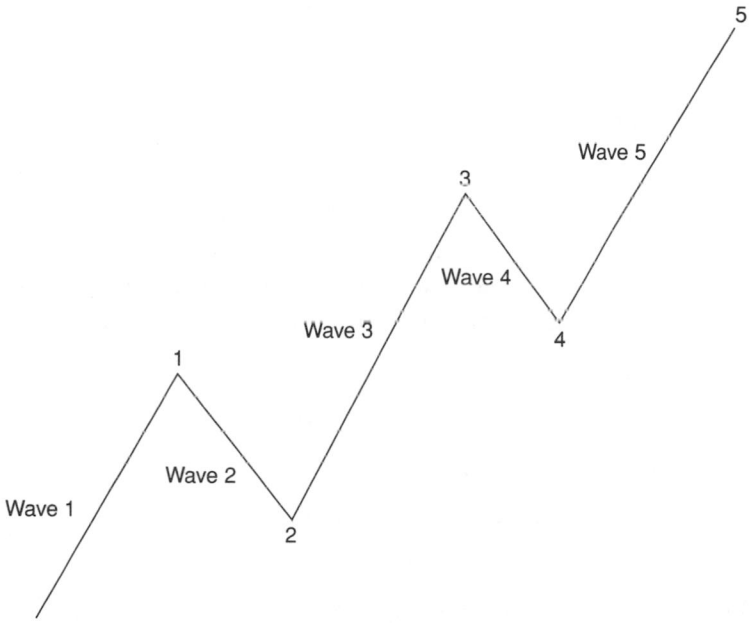

Following a 5-wave impulse, there will be a 3-wave correction (A, B, C). Each wave 1, 3, 5 is an impulse wave that will divide into five smaller waves, and each wave 2 and 4 is a corrective wave that divide into an A, B, C wave.

Diagram 4.5.6 ● Elliott Wave impulse and correction.

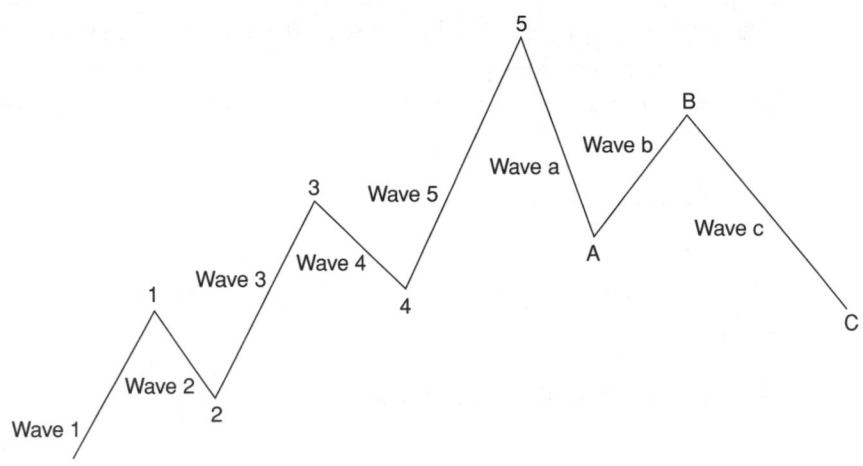

The Basic Rules

This is a very elementary overview of Elliott Wave, and I would strongly recommend further detailed analysis of this topic, particularly in conjunction with Fibonacci. The relationship between the two can already be seen by way of the 5-wave impulse and 3-wave retracement, both being Fibonacci numbers. The basic rules of Elliott Wave can be summarized as follows:

Impulse Waves:

● Wave 1 has five waves (1, 2, 3, 4, 5)

● Wave 2 has three waves (A, B, C)

● Wave 3 has five waves (1, 2, 3, 4, 5)

● Wave 4 has three waves (A, B, C)

● Wave 5 has five waves (1, 2, 3, 4, 5)

Corrective Waves:

● Wave A has three or five waves (1, 2, 3) or (1, 2, 3, 4, 5)

● Wave B has three waves (A, B, C)

● Wave C has five waves (1, 2, 3, 4, 5)

Elliott Wave with Fibonacci

We have already seen an elementary relationship between Elliott Wave and Fibonacci. We can go a little further with this by way of the relationships between the waves themselves. These are not necessarily definitive, but where they do occur can be helpful to our overall analysis. Here are just a few of the major rules defining the relationships between the waves:

The Impulse Waves:

● Wave 2 will be a Fibonacci retracement of Wave 1.

● Wave 2 cannot retrace more than 100% of Wave 1.

● Wave 3 will usually be a Fibonacci extension of Wave 1.

● Wave 3 is typically the largest wave and is never the shortest.

● Wave 4 will be a Fibonacci retracement of all waves 1, 2, and 3.

● Wave 4 will have a Fibonacci relationship with Wave 2.

● Wave 4 should not typically retrace further than the end of Wave 1.

● Wave 5 will be a Fibonacci extension of Wave 1 or 3 and completes the 5-wave impulse sequence.

The Corrective Waves:

● Wave A, B, C will be a Fibonacci retracement of waves 1, 2, 3, 4, and 5.

● Wave C will be a Fibonacci extension of Wave A or Wave B.

Elliott Wave Summary

As we can see, there is a lot to understand about Elliott Wave and its relationship with Fibonacci. I strongly recommend that you learn more about this by looking at *Dynamic Trading* by Robert Miner at www.dynamictraders.com. Used correctly, Elliott Wave and Fibonacci combined can be the most powerful technical analysis tool in the market.

Gann Levels

It is thought that W. D. Gann was the first trader to use the Fibonacci retracement ratios. The numbers used by Gann are either the same or only fractions away from the Fibonacci numbers, and he believed that highs and lows were all related to each other by these ratios. He also believed that the ratios could be used to make accurate assessments of when price targets would be reached. In essence, Gann theory is based both on time and price.

I've known many people to use Gann successfully with their trading, so if you have the time, it's worth following it up. Bear in mind that the similarities with Fibonacci are no accident, so you'd be wise to make yourself familiar with both techniques and then take your pick. From my experience of using Gann, you can successfully use the numbers to determine price targets alone, without the use of time. Personally, I've had very good experiences trading both Gann and Fibonacci, so I would recommend that you investigate both and see whether you like either of them. As much as anything else, both techniques inherently contain a money-management system, which you can use to ensure that you minimize your losses and take profits.

For now, here is Gann explained simply for you:

● Gann believed that there is a relationship between every low (bottom) and every future high (top). He also believed that there is a relationship between every high (top) and every future low (bottom).

● Gann calculated four levels that appeared to have an unusual significance to trading levels in a price series—these are known as the Major Gann Levels. He calculated others, but for our purposes, here are the principal ones:

The Major Gann Levels

G1 Level $\dfrac{\text{All Time High Price}}{2}$

● This is the most significant Gann Level.
  The rule here is that in a significant downtrend the G1 level acts as support. If the price breaks down below G1, it is likely to go down to G3. If the price has fallen through G1, it now becomes resistance.

G2 Level $\dfrac{\text{(All Time High Price + All Time Low Price)}}{2}$

G3 Level $\dfrac{\text{All Time High Price}}{4}$ or $\dfrac{\text{G1}}{2}$

● This is the second most significant Gann Level.

The rule here is that if the price falls below G1, then G3 should act as support if the price falls that far. If the price then falls below G3, then G3 will act as resistance.

G4 Level $\dfrac{\text{(All Time High Price - All Time Low Price)}}{4}$ + All Time Low Price

Diagram 4.6.1 ● Major Gann Levels on a standard price chart.

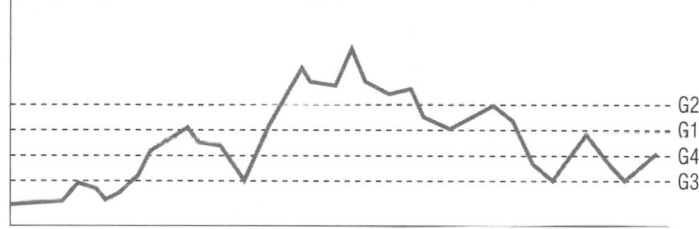

Gann Percentages and Angles

Gann believed that the relationship between price highs and lows was determined by certain percentages. These percentages could be used to determine either the price or the time of establishing a future target. Such a future target could be established by projecting a price level, a time, or an angle from a significant high or low.

For a more in-depth study on Gann (which I wholeheartedly recommend), visit the Web sites mentioned previously. Gann is not something for the fly-by-night student and will require at least a weekend of your time to understand it fully. Thereafter, Gann theory is best applied using specialist software.

Gaps

A gap occurs when a price series experiences an explosive jump either up or down between price bars. We usually refer to Gaps occurring on a daily or weekly bar basis. Gaps are essentially points of exceptionally high or low demand. The theory is that the pent-up buying or selling pressure that forms the gap in the first place will follow through with more buying or selling. For this reason, gaps are believed to be good indicators in a continuation of a move in the same direction.

There are four main types of Gap.

Gap	Identification	Comment
Breakaway Gap	Occurs at the end of a move and goes in the opposite direction.	High significance and usually the easiest to identify and most profitable to trade.
Measured Gap	Occurs in the middle of a trend, hence giving us a target for the end of the move.	The Measured Gap is thought to signify the mid point (50% point) of a move.
Exhaustion Gap	Occurs at the end of a move. Only identifiable by watching the price action after the gap itself. If the price moves back into the gap area, then you can recognize the gap (with the benefit of some hindsight) as an Exhaustion Gap.	High significance even though it is only recognizable after a price reversal. Usually exhaustion gaps will occur at the end of a significant move up or down, suggesting a final flurry of activity before reversing direction.
Island Reversal Gap	You can spot an Island Reversal Gap by the fact that it usually follows an upward Exhaustion Gap or upward Measured Gap, hence leaving an "island" behind.	This is thought to be a strong signal that stock is on its way down.

Diagram 4.7.1 ● Gaps.

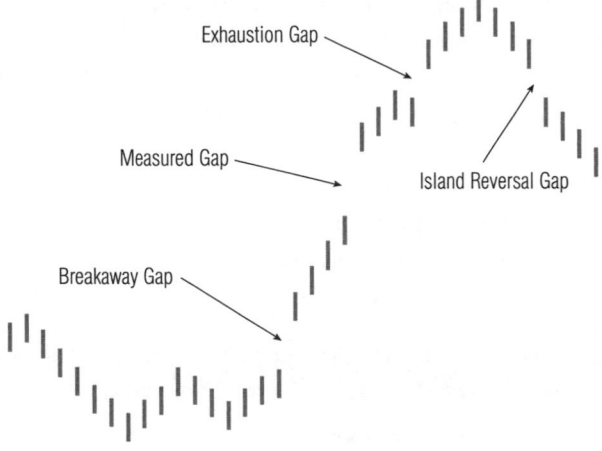

Chart 4.6.1 ● **Gaps for PMC Sierra Inc. (2000–2001).**

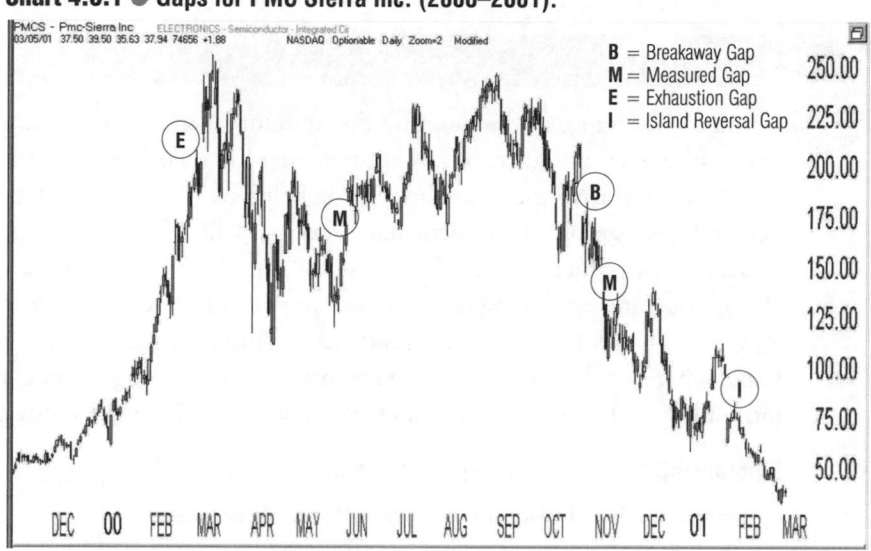

TC2000®.com. Courtesy of Worden Brothers Inc.

In Chart 4.6.1, the Exhaustion Gap in February 2000 is easy to spot, although it is only truly identifiable once the price has returned to not only fill in the gap but break down through it.

The Measured Gap in May 2000 is identifiable by the period of consolidation immediately after it. Although the gap is filled twice in the following month, it is never breached to the downside, and at the end of June the uptrend continues.

The Breakaway Gap in October 2000 can be identified by the end of the upward retracement move. The trend is now firmly established as downward.

The Measured Gap at the end of October 2000 confirms the previous Breakaway Gap and the underlying downward trend of the stock. Notice how in December there is an upward retracement, which does not fill the gap before resuming the downtrend.

The Island Reversal Gap in January 2001 could also be identified as a Breakaway Gap, but you should notice that there is a small Exhaustion Gap just a few days before.

I know of many people who swear by gaps. The problem with gaps is that they are often best identified after the event, and this can make them tricky to trade without the benefit of hindsight. For my own trading style I prefer to be able to set targets, and if they are not reached I can simply exit with a small loss. You can do this with gaps too, but I would recommend paper trading gaps for some time and recording your performance very honestly. Remember also that gaps do not always fill, but "nature hates a vacuum," hence the reason they do fill so often. Gap filling can be rationally explained by the fact that unfilled orders are outstanding after a gap, and brokers are in business to fill those orders.

Volume

Volume is a term used to describe the amount of units traded in a particular stock, future, commodity, or any security that has its own price series.

It's a significant indicator because it helps us to understand the levels of demand and supply in a particular security. Falling prices are generally an indication of reduced demand for a stock and vice versa. Using a volume bar chart, you can start to make other interpretations as well. In general, a move may not last too long if there's no decent volume to go with it. On the other hand, where a move is accompanied by high and increasing volume, the move is more likely to be one that is sustainable. Volume makes prices move.

Diagram 4.8.1 ● Volume and price patterns.

If volume and price move together (up or down), this is a *bullish* sign.

- If the price is moving up and volume is increasing, there is clearly more buying pressure stimulated by an increasing number of orders, hence the price is likely to continue rising in the short term.

- If the price is falling but volume is also falling, this represents a lack of conviction in the markets and a price reversal to the upside could be likely.

If volume and price have a trend divergence, this is a *bearish* sign.

- If the price is rising but on falling volume, this represents a lack of conviction in the markets and a price reversal to the downside could be likely.

- If the price is falling with increasing volume, this is a clear sign of increasing selling pressure, which is likely to drive the price further down at least in the short term.

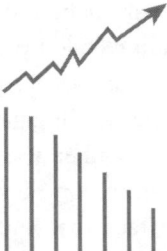
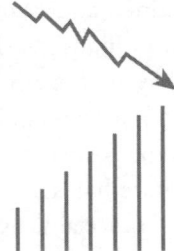

Volume Climaxes (Volume Spikes)

A Volume Climax occurs when a security has been trending for a lengthy period of time. In the Amazon chart here, you can clearly see that the stock is in a downtrend from December 1999 onward. Notice that whenever it makes a rclief rally or upward retracement, it is usually pre-empted by a volume surge on the creation of a new bottom. On this chart, volume climaxes also are occurring when new peaks are formed in the midst of the downtrend. In short, Volume Spikes are often indications of a change in direction in the price.

Chart 4.7.1 ● Volume Climaxes for AMZN (2000).

TC2000®.com. Courtesy of Worden Brothers Inc.

Point	Description
A	End of long-term up trend signalled by significant volume climax
B	Recovery retracement ends with a volume spike
C	New low formed with a volume climax—notice the short-term relief rally (upward retracement afterward)
D	New low formed with a significant volume climax followed by upward retracement
E	Small volume spike heralding end of rally and resumption of dominant downtrend
F	New low formed followed by upward retracement

As you can see, there are a number of volume spikes on the chart, and they nearly all correlate closely with the end of a move upward or downward, followed closely by a price reversal. Amazon is a volatile stock anyway, and in part it is the high volume and volume surges that are responsible for this volatility.

Technical Analysis Indicators

In addition to all the various price chart patterns, Technical Analysts use a host of Technical Indicators. These are typically mathematical formulas, which are derived from price action and in some cases volume as well.

As with all aspects of Technical Analysis, I should warn you that it's easy to get lost in all the jargon and different techniques that exist. Personally I only use a few patterns or indicators, but I know many traders who use different ones both very successfully and unsuccessfully. This chapter is all about making you aware of some of the different techniques and indicators that exist. Follow-up is essential.

Moving Averages

Moving Averages are the most widely known and used technical indicators. They are also the simplest. A *Moving Average* is simply the average closing price of a period of bars on a price chart. So, on a daily chart, a 40-period moving average is the average of the last 40 days' prices. Tomorrow's Moving Average will include what happened today (but not tomorrow), and, similarly, today's Moving Average includes what happened yesterday (but not today!). Moving Averages are most useful for the way in which they smooth price action and cut out the "noise," that is, the peculiar bar by bar data that often results in trading whipsaws.

> A Moving Average is simply the average closing price of a period of bars on a price chart.

The most popular way of using Moving Averages is to have two of them, one short term and one longer term. The idea is that when the short Moving Average rises up through the longer-term Moving Average, this is a bullish signal. When the short-term Moving Average falls down through the longer-term Moving Average, this is seen as a bearish sign. One major caveat that I would add is this: this type of Moving Average analysis works best with trending price series. In this way the Moving Average crossovers can help you to determine whether or not a trend has finished and a reversal is in place. This is not a sensible technique to use with tightly oscillating stocks.

Chart 4.8.1 ● 10 and 40 -week Moving Averages for AMZN (1997–2001).

TC2000®.com. Courtesy of Worden Brothers Inc.

Notice how the ten-period Moving Average (the shorter one) moves much faster and closer to the actual price bars, and notice how the longer Moving Average is so much more smoothed.

You can see that on the basis of Moving Average crossovers, a buy signal would have occurred at sometime in 1998 and that it didn't reverse into a sell signal until roughly March 2000. Despite the huge swings in price, this would have been a very successful trade by any standards. However, the success is mostly down to having selected a stock that literally flew to the stars from nowhere. The daily chart of AMZN is not quite as clear:

Chart 4.8.2 ● 10 and 40 -day Moving Averages for AMZN (1998–1999).

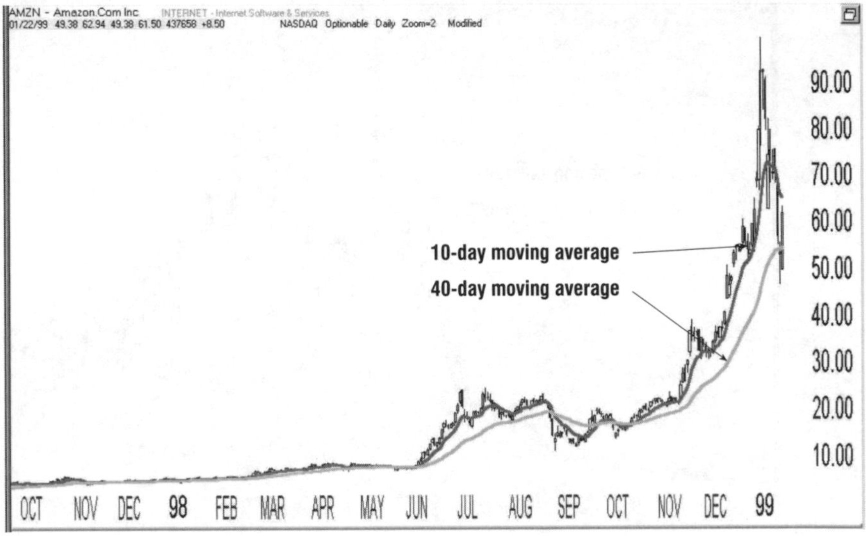

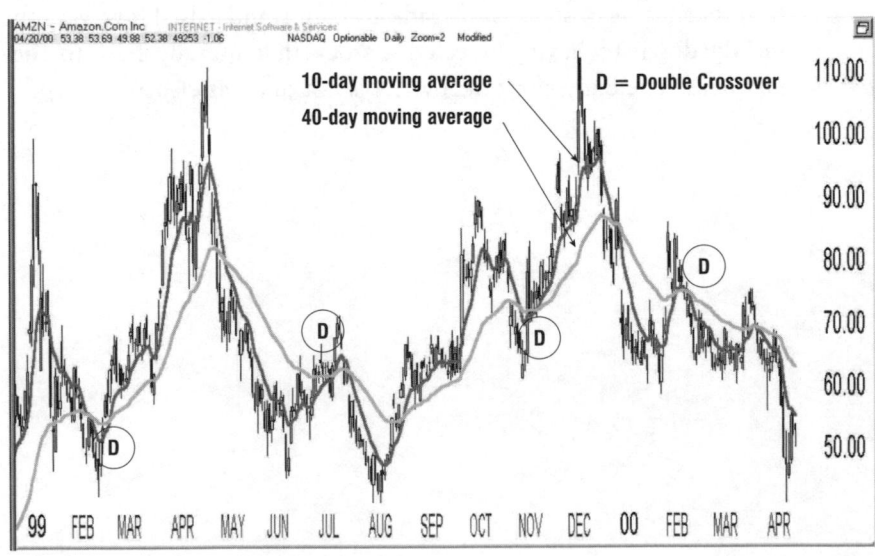

TC2000®.com. Courtesy of Worden Brothers Inc.

Now we have a daily chart of AMZN covering the uptrend. Notice that the Moving Averages cross over in August, September (twice), and October 1999, even during a strong uptrend. These crossovers could be interpreted as signals, which in the preceding graph, wouldn't have been too damaging to your profits.

Let's have a look at what happened after this:

Chart 4.8.3 ● 10 and 40 -day Moving Averages for AMZN (1999–2000).

TC2000®.com. Courtesy of Worden Brothers Inc.

Now we're looking at the time when Amazon had stopped trending upward and was making a beautiful double top. But look at the Moving Averages. They are now crossing over with increasing frequency and because the stock has stopped trending, the Moving Averages are giving bad signals or double signals (D), which at best are confusing.

Chart 4.8.4 ● 10 and 40 -day Moving Averages for AMZN (2000–2001).

TC2000®.com. Courtesy of Worden Drothers Inc.

Notice now that we're back into a trending situation, this time the trend is downward, there are fewer double crossovers, and the position is clearer.

The rule for Moving Averages is that they work best in trending markets.[1] They do not work very well at all in sideways moving markets. Just as an illustration, how would you have liked to have been trading FNM on the basis of moving averages in 1999 (see Chart 4.8.5)? Pretty confusing!

---

[1]Personally, I would recommend using displaced moving averages (DMA). The advantage of using DMAs is that not only can you choose a faster moving average time period, but it also cuts out the "noise" of unusual price bars. The most popular Moving Averages are 200, 50, 40, 20 and 10 - day moving averages—although I don't use them myself.

Chart 4.8.5 ● 10 and 40 -day Moving Averages for FNM (1999).

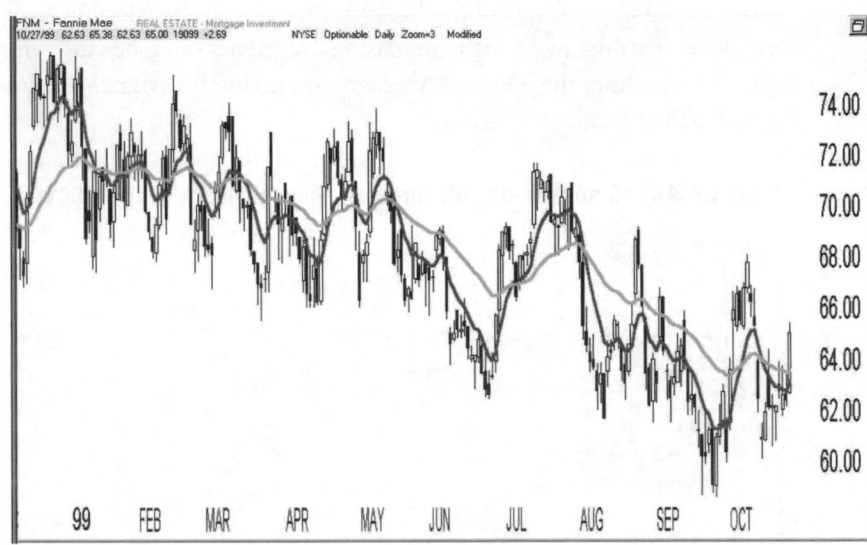

TC2000®.com. Courtesy of Worden Brothers Inc.

Moving Average Convergence Divergence (MACD)

MACD is simply a measure of the relationship between two Moving Averages of the same price series. MACD is a Moving Average of the difference of two Moving Averages of price. As such, it is a measure of momentum in the price movement (Appel, 1979). As the Moving Averages move further apart, this is a sign of increasing momentum. Because MACD is a measure of the relationship of two Moving Averages, it stands to reason that it can be used as a trend-indicative indicator. This follows from the fact that Moving Averages are best used to identify trending patterns as opposed to consolidation price movements.

MACD can be read and interpreted in all kinds of ways. Some traders prefer to look at it as a histogram and to interpret it as a divergence indicator. Others prefer a line version. There are three main ways to interpret MACD, namely simple crossovers, overbought/oversold, and divergence.

● **Simple Crossovers**
When MACD crosses the zero line, this is seen as a signal. The basic idea is that when MACD breaks up through the zero line, this means the Moving Averages have crossed upward and vice versa.

● **Overbought/Oversold**

The further the *shorter Moving Average* moves away from the *longer Moving Average*, the more the security becomes overbought or oversold. In these instances it is likely that the security price is overextended and will pull back to less extreme levels.

● **MACD Divergence (Elder, 1993)**

A divergence occurs where price action is not reflected in the MACD behavior and vice versa. A popular method of analyzing MACD is to look for where the security is making a new high, but the MACD is failing to surpass its own previous high (or vice versa).

There are two main ways to look at MACD divergence:

(a) Where MACD is making new lows but the price is not, there is a *bearish* divergence. Where MACD is making new highs but the price is not, there is a *bullish* divergence. These divergences are most significant where MACD is at overbought and oversold levels.

(b) Where the MACD peaks and troughs are differing with those of the underlying price action. One rule is that if the price peaks are rising but the MACD peaks are falling, a divergence is occurring, and you should be prepared for a change in direction in the trend.

Chart 4.8.6 ● MACD bar chart for PMCS (2000).

TC2000®.com. Courtesy of Worden Brothers Inc.

In Chart 4.8.6, the simple crossovers are easy to spot because the MACD histogram simply moves from either side of the horizontal line.

Overbought and oversold levels are occurring consistently with dramatic price movements, so these too are easy to spot.

We can also identify one of the divergence criteria with ease. Notice how if you draw a line between the two price peaks, the line would be sloping upward while drawing a line between the corresponding MACD peaks would result in a downward slope. This is divergence and can be interpreted as an indication that the price direction is about to change. Be aware that no one pricing pattern or indicator works all the time and that we are simply conducting an overview here.

An alternative way of looking at MACD is simply looking at a line of MACD itself and an average of MACD. As MACD crosses its average down this could be interpreted as a bearish signal, while MACD crossing its average upward could be seen as a bullish sign.

Chart 4.8.7 ● MACD lines for PMCS (2000).

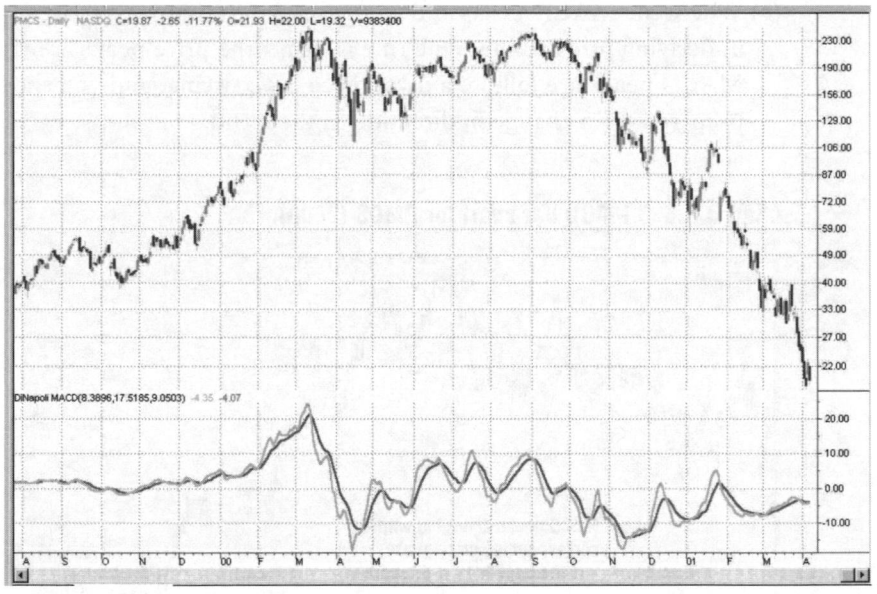

Chart created on TradeStation®, the flagship product of Tradestation Technologies Inc.

Stochastics

A *stochastic* is an oscillator, which is used to determine whether a market is overbought or oversold. As with many of the Technical Analysis indicators, it is best used not in isolation but in conjunction with other indicators and chart patterns, which may outline whether a market is moving up or down, with or against the underlying trend (see Joe DiNapoli's book, *Trading with DiNapoli Levels* (1998) www.fibtrader.com).

The Stochastic Oscillator measures the relationship of a security's closing prices (on given price bars) with its highs and lows. It consists of two lines, %K and %D, and ranges between 0% and 100%. A reading of 0% shows that the security's close was the lowest price that it has traded during the preceding x-time periods. A reading of 100% shows that the security's close was the highest price that the security has traded during the preceding x-time periods.

> I would recommend further investigation into stochastics if you want to develop a real understanding of it. This is an instance of a little information being dangerous.

Many traders will identify the 25% and 75% bounds of the stochastic as being oversold or overbought. The problem with this approach is that you may miss a large part of the down move or up move (depending on whether you are playing the market long and short). The other problem with playing the stochastic signals at these levels is that often a protracted, and consistent trend may not trigger the stochastic to breach the 25% or 75% levels at all, thus preventing you from taking advantage of a so-called signal. As such, the stochastic is an often-misinterpreted indicator.[2]

Another popular interpretation made by traders is that a signal is given when the lines cross each other. When the fast line breaks upward through the slow line, this is a bullish signal, and when the fast line breaks down through the slow line, this is a bearish signal. The trick is to select the appropriate time frames and stochastic parameters, which alone could be a book in itself.

I would recommend further investigation into stochastics if you want to develop a real understanding of it. This is an instance of a little information being dangerous. Many traders simply have a passing knowledge of stochastics and use it misguidedly and unprofitably. Our aim in this chapter is simply to give you a flavor for the various tools that exist to help you determine likely price movements so you can then select the appropriate options strategy. Technical

---

[2] For further reading on stochastics, take a look at Bernstein (1987) or Lane (1984).

Analysis is a vast subject, and the first step is to get an idea of the main chart patterns and indicators. To some of you, this chapter will be just the first step.

The Relative Strength Index (RSI)

Created by Welles Wilder, the RSI[3] is another measure for overbought/oversold analysis. Using a horizontal 50% mid line most followers of RSI take a buy signal above the mid line and a sell signal below the mid line.

The RSI measures the internal strength of a single security and does not compare the relative strength of two securities.[4] It is a price-following oscillator that ranges between 0 and 100. Much like the MACD Divergence interpretation, a popular method of analyzing the RSI is to look for a divergence where the security itself is making a new high, but the RSI is failing to exceed its own previous high. This divergence is interpreted as an indication of a likely reversal.

It is thought that the RSI itself also forms chart patterns such as support and resistance, Head and Shoulders, or Triangles (as described earlier in this chapter) that may not actually be visible on the price chart.

RSI usually makes its own tops above 70 and bottoms below 30, usually preceding the underlying price chart. The problem with the RSI is that because its maximum is at 100 it can be misleading for strong market moves. So if the RSI is, say, just 10 and a significant down move continues, then the RSI only has 10 more points to go, whereas the market may well have much further to go down. The same would apply if the RSI is in the 90s and a strong upswing keeps going.

Different Time Frames

This is a vital concept for you to understand. Chart patterns and indicators can vary substantially when you view charts over different time frames. Because of this, their signals will also vary, and your interpretation must therefore take into consideration the time frame you are looking to trade.

---

[3] See Welles Wilder (1978).

[4] The comparison analysis tool is called the Comparative Relative Strength (or Comparative Strength), which measures one security's performance against another's. The Comparative Strength is a useful indicator to compare how, say, a stock is performing compared with its sector or an index or another security within the same industry or sector. Comparative Strength is simply calculated by dividing one security's price by another's (the comparison security), thus forming a ratio that forms the basis of the Comparative Strength.

For example, consider the following price charts:

Chart 4.8.8 ● **Time frames—daily chart over six months for Citigroup (2000–2001).**

TC2000®.com. Courtesy of Worden Brothers Inc.

To the naked eye, Chart 4.8.8 appears to suggest that price action is range-bound. The October low has been breached, but the March 14 close has finished above the October low. Not a great prognosis overall, but I'd prefer some more clarity on the situation.

A look at the weekly chart over 12 months could shed some light on what's going on here:

Chart 4.8.9 ● Time frames—weekly chart over 12 months for Citigroup (2000–2001).

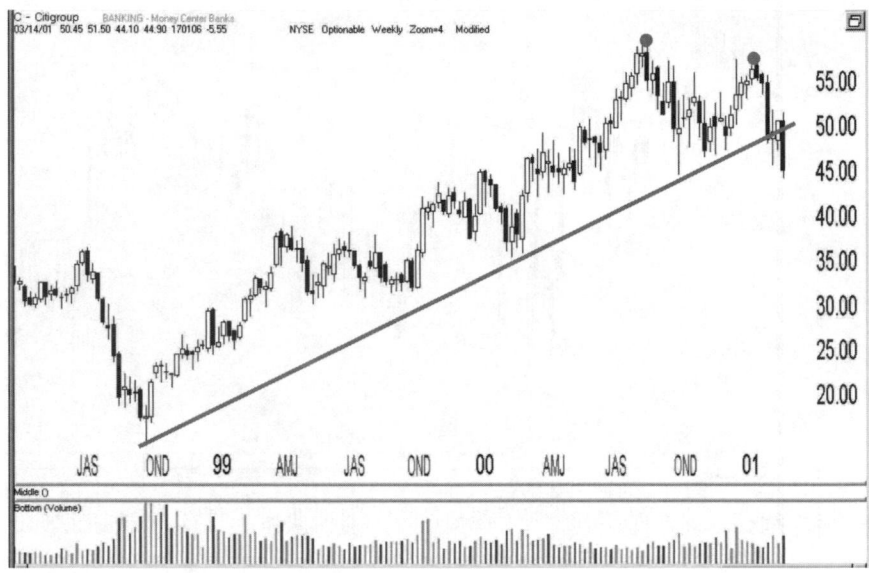

TC2000®.com. Courtesy of Worden Brothers Inc.

Here we can clearly see that between September and January a clear Double Top has formed, and although nothing else is necessarily jumping out of this particular chart, the double top alone would put me on alert since early January if I were trading this stock. The suspicion is that it could decline further to a major degree although I would look for a very short-term retracement before prices decline further. By the time you read this book, you'll be able to see for yourself what's gone on here.

Remember that the longer the time period that the pattern takes, the stronger and more important the pattern becomes. A two-month identifiable pattern is a far more powerful indicator than a ten-minute identifiable pattern.

For now, it's important that you grasp the concept that you should always look at charts over different time periods. The following table will give you an idea of what to look at and what to trade off for the different types of trader:

Type of trader	Time frames to look at	Time frames to trade off
Day trader	Tick	5 minute
	5 minute	30 minute
	30 minute	60 minute
	60 minute	
	Daily	
	Weekly	
End of day	60 minute	Daily
	Daily	Weekly
	Weekly	
	Monthly	
End of week	Daily	Daily
	Weekly	Weekly
	Monthly	Monthly

More Technical Analysis Terminology

Name	Meaning	Comments
Advance/Decline Line	The A/D Line is a measure of market breadth. It is simply the cumulative total of the Advancing/Declining Issues Indicator, which measures the number of advancing "issues" versus the number of declining "issues" on the NYSE.	When more stocks are rising than falling, the A/D Line will be positive and vice versa. As such, it is a useful measure of market breadth. The Dow Jones Industrial Average (DJIA) is an index of just 30 stocks. While it is viewed as a total market bellwether, 30 stocks is hardly representative. The NASDAQ is weighted toward technology stocks, again, hardly a representative sample. Therefore, the Advance/Decline Indicator is seen as a useful tool to gauge market strength or weakness as a whole.

Name	Meaning	Comments
Bollinger Bands	Bollinger Bands are lines that are plotted at standard deviation levels above and below a moving average. Because standard deviation is a measure of volatility, Bollinger Bands are seen as self-adjusting (for volatility) and, when placed over a price chart, the basic interpretation is that the price will stay in between the two bands.	Bollinger Bands will expand during high volatility times and contract during phases of low volatility. Some observations have shown that sharp price movements can be expected when the bands have tightened to extreme levels. There are a number of other observations, which we won't go into here. For more information on Bollinger Bands, take a look at the tutorial on the Web site: www.bollingerbands.com.
Momentum	Momentum is a measure of how much a security's price has changed over a given time span.	
Standard Deviation	Standard Deviation (SD) is a statistical measure of volatility. In Technical Analysis, it is typically used as a component part for other indicators, such as Bollinger Bands.	High SD values will occur when prices have been moving dramatically and vice versa. Watch out for major tops and bottoms to coincide with high levels of volatility.
Put/Call Ratio	Another measure of market breadth and a contrarian indicator, the P/C ratio reflects the number of puts and calls bought on the CBOE. The indicator assumes that put buyers are bearish and call buyers are bullish. Later you'll see that this is not always necessarily the case, given that calls and puts can be bought and sold in different combinations to set up hedged trades.	The higher the P/C ratio, the more bearish the market is feeling. As a contrarian indicator, you might interpret a high P/C ratio as a good time to buy. Obviously, you'd combine this indicator with others.
New Highs/New Lows	This indicator displays the number of stocks making 52-week highs against the number making 52-week lows.	
On Balance Volume	OBV is a measure of volume but assumes that on an up day, all the volume is up volume and on a down day all the volume is down volume. The theory is that OBV is a leading indicator in that it shows where the smart money is flowing before prices confirm the move. A price surge without the requisite OBV move would be considered as unconfirmed.	

Name	Meaning	Comments
Open Interest	Open Interest is simply the number of options or futures contracts unexercised or open at a given point in time. An open contract is simply one that has not been exercised, closed out, or allowed to expire. Open Interest increases when two parties enter into a new options or futures contract (remember there are always two parties to a trade) and decreases if the existing contract is liquidated.	In its own right open interest is purely a measure of liquidity or, rather, activity in a particular underlying security's options or futures series. Some followers believe that rising open interest coupled with rising volume is a confirmation of the current trend direction. On the other hand, falling volume and falling Open Interest is thought to be a sign that the current trend is about to reverse.
VIX	The VIX is a volatility index as measured from the Standard and Poors 100 index.	Generally when the market is rising, the VIX will be low, but when prices are experiencing fast falls the VIX will be high, reflecting increased panic among traders and investors. Contrarian traders look at the VIX for a guide to investor sentiment. They surmise that when the VIX is high most of the sellers will have left the market, and so it may be a good time to buy. Hence the expression, *"When the VIX is high, time to buy; when the VIX is low, time to go."*
12-month high	The highest price reached by the stock in the last 12 months.	
12-month low	The lowest price reached by the stock in the last 12 months.	

This list is simply an outline of the better-known technical indicators and is by no means exhaustive. There are any number of Web sites containing detailed descriptions of many technical indicators and chart patterns. Try out www.stockcharts.com for a start.

Chapter 4 Major Learning Points

I cannot stress more strongly about the need to delve further into the realms of Technical Analysis for you to improve your trading consistency. I once heard someone say that the best options strategy was getting the market/security direction (or lack of it) right! Well, that's only partly true, but let's face it, if you get the direction badly wrong and don't act appropriately when you've made that error, there'll nearly always be a problem. We want to concentrate on improving your chances of success. This takes work, so don't be fooled. The beauty is that this is such a compelling and fascinating area, I consider it more of a hobby than work.

Many speculators take a fleeting interest in the hard work side to investing and trading stocks and commodities. This makes it no better than guesswork or gambling. What we've shown you here is just a start. Many Technical Analysts use different indicators and chart patterns to varying degrees of success. While you don't have to be a Nobel Prize mathematician to trade successfully, most of the successful technical traders do have a deep understanding of the indicators they follow. That's what I want you to start to develop too.

Here's a summary of the chart patterns and indicators we've just been through and my ratings of them as lagging or leading indicators:

Chart pattern	Breakout or Reversal	Lagging or Leading	Rating (A–E)
Support and Resistance	Both	Both	A
Double and Triple Tops and Bottoms	Reversal	Lagging	A
Head and Shoulders	Reversal	Lagging	D
Pennants and Triangles	Both	Leading	B
Flags and Wedges	Breakout	Both	D
Trendlines	Both	Both	B
Fibonacci Retracement and Expansion	Both	Leading	A
Elliott Wave	Both	Leading	A*
Gann	Both	Leading	A/B
Gaps	Both	Lagging	B
Volume	Both	Leading	A

* Where used properly and in conjunction with Fibonacci.

Indicator	Breakout or Reversal	Lagging or Leading	Rating (A–E)
Displaced and standard Moving Averages	Both	Lagging	A*
MACD	Reversal	Lagging	B**
Stochastics	Reversal	Lagging	B***
RSI	Both	Lagging	B

* Displaced Moving Averages merit an A here; normal Moving Averages merit only a C for me!

** This depends on how MACD is being interpreted. I like to use it in conjunction with other indicators, and the typical reading of MACD is not one that I follow, hence the modest rating of a B.

*** Again, this all depends on the interpretation of the Stochastic and the way in which the other indicators are being used.

Two Popular Strategies and How to Improve Them

- Have you ever bought a stock with the view of holding it for some time, but you wanted to ensure against a downturn, just in case?

- Have you ever bought a stock with the view of holding it for some time, but where you wanted to receive a "dividend-like" payment every month for owning it?

- Have you ever bought a stock with the view of holding it for some time, where you wanted to receive the dividend-like payments but also wanted to ensure against the downside?

Well, the answer to all three questions is that you can do them all!

Example 5.1

Let's look at buying a stock again:

Chart 5.1 ● Risk profile of buying a stock.

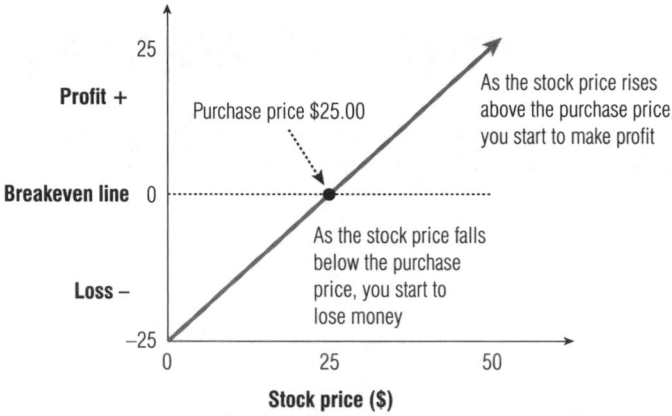

As you can see, your risk is what you pay for the stock in the first place, in this example, $25.00.

The Synthetic Call

Question: When we buy the stock, we want to ensure against it falling fast, so what can we do about that?

Answer: Buy a put option as well. The combination of buying the stock and a put is known as a *Synthetic Call*.

Question: Which exercise price for the put should we choose?

Answer: It depends on your appetite for risk. Generally you should buy the puts one or two strike prices Out of the Money—OTM (that is, below the price you paid for the stock).[1] If you are highly risk averse, here you'd choose the $25 strike price, but if you're only concerned about a level of support, say at $20, then you'd choose the $20 strike put.

---

[1] Remember that for puts OTM will be below the current stock price and for calls, OTM will be above the current stock price.

With respect to American stocks, remember that you'll need to buy 100 shares for every put option you buy. In other words, you'll need to buy one put contract for every 100 shares that you buy. Remember that every US stock options contract represents 100 shares.

Let's have a look at what we're doing here and then compare the Risk Profiles of buying the $25 strike puts versus buying the $20 strike puts.

A recap of our strategy shows us that we're buying the stock and also buying put options for insurance against a downturn.

Diagram 5.1 ● Synthetic Call.

Buy stock   Buy put   Synthetic Call

Steps to Trading a Synthetic Call

1 Buy the stock.

2 Buy puts with a strike price close to the price at which you bought the stock.

● Notice that you have created the same shape of Risk Profile as that of a long call option (but you have paid a lot more for it here). What you are actually doing here is capping your downside risk by buying the put option having bought the stock.

Notice how the Risk Profile we're creating here is the same shape as that of a bought call option, hence the name, Synthetic Call. The difference is that with a Synthetic Call, you are paying a lot more money up front (than with a straight call option), since you're paying for both the stock and the put option. A Synthetic Call is also less risky in terms of your entire net debit (what you pay for the strategy), given that the total of what you can lose is restricted to the stock price plus the put premium less the put exercise price. A Synthetic Call is therefore safer in terms of your percentage possible loss from the amount of money you spend on the trade (net debit).

Comparing the Risk of a Synthetic Call Versus a Long Call

Example 5.2a

Here are our choices:

A. Straight call—buy the November 2001 $25 strike call options for $5.25.[2]

B. Synthetic Call—buy the stock (Dell) for $25, and buy the November 2001 $25 strike put options for $4.50.

	Synthetic Call (Strike $25)	Simple Long Call (Strike $25)
You pay	Stock price + put premium **$25 + $4.50 = $29.50**	Call premium **$5.25**
Risk	Stock price + put premium—put strike **$25 + $4.50 − $25 = $4.50** Risk of $4.50 is only 15% of your total cost	Call premium **$5.25** Risk is 100% of your total cost
Reward	Unlimited to the upside	Unlimited to the upside
Breakeven	Stock price + put premium **$25 + $4.50 = $29.50**	Call strike + call premium **$25 + $5.25 = $30.25**

Which one would you choose to do? Well, the answer will all depend on your appetite for risk and the amount of money you're willing to spend. Note that the price you pay (net debit) for a Synthetic Call is not equal to your risk for that trade. This makes the Synthetic Call considerably less risky than simply buying the call, however, this is balanced by the fact that the Synthetic Call is so much more expensive as well.

Now let's look at another example where we are looking at a lower strike price for the put options:

---

[2] Real prices taken from Dell option Series on April 5, 2001, at 11:30 a.m. EST. I've selected this as an example purely because of the simplicity of the numbers.

Example 5.2b

C. Straight call—buy the November 2001 $20 strike call options for $8.00.[3]

D. Synthetic Call—buy the stock (Dell) for $25, and buy the November 2001 $20 strike put options for $2.38.

	Synthetic Call (Strike $20)	**Simple Bought Call (Strike $20)**
You pay	Stock price + put premium **$25 + $2.38 = $27.38**	Call premium **$8.00**
Risk	Stock price + put premium—put strike **$25 + $2.38 – $20 = $7.38** Risk of $7.38 is 27% of your total cost	Call premium **$8.00** Risk is 100% of your total cost
Reward	Unlimited to the upside	Unlimited to the upside
Breakeven	Stock price + put premium **$25 + $2.38 = $27.38**	Call strike + call premium **$20 + $8 = $28.00**

Again, the risk of the Synthetic Call is less than that of simply buying the call options, but the Synthetic Call is a much more expensive strategy (compare $27.38 versus $8.00).

Let's compare the two Synthetic Calls we've just looked at (B and D):

Example 5.2c

	Synthetic Call B (Strike $25)	**Synthetic Call D (Strike $20)**
You pay	Stock price + put premium **$25 + $4.50 = $29.50**	Stock price + put premium **$25 + $2.38 = $27.38**
Risk	Stock price + put premium—put strike **$25 + $4.50 – $25 = $4.50** Risk of $4.50 is only 15% of your total cost	Stock price + put premium—put strike **$25 + $2.38 – $20 = $7.38** Risk of $7.38 is 27% of your total cost
Reward	Unlimited to the upside	Unlimited to the upside
Breakeven	Stock price + put premium **$25 + $4.50 = $29.50**	Stock price + put premium **$25 + $2.38 = $27.38**
Comparison	• More expensive • Lower maximum risk • Higher breakeven	• Cheaper • Greater maximum risk • Lower breakeven

[3] Real prices taken from Dell option Series on April 5, 2001, at 11:30 a.m. EST. I've selected this as an example purely because of the simplicity of the numbers.

What this table clearly shows is that the higher the put strike price you select for your Synthetic Call Strategy, the lower your risk will be. However, you'll have to pay more up front for that added insurance, and therefore your Breakeven Point will generally be higher as well.

Chart 5.1.1 ● Synthetic Call comparison between B and D.

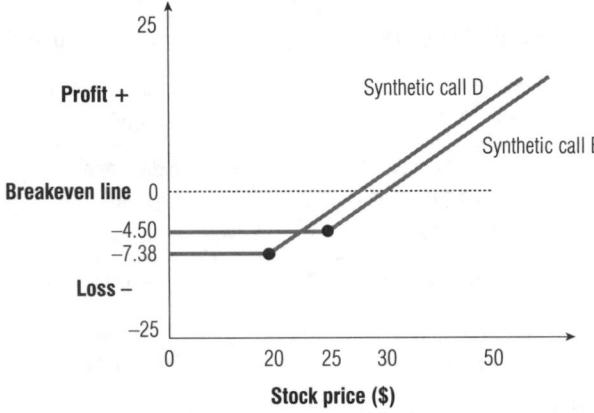

The lower the breakeven point, the better your chances are of being profitable here, but the price you pay is the fact that you're risking more on the downside.

To ask which one to choose is a very personal question that consists of a number of issues:

● What's my own appetite for risk here?

● How does the stock behave?

● Where is the strongest support for the stock price?

● What are the charts telling me?

● What is the market telling me?

These questions will lead you to formulating a trading plan. There is strong support here at the $20 level, and that may well impact upon your eventual decision. The stock has just gapped up almost $2 this morning, and the market has also just gapped up this morning. If I had to make a choice here, I'd choose D because the breakeven is lower. The maximum risk is greater, but the stock price has to fall to $20 for that to happen—and I am happy to take that risk between for the next 71/2 months. (I would also exit my long position on a breakdown below $24.00, but that is a moot point here!)

In conclusion, we can see how we can insure ourselves when we buy a stock for the medium term, by buying a put option. As with any type of insurance policy, the more insurance you pay, the lower your risk exposure should be.

The Covered Call (Covered Write or Buy Write)

Question: When we buy the stock, we want to get some income back while we're holding it over the medium term—is that possible?

Answer: Yes. Sell a call option as well. The combination of buying the stock and selling a call is known as a *Covered Call*.

Question: Which exercise price and expiration date for the call should we choose for this strategy?

Answer: In general, you should sell call options one or two strike prices Out of the Money (OTM) (that is, higher than the price you paid for the stock), and with approximately one month left to expiration.

With respect to US stocks, remember that to be covered, you'll need to buy 100 shares for every call option you sell. And remember that every US stock options contract represents 100 shares.

Diagram 5.2 ● Covered Call.

Buy stock   Sell call   Covered Call

Steps to Trading a Covered Call

1 Buy the stock.
2 Sell calls one or two strike prices OTM (that is, calls with strike prices one or two strikes higher than the stock).
● Notice that you have created the same shape of Risk Profile as a short put option. The difference here is that you've bought the stock and have therefore had to part with cash to execute the purchase. Having bought the stock, you partially offset that purchase cost by selling short-term calls (say, on a monthly basis).

Remember that when you sell options, you generally want to sell them with short-term expirations only. There are two main reasons for this:

1. Selling options is dangerous because of the unlimited Risk Profile that

accompanies the strategy. This can be mitigated when the transaction forms a part of combination (spread) order.

2. Shorter-term options are more expensive on a per-day basis than longer-term options. As an assignment, just compare two ATM options of the same stock, one with two weeks left to expiration and one with one year left to expiration. Then divide the option premiums by the respective number of days left until expiration. You'll find, without exception, that on a per-day basis, the shorter-term options are more expensive even though the nominal dollar amount is lower.

When you buy options premium, you want to give yourself as much time as possible to be right. This means that you should take advantage of buying the better value longer-term options. Even though they're more expensive in nominal dollar terms, they're much better value in terms of a per-day value. And there's not much point in not giving yourself adequate time to be right. At the same time, when you're selling options premium, you generally want to have as little time as possible to be wrong. When you think about it, this is all logical stuff.

Now that you can see that a Covered Call is the same shape of Risk Profile as that of a Short (Naked) put, let's compare the two strategies:

● Selling a naked put requires you to have an advanced trading account with your options broker. You'll also have to provide margin in your account to cover the potential risk.

● With a Covered Call, the call that you sell is "covered" by the fact that you have bought the stock. How is this so? Let's go through the process step by step:

(a) When you sell the call, you are the one who is obligated to deliver the stock if the stock rises above the strike price. Of course, this is just logical. The person who bought the call from you has the right, *not* the obligation to buy the stock from you (if the call is ITM, that is, greater than the strike price).

(b) You're "covered" from unlimited risk in the eventuality that the call buyer could exercise you because you already own the stock, which you would have to deliver if you are exercised. The word "covered" only means that you are protected from unlimited risk. Had you sold the call option naked, then you would have been exposed to unlimited risk.

Remember what you're doing here:

Profile	Description	Risk	Reward	Breakeven
	Buy stock	Purchase price	Unlimited to the upside	**Purchase price**
	Sell call	Unlimited to the upside	Limited to the call premium received	**Strike price plus premium paid**
	Covered Call	Cost of stock less call premium received	Limited to the call premium received plus the call strike price less the stock price paid	Stock price paid less the call premium received

Example 5.3 **A Covered Call**

Let's say BORT is trading at $28.10 on March 27. The $30 strike calls are trading at $0.85.

We want to sell eight calls but have to be covered. How many shares do we need to buy to cover the calls we want to sell?

8 x 100 = 800 shares.

Here are the steps:

buy 800 BORT shares at **$28.10**	**$22,480**
sell 8 BORT $30 strike April calls at **$0.85**	**$680**
Net investment	**$21,800**

Let's take a closer look at what we've done here and see what happens in various scenarios:

Scenario 1—stock falls to $0.00

Stock now at $0.00	loss	$0.00 - $28.10 =	-$28.10
Short calls expire worthless	profit	$0.85	$0.85
	Total loss		**$27.25**

Scenario 2—stock falls to $25.00

Stock now at $25.00	loss	$25.00 - $28.10 =	-$3.10
Short calls expire worthless	profit	$0.85	$0.85
	Total loss		**$2.25**

Scenario 3—stock falls to $27.25			
Stock now at $27.25	loss	$27.25 - $28.10 =	-$0.85
Short calls expire worthless	profit	$0.85	$0.85
	Breakeven		**$0.00**

Scenario 4—stock remains at $28.10			
Stock now at $28.10	→	$28.10 - $28.10 =	$0.00
Short calls expire worthless	profit	$0.85	$0.85
	Total profit		**$0.85**

Scenario 5—stock rises to $30.00			
Stock now at $30.00	profit	$30.00 - $28.10 =	$1.90
Short calls expire worthless	profit	$0.85	$0.85
	Total profit		**$2.75**

Scenario 6—stock rises to $30.95			
Stock now at $30.95	profit	$30.95 - $28.10 =	$2.85
Short calls sold	profit	$0.85	$0.85
Short calls exercised at $30.00	loss	$30.00 - $30.95	-$0.95
	Total profit		**$2.75**

Scenario 7—stock rises to $35.00			
Stock now at $35.00	profit	$35.00 - $28.10 =	$6.90
Short calls sold	profit	$0.85	$0.85
Short calls exercised at $30.00	loss	$30.00 - $35.00	-$5.00
	Total profit		**$2.75**

We can summarize our BORT Covered Call at expiration as follows:

Diagram 5.1a ● BORT Covered Call.

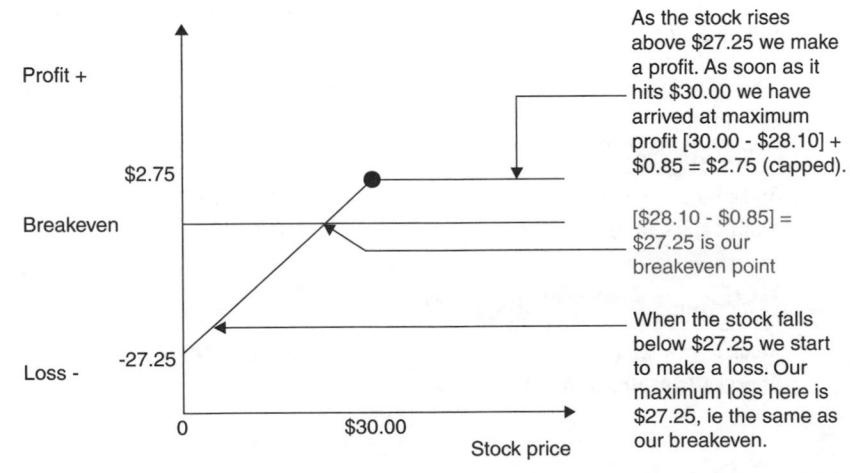

As the stock rises above $27.25 we make a profit. As soon as it hits $30.00 we have arrived at maximum profit [30.00 - $28.10] + $0.85 = $2.75 (capped).

[$28.10 - $0.85] = $27.25 is our breakeven point

When the stock falls below $27.25 we start to make a loss. Our maximum loss here is $27.25, ie the same as our breakeven.

There are a couple of important things to realize about the trade in Example 5.3:

● The strike price of the call we sold is higher than the price we paid for the stock.

● Having our calls exercised wasn't a problem because we already owned the stock at a lower purchase price. This meant we made a profit on the stock (because the call strike was higher than what we originally paid for the stock) and also got to keep the entire call premium.

The summary of the BORT April $30.00 Covered Call Risk Profile is as follows:

Max risk	[stock price paid – call premium]	$28.10 - $0.85	**= $27.25**
Breakeven	[stock price paid - call premium]	$28.10 - $0.85	**= $27.25**
Max reward	[call strike – stock price paid] + call premium	$30.00 - $28.10 + $0.85	**= $2.75**
Initial yield			**3.02%**
Max yield			**9.79%**

What would happen if we had written the $25.00 strike call when BORT was trading at $28.10? In other words, what happens if we write an ITM covered call?

Assuming the $25.00 strike April calls are trading at $3.55, then here's what would happen:

Max risk	[stock price paid – call premium]	$28.10 - $3.55 **= $24.55**
Breakeven	[stock price paid - call premium]	$28.10 - $3.55 **= $24.55**
Max reward	[call strike – stock price paid] + call premium	$25.00 - $28.10 + $3.55 = **$0.45**
Initial yield		**12.63%**
Max yield		**1.60%**

Covered Call Comparison

	$30.00 strike (OTM)	$25.00 strike (ITM)
You pay	$28.10 - $0.85 = **$27.25**	$28.10 - $3.55 = **$24.55**
Max risk	$28.10 - $0.85 = **$27.25**	$28.10 - $3.55 = **$24.55**

	$30.00 strike (OTM)	$25.00 strike (ITM)
Breakeven	$28.10 - $0.85 = **$27.25**	$28.10 - $3.55 = **$24.55**
Max reward	$30.00 - $28.10 + $0.85 = **$2.75**	$25.00 - $28.10 + $3.55 = **$0.45**
Initial yield	**3.02%**	**12.63%**
Max yield	**9.79%**	**1.60%**

By trading an ITM Covered Call, the chief benefit is that of more cushion to your breakeven point. Here the ITM Covered Call gives you $2.80 more cushion. The initial yield looks promising too, doesn't it. A whopping 12.63% compared to the OTM initial yield of only 3.02%. However, look closer and see what the maximum yield on the trade is, and you'll start to realize that, despite the high initial yield, your maximum yield on the ITM Covered Call is only 1.60%. This is because you're obligated to sell the stock at $25.00, yet you bought the stock for $28.10. That's a $3.10 immediate loss on your trade. You sold those ITM calls for $3.55, giving you a maximum profit for the trade of only $0.45.

Compare these figures to the OTM Covered Call, and we can see that the OTM Covered Call gives us much more scope to the upside with an attractive 9.79% maximum yield. Even the 3.02% initial yield is attractive. Do you realize that if you made 3.19% every month that would translate to compounded yield of more than 42% per annum?

If we had tried to choose the $35.00 OTM strike, we'd see that the calls were only trading at $0.10 on the bid (remember, we sell at the bid), and that wouldn't be worth our while, so the optimum strike for a BORT March Covered Call is the $30.00 strike.

Remember, the reason for getting into a Covered Call is because you're bullish. You don't mind having a capped upside because it's a short-term income trade lasting only about one month.

Comparing the Risk of a Covered Call Versus Selling a Naked Put

Example 5.4[4]

E Covered Call—buy the stock for $25 and sell the May 2001 $30 (strike) call for $0.75.

F Naked Put—sell the $20 (strike) May 2001 put for $0.75.

---

[4] Using real prices for Dell on April 6, 2001.

	Covered Call (E) (Strike $30)	**Naked Put (F) (Strike $20)**
You pay/receive	Stock price – call premium **$25 – $0.75 = $24.25 (you pay)**	Put premium received **$0.75 (you receive)**
Risk	Stock price – call premium received **$25 – $0.75 = $24.25** Risk of $24.25 is 100% of your total Cost	Put exercise price less put premium received **$20 – $0.75 = $19.25** Risk of $19.25 is more than 25 times what you received for the put premium
Maximum reward	Limited to the call premium received, plus the call strike price less the stock price paid **$0.75 + $30 – $25 = $5.75** You only receive this maximum reward if the stock price appreciates to $30 or more at expiration. This represents a maximum return on maximum risk of 23.7% but the stock must reach $30 at expiration for this to happen.	Limited to the put premium received **$0.75** Provided the stock remains above $20, you will receive $0.75 as your maximum reward. You didn't have to put any money down for this trade, but you did have to provide liquid funds in your account as margin for the trade. Your return on maximum risk is only 3.9% but the stock has to plummet to below $19.25 for you to start to lose money.
Breakeven	Stock price–call premium received **$25 – $0.75 = $24.25**	Put strike–put premium received **$20 – $0.75 = $19.25**
Comment	As you can see, a straightforward comparison can be a little misleading and although these two strategies share the same **_shape_** of risk profile, they actually require totally different risk perspectives from the trader. A Covered Call trader will not necessarily fancy Naked Puts and vice versa. The danger with both these strategies is if the stock plummets. For this reason, you should never trade them before a major news item is due out on the stock (for example, earnings). Furthermore, these strategies should only really be played in up-trending markets.	

Chart 5.2.1 ● Covered Call compared with Naked Put.

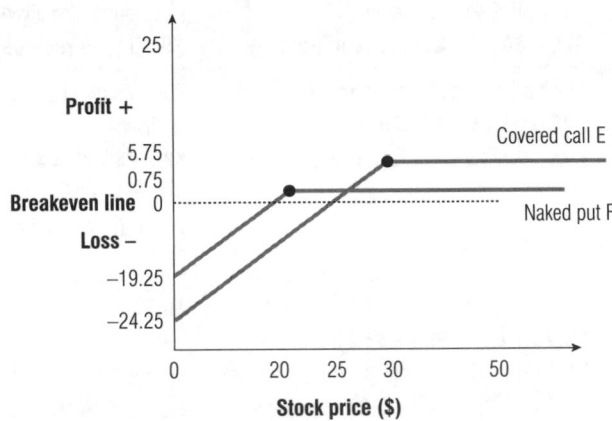

We now need to compare different Covered Calls so we can analyze the best way to play this strategy. The thing with options is that you have so much choice in terms of exercise prices and expiration dates.

Let's compare Covered Call E with another two, G and H. There's no room for maneuver on the expiration dates; we don't go beyond one month unless it's by just a week or so.

E. Covered Call—buy the stock for $25 and sell the May 2001 $30 (strike) call for $0.75.

G. Covered Call—buy the stock for $25 and sell the May 2001 $27.50 (strike) call for $1.30.

H. Covered Call—buy the stock for $25 and sell the May 2001 $25 (strike) call for $2.40.

	Covered Call (E)	Covered Call (G)	Covered Call (H)
You pay/ receive	Stock price – call premium $25 – $0.75 = $24.25 (you pay)	Stock price – call premium $25 – $1.30 = $23.70 (you pay)	Stock price – call premium $25 – $2.40 = $22.60 (you pay)
Risk	Stock price – call premium received $25 – $0.75 = $24.25 Risk of $24.25 is 100% of your total cost	Stock price – call premium received $25 – $1.30 = $23.70 Risk of $23.70 is 100% of your total cost	Stock price – call premium received $25 – $2.40 = $22.60 Risk of $22.60 is 100% of your total cost

	Covered Call (E)	Covered Call (G)	Covered Call (H)
Maximum Reward	Limited to the call premium received, plus the call strike price less the stock price paid **$0.75 + $30 − $25 = $5.75** You only receive this maximum reward if the stock price appreciates to $30 or more at expiration. This represents a maximum return on maximum risk of **23.7%**, but the stock must reach $30 at expiration for this to happen.	Limited to the call premium received, plus the call strike price less the stock price paid **$1.30 + $27.50 − $25 = $3.80** You only receive this maximum reward if the stock price appreciates to $27.50 or more at expiration. This represents a maximum return on maximum risk of **16%**, but the stock must reach $27.50 at expiration for this to happen.	Limited to the call premium received, plus the call strike price less the stock price paid **$2.40 + $25 − $25 = $2.40** You only receive this maximum reward if the stock price remains at $25 or more at expiration. This represents a maximum return on maximum risk of **10.6%**, but the stock must be at $25 at expiration for this to happen.
Interim reward	If the stock remains at its current level of $25, what are our respective yields then? Because we are presuming there is no uplift in the stock price whatsoever, the calculation is simply the call premium received divided by the maximum risk of the trade.		
	($0.75/$24.25) = 3.1%	**($1.30/$23.70) = 5.5%**	**($2.40/$22.60) = 10.6%**
Breakeven	Stock price − **call premium** received **$25 − $0.75 = $24.25**	Stock price − **call premium** received **$25 − $1.30 = $23.70**	Stock price − **call premium** received **$25 − $2.40 = $22.60**
Comment	Which one would you choose? Well there is no right or wrong answer *per se*, but remember why you would choose a Covered Call strategy. It's because you believe the stock will appreciate in value steadily over the medium term. Bearing this in mind, H doesn't fit in because you're not allowing for any of the expected rise in the stock value. You're then left between E and G. If you're anticipating a large move to the upside before expiration, then E would be the better choice because your maximum reward is higher. If you're more conservative, then G would be the better choice, since your risk and breakeven are lower (as is your maximum profit).		

Chart 5.2.2 ● Covered Calls E, G, and H (not to scale).

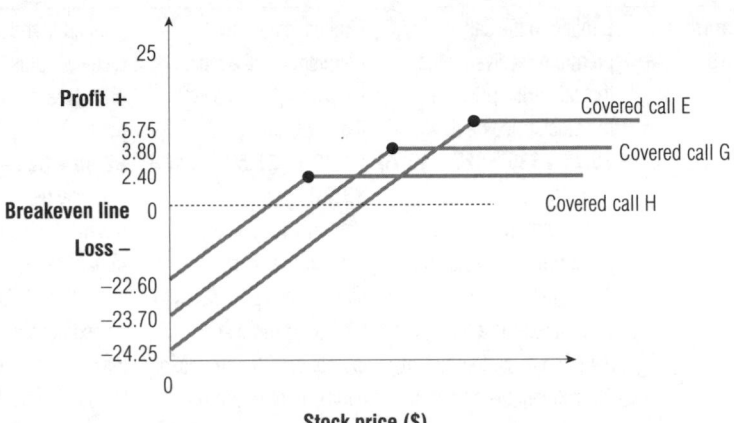

How to Improve the Covered Call

The slight weakness with a Covered Call is the risk profile to the downside. I generally don't like to see that diagonal line going all the way down, although with a Covered Call that diagonal line element only represents the actual stock risk profile as opposed to a leveraged options position. Generally, we should only be trading Covered Calls on up-trending stocks. However, up-trending stocks often have low volatility and low call premiums, making them unattractive as an income strategy. That lures many traders into the higher volatility, riskier stocks with higher call premiums. If you're that type of trader and can't resist the added risk, you should consider some serious downside protection. By "serious" I mean more protection than a stop, which won't protect you from a severe gap down.

So how do you suppose you could cap a catastrophic risk on the downside? The answer is to buy a protective put. This is an advanced strategy, outside the scope of this book, known as a Collar. There are several ways to play a Collar but for now, we're just going to look at the protective put option as an additional leg to the Covered Call.

If you're a fan of trading Covered Calls but would like to have some protection on the downside, then you might want to look at this approach:

Step 1   Understand the context of your trade and how long you're looking to hold the stock for (say, six months).

Step 2   Buy the stock.

Step 3   Sell the calls on a monthly basis.

Step 4   Buy a protective put for half the period of time you're looking to hold the stock for.

What you're doing here is akin to a finance deal. You're buying an asset, financing it (by selling calls every month) and insuring the transaction (by buying the protective put). I have suggested only insuring the deal for half your expected investment time frame because the bought put will increase your Breakeven Point, maybe excessively if you buy the put with too long to expiration. By the time the put is approaching expiration (say, in three months) you should be able to tell if your stock is behaving in the way you anticipated, and if it's weaker than you thought, you might want to reconsider your analysis on the stock.

Which put strike price do you buy? This depends on how much insurance you're looking for. For me, this put is insurance against a calamity, so I would choose a strike price around a clearly defined support area, which I'd have identified beforehand. Generally this will be below the current stock price. You must plan your trades and identify the areas of Support and Resistance that concur with the time frame you are trading. Every trade is a business transaction, and you should plan each one with the same kind of due diligence. Good trading and investing is all about stacking the probabilities in your favor. Pre-planning enables you to take the right approach.

Warning!

The net result of buying the protective put will have the effect of capping your downside until the put expires. However, the three-month protective put is likely to be more expensive than the one-month call you're selling. This means that this is a strategy that requires ongoing maintenance (that is, you need to be selling the calls every month for at least the period of the bought put in order for it to make financial sense). This is why you need to assess your context for placing the trade in the first place.[5]

---

[5] An alternative to this is if you trade a traditional Collar. A traditional Collar is a long-term trade, best suited to in excess of a year till expiration. It involves buying the stock (or going long a Future), selling a long-term OTM call option, and buying the same expiration long-term put option very close to the Money (that is, as close to the stock price as possible). In this way, it is actually possible to create a technically risk-free strategy albeit with limited upside.

The Collar (or Protected Buy-Write)

The Collar is designed to produce an extremely low risk strategy where, in certain cases, the trader can even enjoy a virtually riskless trade.[6] It may sound too good to be true, but it is possible—although I recommend that you enter in two separate orders for buying the stock and trading the calls and puts. Floor traders do not like the idea of you successfully executing a trade like this, even if the potential returns aren't spectacular.

For the strategy to work in this way, it needs to be a long-term strategy, with the options expiring at least one year out, that is, Long-term Equity AnticiPation Securities (LEAPs®). LEAPs are basically long-term expiration options.[7]

Here's how such a strategy would work:

1. Buy the stock.	✓ Buy the asset
2. Buy LEAP puts very close to the stock price.	✓ Insure it
3. Sell LEAP calls above the stock price.	✓ Finance the trade

Collar

Buy stock	Buy ATM put	Sell OTM call	Collar

The Art to Creating a Successful Collar

Risk

For a "riskless" trade[8] you will need to ensure that the call premium you receive less the put premium you pay, plus the stock price you pay less the put strike price is either zero or negative. In this way, your risk is limited as follows:

[stock price + put premium – put strike price – call premium]

---

[6] The risk-free position generally only applies to the position at expiration.

[7] Equity LEAPs are long-dated options on common stock or ADRs of companies that are listed on securities exchanges or trade over-the-counter. Equity LEAPs expire in approximately two to three years from the date of initial listing; equity LEAPs roll into the standard option after the May, June or July expiration depending upon whether the standard option associated with the LEAP is on the January, February, or March expiration cycle.

[8] This does not take account of the opportunity cost of money.

If this equation gives you a zero or negative figure, then you have a riskless trade.

Reward

Your maximum reward for a Collar is limited to the call strike price less the put strike price less the risk of the trade (as described above).

[call strike price] − [put strike price] − risk of trade

Breakeven

Stock price paid − [call premium received − put premium paid]

Likely Returns and When to Trade a Collar

Don't expect massive returns if you're looking for a zero or low risk strategy. There's always a trade-off between risk and reward, and this is also the case for Collars. In my experience and as a rule of thumb, you can certainly find high volatility stocks to yield you a maximum return in excess of 20% over 18 months for a "zero risk" Collar. If you want a guaranteed minimum return, then your maximum upside will be reduced. Obviously, the more risk you're willing to take on, the higher your maximum upside will be.

The criteria for finding appropriate stocks to Collar are

● high volatility,

● LEAPs over one year till expiration, and

● stock prices at strong support levels.

Collars are particularly useful when you cannot afford a loss on a trade but you'd still like to give yourself a chance of returns in the markets. It is extremely hard to find a zero risk Collar with expirations of less than one year. Around 18 months to expiration is optimal and gives you a chance to find the appropriate stocks. You must accept that this is a trade, which you cannot unravel long before expiration. Because of the way Time Value works, your zero Risk Profile on the Collar only really reveals itself when you are close to expiration. Even if the stock appreciates beyond the call strike price, then it is unlikely that you'll be exercised with more than one month left to expiration.

Example 5.4a

Have a look at the following options chain for YHOO on April 20, 2001, and let's create a Collar:

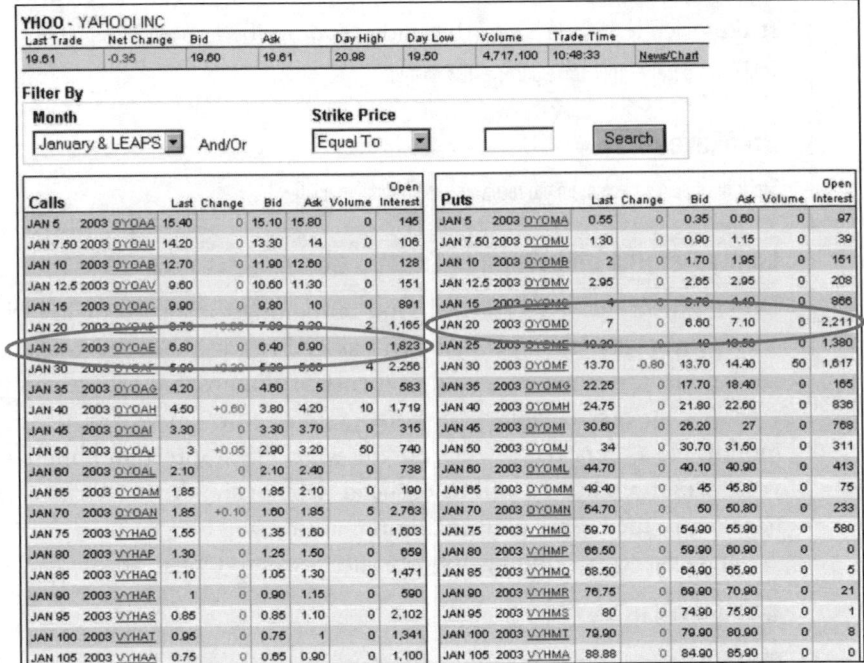

We're going to do the following:

---

1. Buy the stock at the market ask ($19.61).   ✓ Buy the stock

---

2. Buy the January 2003 $20 strike put at the ask ($7.10).   ✓ Insure it

---

3. Sell the January 2003 $25 strike call at the bid ($6.40).   ✓ Finance the trade

---

"Low Risk" Collar Risk Profile

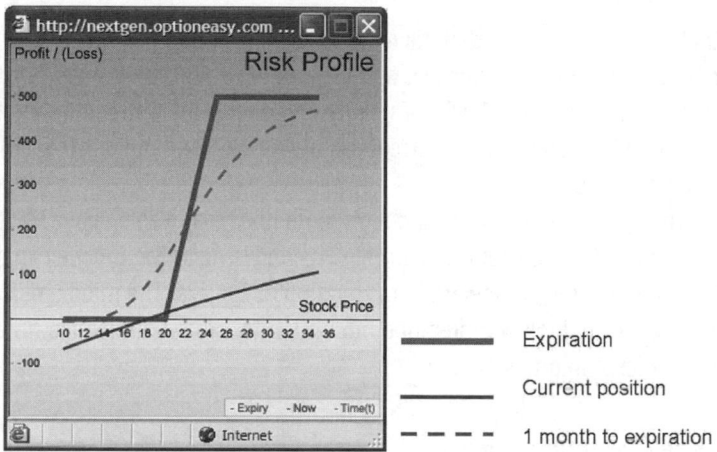

Expiration

Current position

1 month to expiration

"Low Risk" Collar Example 5.4a

Net debit	$20.31
Maximum risk	$0.31
Maximum reward	$4.69
Breakeven	$20.31
Maximum yield on risk	1,512.9%
Maximum yield on net debit	23.1%
Minimum yield on risk	
Minimum yield on net debit	N/A*

Note that the Maximum Risk, Reward, and Breakeven figures are calculated in terms of the expiration position.

* Minimum yields here would be negative.

As we can see, our maximum yield in terms of risk is enormous (1,512.9%) although our maximum yield on our net debit (that is, the money that we're spending on this trade) is only 23.1%. On an annual basis, this would only be 12.62% p.a., but the stock only has to move a little over five points and we're taking very little risk here indeed (just 1.5% of our total net debit).

Example 5.4b

Note that we took the prices that the market would give us (that is, buying at the ask and selling at the bid). Even so, our risk was very low at $0.31. With a limit order, we could realistically extinguish that $0.31 of risk by combining the options trades together at a net debit of $0.39 instead of the current call bid ($6.40) and put ask ($7.10) which gives a net debit of $0.70.

The trade becomes risk free, although remember that we still have to hold the stock during this time. Our "Current" risk profile Position is negative, but we can see over time that it will migrate upward toward our expiration risk curve. The middle risk curve is how our risk profile will look with just one month left to expiration. Notice how it is getting closer to the expiration risk curve.

"Zero Risk" Collar Risk Profile

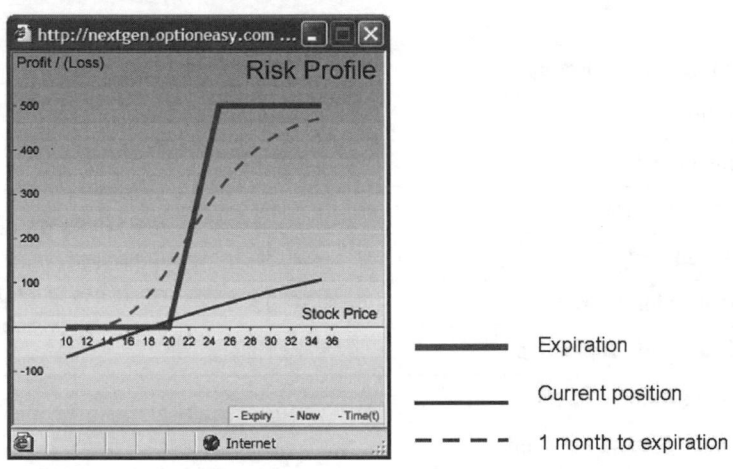

———	Expiration
———	Current position
– – – –	1 month to expiration

"Zero Risk" Collar Example 5.4b

Net debit	$20.00
Maximum risk	$0.00*
Maximum reward	$5.00
Breakeven	N/A
Maximum yield on risk	N/A
Maximum yield on net debit	22.6%
Minimum yield on risk	N/A
Minimum yield on net debit	N/A

Note that the Maximum Risk, Reward, and Breakeven figures are calculated in terms of the expiration position.

* We have ignored commission here.

Example 5.4c

Finally, let's take a look at what would happen if we were able to set a limit order based on the "last prices" achieved:

1. Buy the stock at $19.61.	✓ Buy the stock
2. Buy the January 2003 $20 strike put at $7.00.	✓ Insure it
3. Sell the January 2003 $25 strike call at $6.80.	✓ Finance the trade

In other words, we're going to enter in a Limit Order to buy the stock at $19.61 and combine the bought put and sold call at a net debit limit of $0.20.

"Guaranteed Return" Collar Risk Profile

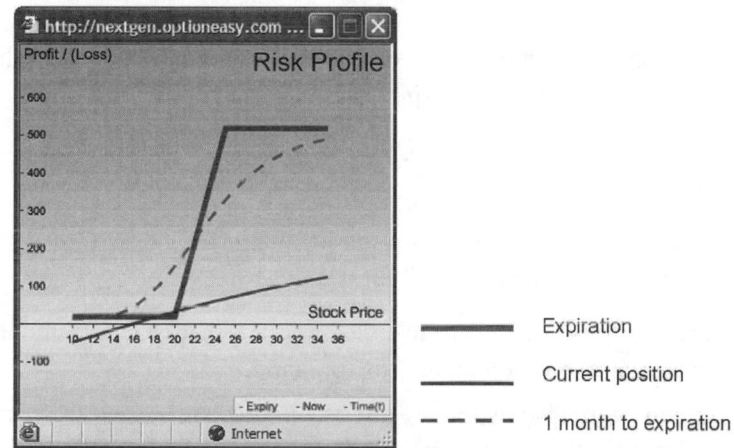

Expiration

Current position

1 month to expiration

Notice how the risk profile (expiration) is entirely above the breakeven line. This signifies that not only is this a "zero risk" trade but also one where we can have a small guaranteed positive return if we are filled.

"Guaranteed Return" Collar Example 5.4c	
Net debit	$19.81
Maximum risk (none here)	($0.19)*
Maximum reward	$5.19
Breakeven	N/A
Maximum yield on risk	N/A
Maximum yield on net debit	23.70%
Minimum yield on risk	N/A
Minimum yield on net debit	1.00%

Note that the Maximum Risk, Reward, and Breakeven figures are calculated in terms of the expiration position.

* Brackets denote that there is no risk (or negative risk) and that our minimum guaranteed return would be $0.19 at expiration.

It is highly unlikely that we'll be executed on the shorted call when there is more than one month left to expiration.

Futures

There are two major differences trading Collars, Synthetic Calls, and Covered Calls on stocks as compared with futures.

(a) Futures options are European-style options—that is, they can only be exercised at expiration and not beforehand.

(b) You don't actually pay money out of your account when you take a long position on a Future. This means that you can trade a Collar at little or no net debit whatsoever, or even in special circumstances at a net credit.

The conclusion is that Collars with futures options can be an exceptionally useful strategy if you can find the appropriate prices to make it work.

Chapter 5 Major Learning Points

In this chapter we've learned about Synthetic Calls and Covered Calls. Let's compare the two strategies:

	Synthetic Call	**Covered Call**
Strategy	Buy stock + buy put = Synthetic Call	Buy stock + sell call = Covered Call
Outlook	*Bullish*, although you are insuring your stock purchase.	*Mildly bullish*. You expect a steady rise.
Rationale	• To buy a stock for the medium or long term with the aim of underwriting your downside in the meantime. • If the stock price rises more than the cost of the bought put option, you will make profit. • If the stock falls, you will lose money, but your losses will be capped at the level of the put strike price.	• To buy a stock for the medium or long term with the aim of capturing monthly income by selling calls every month. This is like collecting rent for holding the stock and will have the effect of lowering your cost basis of holding the stock. • If the stock rises, you short call may be exercised, in which case you will make some profit. If the stock falls, your sold call will expire worthless, you will keep the premium, thus enabling you to have bought the stock cheaper (because you offset the received premium against the price you paid for the stock).
Net position	• This is *net debit* transaction. • Your risk is *limited* if the stock falls.	• This is a *net debit* transaction because you are paying for the stock and only taking in a small premium for the sold call options. You can increase your yield by purchasing the stock on margin, thereby doubling your yield if you use 50% margin. • Your risk is the price you paid for the stock less the premium you received for the call.

In the Strategy row:

Synthetic Call: Buy stock + Buy put = Synthetic Call

Covered Call: Buy stock + Sell call = Covered Call

Effect of time decay	• Time decay is *harmful* to the value of the put you bought.	• Time decay is *helpful* to your trade here because it should erode the value of the call you sold. Provided that the stock does not reach the strike price at expiration, you will simply retain the entire option premium for the trade, thus reducing your original cost of buying the share. If the stock price does reach the strike price of the call, then you will either be exercised early, in which case you'll sell the stock at the higher price (that is, the strike price), or you'll be exercised at expiration, where the same thing will happen.
Safest time period to trade	• Buy the puts with expirations with at least half the period you want to invest in the stock.	• Sell the calls on a monthly expiration basis.

We've also learned how to improve a Covered Call and reduce our risk, while accepting that our maximum upside would be reduced too. Collars are advanced strategies, which require trading experience to achieve the appropriate execution. This is why we suggest separating the options order entries from those of buying the stock. Example 5.4 (parts a, b, and c) is included to demonstrate the flexibility of using options to hedge your positions and achieve minimum levels of returns.

Because the following chapter covers the Greeks, we haven't yet covered how the various sensitivities respond to the above strategies. Please read the next chapter, and then you can return to the table footnoted below[9]

[9]Greek	Synthetic Call	Covered Call
Delta	Delta will assume the same shape as that for the delta of a long call. The stock delta is more powerful than the put delta, and the net profile follows that of a simple call option. Therefore, the Synthetic Call delta will increase as the stock price rises, demonstrating that a higher stock price will increase the value of the Synthetic Call position.	Delta (speed) is positive and falls to zero as the asset price rises above the strike price. The lower the stock price is, the higher delta is (remember for one contract delta's maximum is +1 and minimum is -1). This indicates that as the stock price increases, so does the value of the Covered Call. As the stock price rises through past the strike price, delta decreases in value and effectively rests at zero when the stock price exceeds the strike price plus the sold call premium. This mirrors the way in which a Covered Call has a maximum upside at this level, no matter how far the stock increases.
Gamma	Gamma (acceleration) is always positive with this position (because you are a net buyer of options) and peaks when the position is ATM.	Gamma is always negative with this position (because you are a net seller of calls) and peaks inversely when the position is ATM.
Theta	Because theta is irrelevant for stock positions (you buy a stock in perpetuity, therefore there is no time decay), the theta position here solely reflects that of the bought put option. Therefore, as you'd expect, theta is negative, bottoming at the strike price, indicating that the time decay is hurting the Synthetic Call strategy, particularly around the strike price.	Theta is positive, illustrating that time decay is helpful to the position. Theta is positive because we have sold premium and peaks around the strike price. As we approach expiration, theta's helpful impact becomes more prominent.
Vega	Volatility is helpful to the position. Vega peaks at the strike price indicating that small increases in volatility will have the most impact on the Synthetic Call position at that level.	Vega is negative, illustrating that volatility is harmful to the position. Vega bottoms at the strike price indicating that increased volatility will be most harmful to the Covered Call position in that price range.
Rho	Higher interest rates are harmful to the position. Rho is negative and becomes more negative the further the stock price falls.	Rho is negative, illustrating that higher interest rates would be harmful to the position. Rho becomes more negative the further the stock price rises.

An Introduction to the Greeks

The Greeks are simply sensitivities to options risk characteristics. The names are taken from actual Greek words. To understand why options have sensitivities to various factors, all we have to do is go back to our original definition of an option:

● The right, not the obligation

● To buy or sell an asset

● At a fixed price

● Before a predetermined date

...and then remind ourselves of the seven factors that affect an option's premium:

(i)   **type of option (call or put)**

(ii)   **the underlying asset price**

(iii)   **the strike price of the option**

(iv)   **the expiration date of the option**

(v)   **the volatility of the underlying asset**

(vi)   **the risk free rate of interest**

(vii) **dividends payable and stock splits**

If these factors affect the pricing of an option, then it stands to reason that option premiums must be sensitive to them. We can distill this further by highlighting the following sensitivities:

Factor affecting option premium	Sensitivity of option to...
Underlying asset price →	...Speed of the underlying asset price movement
Expiration date →	...Time Decay
Volatility of underlying asset →	...Volatility
Risk free rate of interest →	...Interest Rates

Each sensitivity has a corresponding "Greek":

Sensitivity of option to...	Greek
Speed of underlying asset price movement →	Delta Gamma*
Time Decay →	Theta
Volatility →	Vega
Interest Rates →	Rho

* Gamma measures the option sensitivity to Delta, which we will discuss

The Greeks

Greek		Sensitivity to
Delta	**Δ**	Change in option price relative to change in underlying asset price (that is, **Speed**)
Gamma	**Γ**	Change in option delta relative to change in underlying asset price (that is, **Acceleration**)
Theta	**Θ**	Change in option price relative to change in time left to expiration (that is, **Time Decay**)
Vega	**K**	Change in option price relative to the change in the asset's volatility (that is, **Historical Volatility**)
Rho	**P**	Change in option price relative to changes in the Risk Free Interest Rate (that is, **Interest Rates**)

A simple summary of the Greeks defines and explains them as follows:

Greek	Definition	Comment
Delta	Measures the sensitivity of an option price relative to change in underlying asset price (i.e. speed). *A positive delta means that the options position will become more valuable as the stock price rises. A negative delta means that the options value will increase as the underlying asset's value decreases.*	Delta ratio is also known as the Hedge Ratio. We can view delta as the probability of an option expiring In the Money. An ATM option will have a 50:50 chance of expiring ITM. For a call this means a delta of 0.5 and for a put this means a delta of -0.5 (because the put will rise as the stock falls and vice versa).
Gamma	Measures the sensitivity of the option delta relative to the underlying asset price movement (that is, acceleration). Gamma is positive for long call and long put positions and has the same value for equivalent ATM calls and puts. A low gamma means that large shifts in the stock price will be beneficial while a high gamma signifies that even small shifts in the stock price will be beneficial to the options position.	Rate of change of delta, that is, the curvature of delta risk. We can view gamma as the odds of a change in delta. The odds of a change in delta will be highest where there is a turning point in the risk profile chart. So for a long call or put, gamma will peak At the Money.
Theta	Measures the sensitivity of the option price relative to change in time left to expiration. *For long options positions, theta is usually negative, signifying that Time Decay is hurting the long option position and that the passage of time will reduce the value of that long position.* For combination options trades theta can be positive, showing that Time Decay can help the spread position (for example, Covered calls).*	Time decay is fastest during the last 30 days till expiration and when option is ATM.
Vega	Measures the sensitivity of the option price relative to the change in the asset's volatility. *Vega is always positive for long options positions and is identical for equivalent ATM calls and puts. A high positive vega signifies that small increases in volatility will be helpful to the options position while a low vega signifies that high volatility will be required to augment the options position.*	Historical Volatility.

*The one exception to the rule being with Deep In the Money put options.

Greek	Definition	Comment
Rho	Measures the sensitivity of the option price relative to changes in the Risk Free Interest Rate. *Higher interest rates will be beneficial to calls and detrimental to puts. Also, the longer the time to expiration, the greater value (positive or negative) rho will have, since interest rates need time to bite.*	Interest rates.
Zeta	Measures the percentage change in option price per 1% change in implied volatility.	1% implied volatility change.

Let's go through each Greek to make sense from all this.

Delta Δ

The Basics

- The option delta is the rate of change of the option price compared with the price movement of the underlying asset price. In other words, delta measures the *speed* of the option price movement as compared with movement of the underlying asset.

$$\text{Delta} = \frac{\text{rate of change in option price}}{\text{rate of change in underlying asset price}}$$

- You can think of delta as being the probability of the option expiring In the Money. As a general rule, ATM (At the Money) call options have deltas of 0.5. Therefore, for every $1.00 the stock moves, the call will move at approximately $0.5, that is, half the distance of the underlying stock. Inevitably, as the stock price moves away from the ATM position, the delta value will change too, away from 0.5.

- Because US stock options contracts represent 100 shares, the delta value of an ATM call option is represented as 50 instead of 0.5. One individual share has a delta of one—because a contract represents 100 shares, [100 x 0.5 = 50].

- A delta of +/- 50 is saying the option has a 50% chance of expiring In the Money. This makes complete sense because ATM options have a 50% chance of expiring In or Out of the Money.

- ATM = +/- 50 deltas—that is, moves at half the speed of the underlying asset.
- ATM calls have a delta of 0.5 meaning that for every one point the stock rises, the option will increase by 0.5 points.
- ATM puts have a delta of -0.5 meaning that for every one point the stock falls, the option price will increase by 0.5 points.
  - If you buy an ATM call, then you have a delta of 0.5.
  - If you sell an ATM call, then you have a delta of -0.5.
  - If you buy an ATM put, then you have a delta of -0.5.
  - If you sell an ATM put, then you have a delta of 0.5.
  - All bought calls have a positive delta.
- All sold calls have a negative delta.
- All bought puts have a negative delta.
- All sold puts have a positive delta.

Example 6.1.1

If you buy 100 shares of AMZN (+100 deltas), you would need to buy two ATM puts (-50 deltas each) for a Delta Neutral position.

Why Does Speed Matter?

Delta is important because it is an indication of the leverage we have in a position. Let's look at an illustration:

Example 6.1.2

Imagine taking a long position on a stock; say you buy 100 shares of one stock. Each $1.00 your stock rises, you make $100 x $1.00 = $100. Each $1.00 your stock falls, you lose $100.

But how would you feel if by buying call options you now make $300 when your stock rises by $1.00? Well, you'd feel pretty good until I then ask you the question, how do you feel if you could also lose $300 for every point the stock falls? Doesn't feel quite so good, does it! Some of you will simply say, "Well, that's what would happen anyway if I had bought 300 shares." And you're quite right. But you'd be missing a crucial point here, and that's leverage.

Let's say you bought the stock at $50.00. To buy 100 shares costs you $5,000.

And let's compare that to buying the equivalent in call options: one contract (representing 100 shares for US stocks) costs you, say $7.00, for which you'll have to pay a total of $700. (Remember, with just one contract, it's $7.00 for each one of those 100 shares that the contract represents.)

And for illustration purposes, let's say also that your delta is 1, that is, for every one point the stock moves, the call option you've bought also moves by one point.
If the stock *rises to $55:*

● your shares will increase by $5.00 per share, and you'll make $500 in extra profit, a profit of 10%.

● your options will increase by $5.00, and you'll make $500 in profit, a profit of more than 70%.

So far so good, you may say, but let's turn this around and let's see what would happen if the market went against you and *the stock had actually fallen from $50 to $45*:

● your shares will decrease by $5.00 per share, and you'll lose $500, a loss of *10%*. From the $5,000 you started with, you'd now have $4,500;

● your options will decrease by $5.00 and you'll lose $500, a loss of more than *70%*. From the $700 you started with, you've now only got $200.

Can you now see why we might want to do something about the speed of the options price movements and why we might want to offset (or hedge) delta?

Just as we always want enough time to be right when we buy an option, we also want to make sure that modest swings in the stock price aren't causing uncomfortably wild movements in our options position too quickly. This is why we want to hedge delta, or in other words, *slow down the speed* of the *percentage* movement of our position.

Delta Neutral Trading

Delta Neutral trading is a vast topic in itself. It is a method of trading whereby your position delta on the totality of your spread trade is one where the sum of the deltas equals *zero*. The idea is that this conveys a "hedged" position, whereby the risk is reduced because your position speed is slowed down.

Delta neutral traders do this on the basis that they can continually make profitable adjustments to their trade as the asset price fluctuates. The adjustments (usually selling part of the profitable side) bring the spread trade back to a Delta Neutral position (that is, where the sum of the deltas for that position equal zero), while also capitalizing on the profitable side of the trade.

A popular technique is to make the profitable adjustments back to Delta Neutral when the underlying asset has moved by 20% in either direction.

Delta neutral does *not* mean risk free! Deltas are *not* linear, and as the stock price fluctuates, so will your options values and the delta values.

Example 6.1.3

Consider a simple call option of Microsoft captured on April 20, 2001. The stock price is $69, and the $70 strike January 2002 call option is priced at $9.80.

Chart 6.1.1 ● Long Call risk profile—excludes commission.

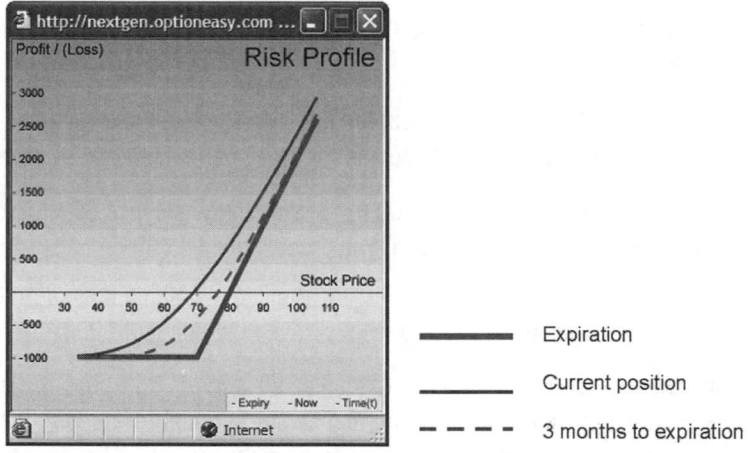

— Expiration

— Current position

- - - - 3 months to expiration

Chart 6.1.2 ● Long Call delta profile.

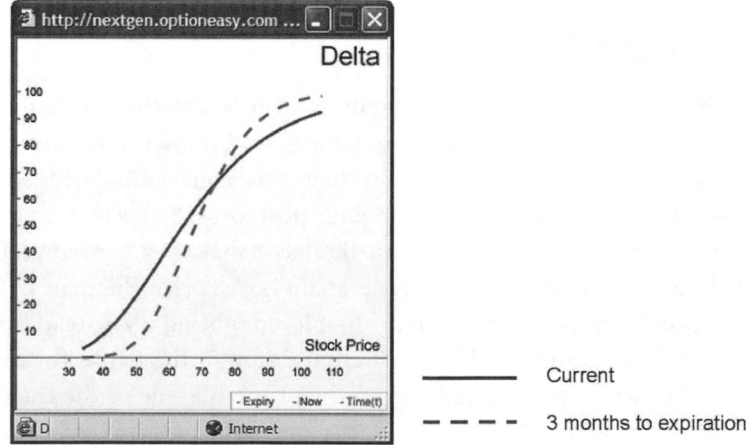

— Current

- - - - 3 months to expiration

See how delta moves as the stock price moves, and notice how the shorter expiration delta curve is that much steeper than the longer expiration delta curve. What this tells us is that delta is more sensitive the shorter the term left to expiration.

A good idea, therefore, would be to try and slow down delta to near zero while at the same time retaining our bullish objectives within the trade. To accomplish this we could sell a higher strike call option with the same expiration date. This would create a Bull Call Spread (see Chapter 7, "Bull Call Spreads and Bull Put Spreads").

Remember that Delta Neutral does *not* mean risk free! Deltas are *not* linear.

Other Points to Remember

- Delta Neutral still requires you to manage the Time Decay.

- Longer-term options will generally have lower deltas than shorter-term options.

- Your position delta on your trade is also known as your "hedge ratio."

- Delta is principally affected by time left to expiration and price of the underlying asset.

- Some futures delta neutral trades can require no margin in certain cases (and with certain brokers).

- With calls, delta increases as the underlying asset price increases. Call deltas are always positive. Note that when you sell a call (naked), your position is delta negative.

- With puts, delta decreases as the underlying asset price decreases. Put deltas are always negative. Note that when you sell a put (naked) your position is delta positive.

Position	Delta (+ or -)	Comment
Buy 100 shares	+100	One share has a delta of 1.
Sell 50 shares	-50	Selling one share gives a -1 delta.
Buy ATM call	+50	One contract represents 100 shares. 100 * 0.5 = +50
Sell ATM call	-50	

Position	Delta (+ or -)	Comment
Buy call	+	A long call always has a positive delta. As the stock price rises, so does the call premium. As the stock price falls, so does the call premium.
Sell call	-	A short call always has a negative delta.
Buy ATM put	-50	One contract represents 100 shares. 100 * 0.5 = +50
Sell ATM put	+50	
Buy put	-	A long put always has a negative delta. As the stock price rises, the put premium will fall. As the stock price falls, the put premium will rise. This inverse relationship results in a negative delta.
Sell put	+	Short put always has a positive delta.
Deep ITM call	+100 (maximum)	One deep ITM call will move roughly 1 for 1 with the underlying stock. It can never move faster than the underlying stock. Where you see numbers higher than this, it's because there must be more than one contract being traded.
Deep OTM call	0	Deep OTM calls will have deltas of almost zero, reflecting that they have very little chance of expiring ITM.
Deep ITM put	-100 (maximum)	One deep ITM put will move inversely roughly 1 for 1 against the underlying stock.
Deep OTM put	0	Deep OTM puts will have deltas of almost zero, reflecting that they have very little chance of expiring ITM.
ATM Straddle	0	
ATM Strangle	0	
Bull spreads	+	Delta is hedged to an extent
Bear spreads	–	Negative delta is hedged to an extent

Example 6.1.4 Bull Call spread

SpreadCo Inc. is currently trading at $100 per share. We're bullish, so we construct a Bull Call Spread trade as follows:

We buy 10 January 100 strike calls and sell 10 January 120 strike calls at the same time.

Buy 10 Jan 100c	Delta =	10 x 100 x 0.5	=	+500
Sell 10 Jan 120c	Delta =	10 x 100 x (−0.43)	=	−430 (say)
		Hedge ratio =		**+70**

Delta with Puts

Let's consider the equivalent Microsoft example but this time with puts captured on the same date, April 20, 2001. The stock price is $69, and the $70 strike January 2002 put option is priced at $8.60.

Chart 6.1.3 ● Long Put risk profile.

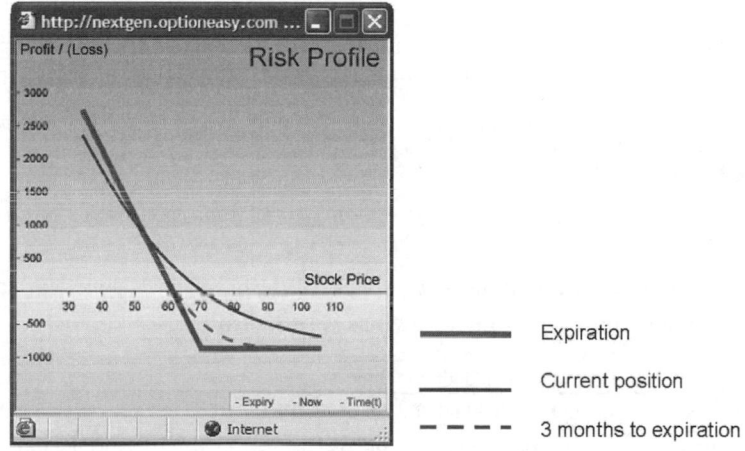

Chart 6.1.4 ● Long Put delta profile.

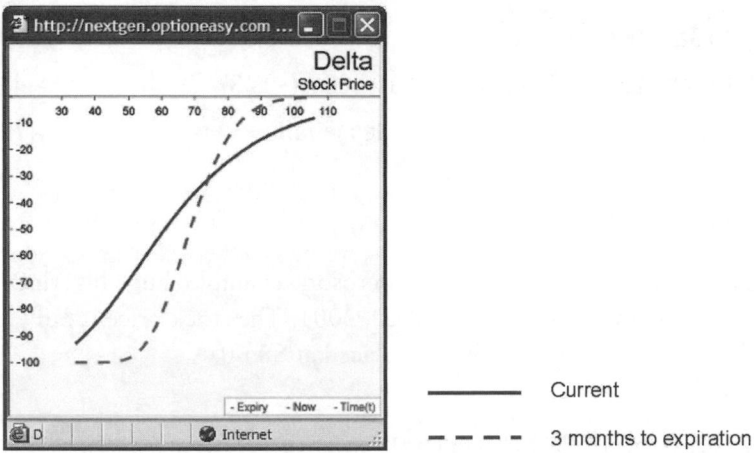

Notice how the Long Put delta profile looks identical to the Long Call delta profile. The difference is, of course, that the Long Put delta is negative.

Gamma Γ

Gamma is the rate of change of delta measured against the rate of change in the underlying asset.

In simple terms, gamma is the speed of delta, or the "speed of speed." The speed of speed is commonly known as *acceleration*.

$$\text{Gamma} = \frac{\text{rate of change in delta}}{\text{rate of change in underlying asset price}}$$

Gamma is significant because it helps the trader measure risk, particularly for Delta Neutral traders. Gamma effectively shows us how quickly the odds are changing of the option expiring In the Money. By knowing the gamma of an option, we know how quickly the delta will change and how quickly we should adjust our position in advance of this.

Summary of how gamma behaves:

ATM	Gamma tends to be high when the option is near the money. This means that the delta is highly sensitive (when the option is NTM) to changes in the stock price. In other words the **odds** of the option changing from being OTM to ITM or vice versa are high when the option is near the money. Therefore, it is logical that ATM options have high gammas.

ITM	When options are deep In the Money (DITM), delta is close to 1 and in itself is not particularly sensitive to changes in the underlying asset price. Therefore, the gamma of DITM options is low.
OTM	Similarly, gamma is low for deep Out of the Money (DOTM) options.
Generally	The gamma for puts and calls is always identical and can be positive or negative.

Mathematically speaking, gamma is the first derivative of delta. Therefore, if delta is a measure of speed, gamma is a measure of acceleration. Gamma can be seen as the acceleration of the option price versus the underlying asset price, or as the speed of delta versus the underlying asset price.

To this end, the gamma for calls and puts is always identical and gamma can be positive or negative.

Gamma tends to be high when an option is near the money. A high gamma simply means that delta is highly sensitive to changes in the stock price around its current level (Kolb, 1997).

Some traders like to hedge their gamma positions so that the delta will not spiral out of control (remember, gamma is a measure of acceleration, so if the acceleration is contained, then the speed, delta, will at least remain constant). Of course, it is also possible to hedge both gamma and delta simultaneously. As with delta, the gamma of near the money calls and puts rises as we get closer to expiration. For Deep In or Out of the Money options, gamma will fall dramatically as time to expiration becomes very close.

If you look now at Chart 6.1.2, you'll see how the delta of a bought call starts to decelerate toward 1 as the stock price rises. This is an obvious clue as to how the gamma of the same trade will behave, that is, gamma will be lower. See Chart 6.2.1 here.

Chart 6.2.1 ● Long Call gamma profile.

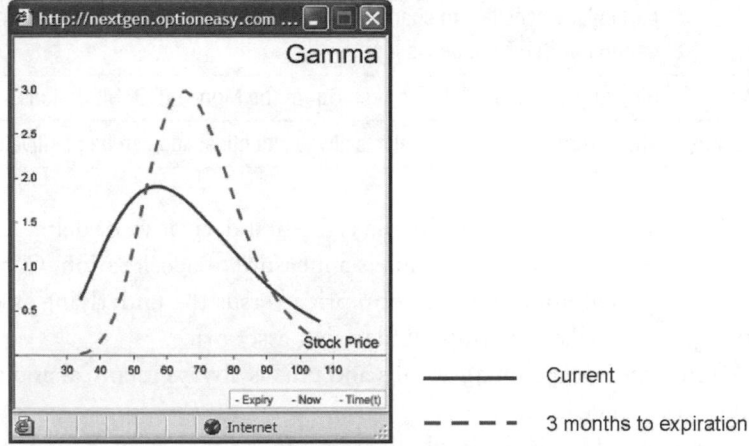

──────── Current

─ ─ ─ ─ 3 months to expiration

Can you see how the Long Call gamma is decelerating at its fastest when the stock price is above $70 (that is to say, In the Money) and continues as the stock price goes Deep In the Money? Similarly, gamma is extremely low when the stock price is Deep Out of the Money, to the left of the chart.

Delta Neutral does not necessarily mean gamma neutral and vice versa, but detailed investigation into this concept does not fall within the scope of this book.

Chart 6.2.2 ● Long Put gamma profile.

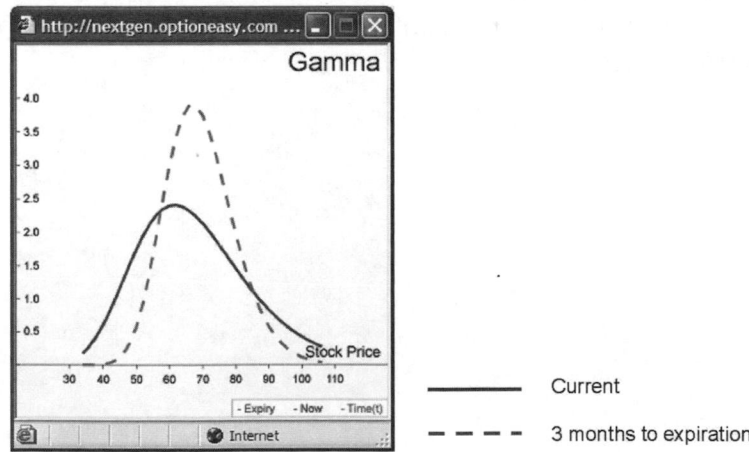

──────── Current

─ ─ ─ ─ 3 months to expiration

As you can see, gamma for puts and calls is identical. *Please note that the charts are scaled such that the stock price is segmented in $10 intervals, and this chart is using unsmoothed lines.*

To Conclude About Gamma

- Gamma measures how sensitive delta is to changes in the stock (or underlying asset) price.

- By knowing the gamma of an option, we know how quickly the delta will change and how quickly we should adjust our position.

- Gamma is significant because it helps the trader measure risk, particularly for Delta Neutral traders.

- Gamma tends to be large when the option is Near the Money. This means that the delta is highly sensitive (when the option is Near the Money) to changes in the stock price.

- When options are Deep In the Money (DITM), the delta will be close to 1 (for calls) or -1 (for puts) and will not be too sensitive itself to changes in the underlying asset price. Therefore, the gamma of DITM options will be low.

- Similarly, gamma will be low for Deep Out of the Money (DOTM) options.

- The gamma of a put and a call is always identical and can be positive or negative.

Asset price	Delta	Gamma
ATM	Around 0.5 (calls) or -0.5 (puts)	High
NTM	Around 0.5 (calls) or -0.5 (puts)	High
Deep ITM	Around 1 (high for calls) or -1 ("high" for puts)	Low
Deep OTM	Low	Low

Theta Θ

Theta is arguably the most important sensitivity of the Greeks and is certainly on a par with delta.

The characteristic of option prices to change purely as a result of the passage of time is known as *Time Decay*. Theta is a measure of how Time Decay affects the option premium. As such, theta is nearly always negative for bought options.[1] This makes sense because Time Decay erodes the option value as time to expiration diminishes.

Example 6.3.1 Time Decay

You pay me $1.00 for an OTM option with 10 days until expiration.

With each day that passes, let's say the option loses $0.10 of Time Value. (Please note this is just an illustration. In practice, Time Decay is not linear.)

So assuming there is no movement in the underlying stock price, the option value will behave as follows:

Day	Option Value	Buyer Profit	Seller Profit
Day 0	$1.00		
Day 1	$0.90	(0.10)	+ 0.10
Day 2	$0.80	(0.20)	+ 0.20
Day 3	$0.70	(0.30)	+ 0.30
Day 4	$0.60	(0.40)	+ 0.40
Day 5	$0.50	(0.50)	+ 0.50
...			
Day 10	$0.00	(1.00)	+1.00

Do you see how Time Decay has helped me (the seller) and hurt you (the buyer)?

Lesson:

Never buy OTM options with less than one month to expiration unless it forms part of a multi-legged spread trade.

The negative value of theta indicates to us that as time gets closer to expiration, Time Decay increases. With options, Time Decay increases exponentially during the last month before expiration. Put another way, **Time Value decreases** exponentially during the last month before expiration.

---

[1] Theta can be positive for Deep In the Money puts in certain scenarios.

The Big Question Is How Can We Mitigate Time Decay?

(i) Sell off any owned ATM or OTM options with 30 days left to expiration—Time Decay accelerates at its fastest during the last 30 days to expiration. Remember that OTM and ATM options have no Intrinsic Value, so they must be made up purely of Time Value. Because we know that Time Value decreases exponentially during the final month before expiration, it makes sense not to hold onto these options.

(ii) Sell options you don't own as an adjustment to existing trades—we're not talking about creating naked positions here; the sold option would be complementary to your existing play (for example, Bull and Bear spreads).

(iii) Buy short-term Deep ITM options, for example, a Deep ITM put or Deep ITM call will have lots of Intrinsic Value and virtually no Time Value. If there is no Time Value, then it can't decay any further, can it?!

Remember about Time Value and Intrinsic Value. Well, here we're talking about there being so little Time Value as a proportion of the option premium because the option is so Deep ITM.

Let's take at look at each one of these points in turn:

(i) Sell off OTM or ATM options with less than 30 days to expiration.

The diagram here gives us a perfect illustration of how theta decay works with options. Notice how the slope falls off at its steepest during the last 30 days.

Diagram 6.3.1 ● Time Decay.

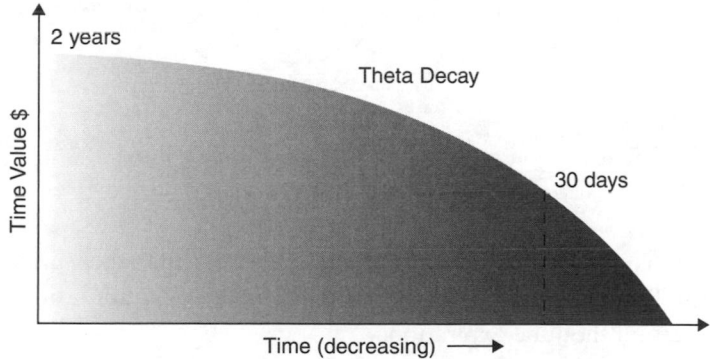

(ii) Sell options you don't own as an adjustment to existing trades.

Note here that we're not advocating selling options naked and exposing yourself to an unlimited Risk Profile. Many people successfully sell OTM options every month and collect a decent premium. However, if the market suddenly jolts against them and they get exercised, then an entire year or more can be wiped out in literally one day. The fact remains that selling options naked is not a businessperson's way to trade. Although there are some high-probability mathematical techniques of naked options selling, if your capital can be wiped out that fast when you're not looking, then that's simply not a sensible way to go about your business. It's far better to be able to sleep at night; that way you'll pass the test of longevity and be able to consistently trade and invest for many years even well into your retirement.

(iii) Buy short-term Deep ITM options.

You can mitigate the effects of Time Decay by buying Deep in the Money (DITM) options, the reason being because Intrinsic Value is vastly outweighing Time Value. If there is little to no Time Value in the option (as compared with Intrinsic Value), then your risk exposure to Time Decay is, by definition, little to none!

Diagram 6.3.2 ● Time Value for Deep ITM options.

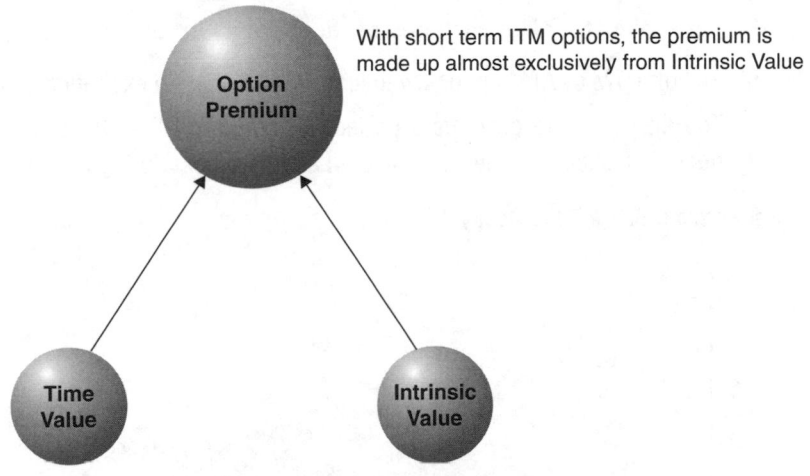

With short term ITM options, the premium is made up almost exclusively from Intrinsic Value

If you look at this options series, you'll see that the stock price is currently $42.10. There are only 18 days left to the May expiration and just over six weeks left till the June expiration.

Question:

How much Time Value and Intrinsic Value is there for the following options? For our purposes here, look at the Ask:

Remember:

- Call option Intrinsic Value = share price—exercise price.
- Call option Time Value = call option price—Intrinsic Value.
- Intrinsic Value minimum = Zero.

See if you can fill in the table below:

Call option		Last ($)	Intrinsic Value	Time Value
May 12.5	2001	30.20	42.10 − 12.50 = **29.60**	30.20 − 29.60 = **0.60**
May 15	2001	27.80		
May 17.5	2001	25.30		
May 20	2001	22.80		
May 22.5	2001	20.30		
May 25	2001	18.00		
May 40	2001	5.50		
June 20	2001	23.20		
June 22.5	2001	20.90		
June 25	2001	18.70		
June 40	2001	8.20		

Answers: (Take note of the percentage of the entire option premium, which is taken up by Intrinsic or Time Value as the option gets Nearer the Money.)

Call option		Last ($)	Intrinsic Value		Time Value	
May 12.5	2001	30.20	29.60	98%	0.60	2%
May 15	2001	27.80	27.10	97.5%	0.70	2.5%
May 17.5	2001	25.30	24.60	97%	0.70	3%
May 20	2001	22.80	22.10	97%	0.70	3%
May 22.5	2001	20.30	19.60	96.5%	0.70	3.5%

Call option		Last ($)	Intrinsic Value		Time Value	
May 25	2001	18.00	17.10	95%	0.90	5%
May 40	2001	5.50	2.10	**38%**	3.40	**62%**
June 20	2001	23.20	22.10	95%	1.10	5%
June 22.5	2001	20.90	19.60	93.8%	1.30	6.2%
June 25	2001	18.70	17.10	91.5%	1.60	8.5%
June 40	2001	8.20	2.10	**25.6%**	6.10	**74.4%**

Do you see how DITM options premiums are heavily weighted by Intrinsic Value and minimally weighted by Time Value, thus reducing the exposure to Time Decay—and how Time Value tends to dominate the short-term ATM options?

Staying with our simple call option of Microsoft (Example 6.1.3), the stock price is $69, and the $70 strike January 2002 call option is priced at $9.80. Let's look at the theta as at April 20, 2001, and compare it with the position of theta with only one month left to expiration:

Notice how both theta lines are negative but especially notice how much more theta decay is harming our long call position when there is only one month left to expiration. Also notice how theta is at its lowest at the $70 level, that is, At the Money (ATM).

Chart 6.3.1 ● Long Call theta profile.

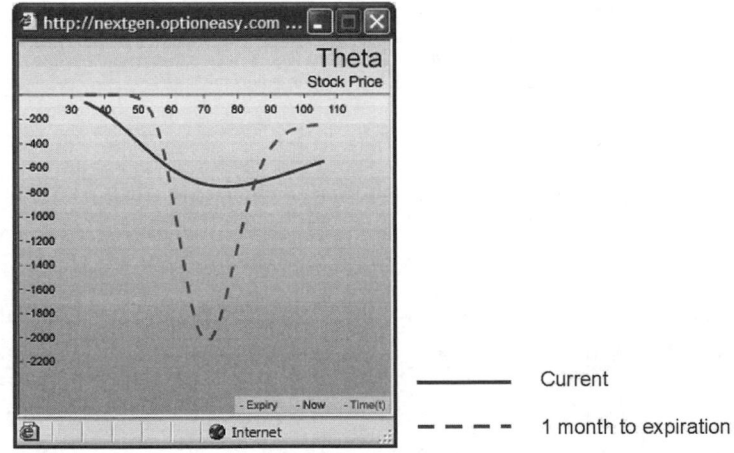

_____ Current

- - - - - 1 month to expiration

The same applies to puts. Let's look at the equivalent example with puts:

Chart 6.3.2 ● **Long Put theta profile.**

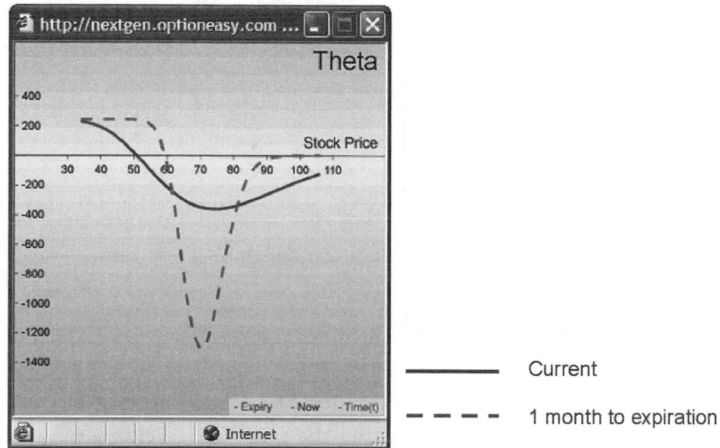

Now have a look at theta decay for the Short Call and Short Put positions. Can you guess what will happen and how they will look?

Chart 6.3.3 ● **Short Call theta profile.**

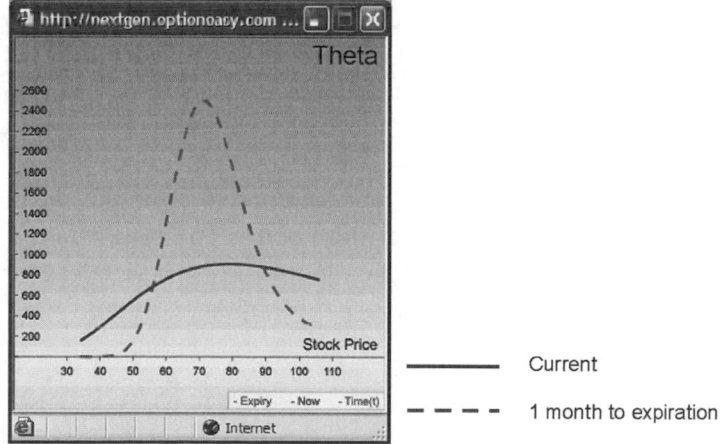

Chart 6.3.4 ● Short Put theta profile.

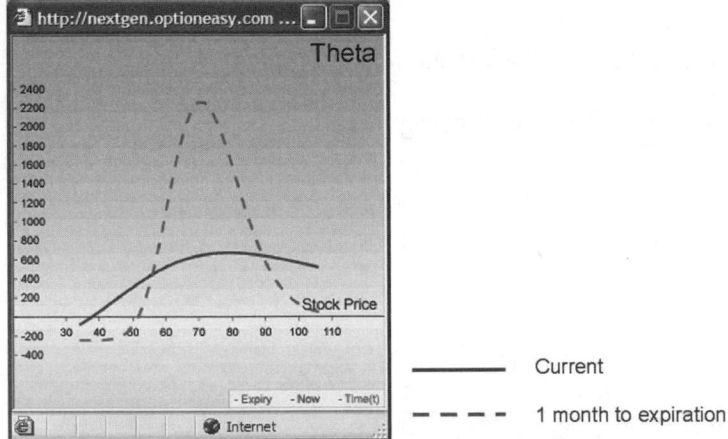

—————— Current

– – – – 1 month to expiration

Generally, when theta is positive, Time Decay is helping the position. When theta is negative, Time Decay is hurting the position. When we buy options, we have a negative theta, indicating that Time Decay hurts our long option position. This makes sense as an option is a wasting asset. When we write options, we would expect the opposite to be the case, which of course it is. When we write an option, its value will decline as we approach expiration. If we write a $1.00 OTM option with 10 days left to expiration, assuming that Time Decay reduces the option by $0.10 per day, then by day 5, we'd only have to pay $0.50 to buy it back, thereby making a $0.50 profit assuming the stock has not moved. In this scenario Time Decay has helped us, the writer of the option. On the other hand, the person who (stupidly!) bought the OTM option from us with only 10 days to expiration has lost 50% within the first 5 days, assuming there is no movement in the stock price.

If Time Decay is unhelpful to your long option positions, then it stands to reason that it will be helpful to your short option positions. You can see this by way of simple graphical representation in that now the theta lines are positive, showing that theta decay is helpful to a short option position.

Diagram 6.3.3 ● Theta Summary.

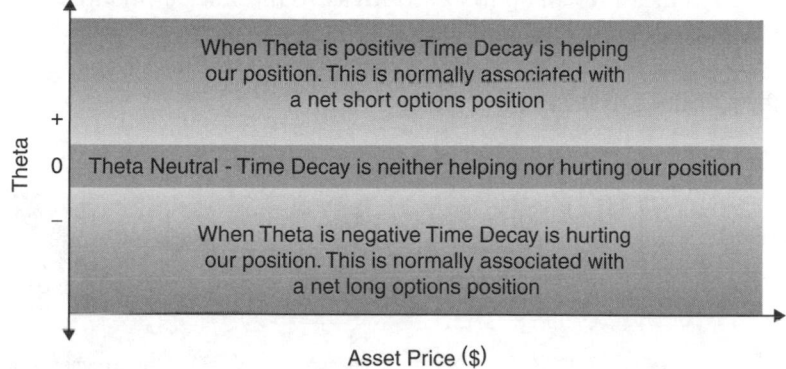

Vega K (also known as Kappa or Lambda)

Remember from Chapter 1, "Introductions to Options," that there are seven factors that influence an option's price:

1. The type of option (call or put)

2. The price of the underlying asset

3. The exercise price (or strike price) of the option

4. The expiration date

5. **Volatility**—Implied and Historical

6. Risk-free interest rate

7. Dividends and stock splits.

> **Memory Tip**
>
> *Vega starts with a **V** and stands for Volatility.*

When you trade stocks, you must be aware of volatility. Volatility is a measure of how a security's price is moving. Volatility is recognized as a measure of risk. If a stock price fluctuates all over the place in wild swings, then you'd find it uncomfortable because you wouldn't have a clue what it was going to do next, and it would feel risky. If a stock price remains static all the time, then you might get a bit bored, but you wouldn't have to reach for the Pepto-Bismol!

So, higher volatility is predicated by wider, faster price fluctuations. This translates into greater risk. The greater the volatility and risk, the more expensive options premiums become.

Volatility is calculated by measuring the standard deviation of closing prices, then expressed as an annualized percentage figure. Volatility is not directional.

If a stock is priced at $100 and has volatility of 20%, then we expect the stock to trade in the range of $80–$120 for the next year.

Vega measures an option's sensitivity to the stock's volatility[2]. This volatility is known as **Historical** or **Statistical** volatility.

Diagram 6.4.a ● Volatility.

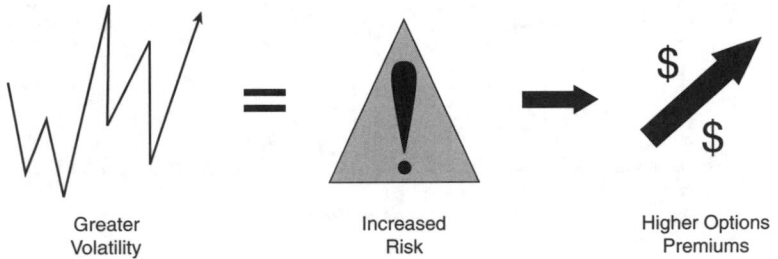

| Greater Volatility | Increased Risk | Higher Options Premiums |

There are two categories of volatility: Historical and Implied.

Historical (or Statistical) Volatility	Derived from the standard deviation of the underlying asset. Price movement over a known period of time.
Implied Volatility	Derived from the market price of the option itself.

Remember that there are seven variables that affect an option's premium. Six of these variables are known with certainty:

(i)   stock price

(ii)   strike price

(iii) type of option

(iv)   time to expiration

(v)   interest rates

(vi)   dividends

(vii) The final variable can be considered not to be known with certainty and is the *expected volatility* of the stock going forward.

Implied Volatility

There are several mathematical models for calculating the *theoretical* value of an option. In the main they manipulate the above seven variables to arrive at the

---

[2] On price charts, Bollinger Bands can provide a visual representation of volatility.

correct *theoretical* option price. I stress the word *theoretical* because the theoretical price is not the market price for the option. Sometimes the figures will be the same; sometimes they'll be different—there's no magic rule.

● The thing to remember is that the theoretical option price uses Historical Volatility (of the stock) to calculate the *theoretical* value of an option. So, all the seven factors go into the pot and we emerge with a theoretical option price.

● The market price of an option premium has a volatility figure *implied* within it. We reverse the theoretical option price model to find out what figure for volatility was *implied*. So, with a real market option where we know what price it is trading at, we mix the six factors (not volatility) into the pot with the actual market option price to work out what the *Implied Volatility* figure must be to create that market price.

Theoretical Option Price

Diagram 6.4.b ● **Theoretical option pricing.**

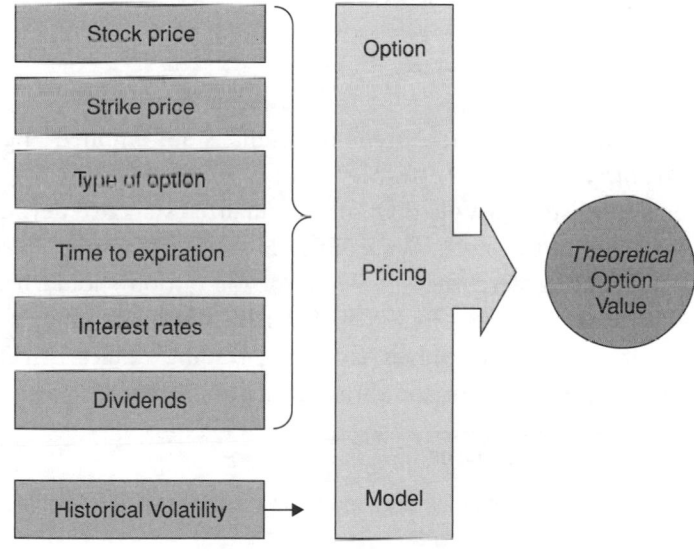

Implied Volatility Calculated from Real Option Prices in the Market

Diagram 6.4.c ● Theoretical option pricing.

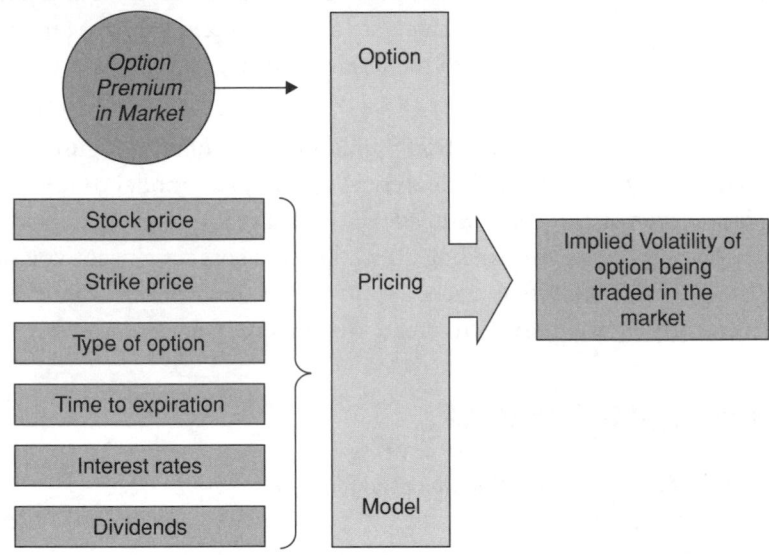

This expected volatility figure is expressed as an annualized percentage and, working back from the option premium itself, is an "implied" figure, hence *Implied Volatility*.

A reminder: Historical Volatility is the annualized standard deviation of *past* price movements of the stock. We can use Historical Volatility as a reference figure for calculating what the *Fair Value* of the option should be, given the stock's Historical Volatility. In the real world, option premiums frequently trade away from their fair values, adopting trading ranges driven more by demand and supply in the cut and thrust of market activity.

Volatility	Based on...
Historical	Underlying **stock** volatility over a period of time, for example the past 20 trading days. Expressed as a % reflecting the average annual standard deviation.
Implied	The volatility derived from the **option's** traded market price using an option pricing model. Expressed as a %.

The mechanical pricing of options involves complex mathematical formulas, which we don't need to explore here. There are also a number of different methodologies available for options pricing models, each with their associated merits. Typically I'll be tacitly referring to the Black-Scholes Options Pricing Model (for stocks and American-style (early exercise) options) and Black's Option Pricing Model (for futures and European-style (no early exercise) options).

What we need to remember is that there are seven major influences for pricing an option (above). We also need to remember that Volatility is one of them. In the actual marketplace the value assigned to an option is determined by market forces. This can give rise to inconsistency between the Fair Value of an option and the actual price of the option in the marketplace. The Fair Value of an option is the mathematically based calculation of the option price, using Historical Volatility as the figure for volatility.

The inconsistency emerges when the market price differs from the Fair Value, which is a common occurrence. Out of all seven factors that influence the option price, the only one that could be subject to any form of debate is Volatility. Let's go through the seven factors again:

Factor influencing option price	Comment
1. The type of option (call or put)	This is fixed and cannot be changed; the option is either a call or a put.

Factor influencing option price	Comment
2. The price of the underlying asset	No room for maneuver here because the option price is directly correlated with the underlying asset price.
3. Strike price	The strike price is fixed for each option.
4. The expiration date	The expiration date is fixed for each option.
5. **Volatility***—Implied and Historic	Although Historical Volatility itself is fixed (with respect to whatever time period we're assigning to it, say, 20 trading days), the choice of time frame can be somewhat arbitrary and doesn't necessarily fit with the time left to the option's expiration. The discretion between the option's market value and its Fair Value is therefore interpreted as an anomaly of volatility (it simply cannot be any of the other six factors). Implied Volatility is a calculated figure arising from the actual market price itself.

| 6. Risk-free interest rate | The risk-free rate is fixed. |
| 7. Dividends and stock splits | This is fixed. |

*Volatility is always expressed as a percentage.

Question: What does Historical Volatility mean?

Answer: Historical Volatility is a reflection of how the underlying asset has moved in the past.

Example 6.4.1[3]

Consider a stock priced at $41.41 on May 1, 2001, and with July $40 strike calls and puts priced at $9.30 and $7.40 respectively.

Option		Option price	Historical Volatility (23 days)	Implied Volatility
Call strike $40	July 2001	$9.30	196.74	111%
Put strike $40	July 2001	$7.40	196.74	111%

If the options were priced in the market according to the Historical Volatility, the call would be worth **$15.41**, and the put would be priced at **$13.51**. Are we getting a bargain here for our options?[4] Well, that would depend on whether Implied Volatility is usually at a discount or premium to Historical Volatility with this particular stock, as well as a number of other factors. Each stock, each underlying asset will have different characteristics with regard to the relationship between Implied and Historical Volatility of their options chains. Just like you have to familiarize yourself with a stock's personality, you also have to familiarize yourself with its option chain's personality and the historical relationship between Historical and Implied Volatility.

For now, just remember that Historical Volatility is a figure derived from the underlying asset price movement, and Implied Volatility is derived from the actual market premium of the option itself.

---

[3] Real life example from May 1, 2001.

[4] The higher the Implied Volatility, the higher the option price will be and vice versa. If Implied Volatility is substantially lower than Historical Volatility, there could be an argument to suggest good value in the option price itself.

Volatility	Based on
Historical/Statistical	Underlying asset volatility over a period of time, for example, the past 20 trading days. Expressed as a percentage reflecting the average annual range (that is, standard deviation).
Implied	The volatility derived from the option's traded market price using an option pricing model. Expressed as a percentage and based on the perception of where market will be in the future. This is the volatility figure derived from the Black-Scholes Options Pricing Model.

In terms of trading, if you can recognize how Implied and Historical Volatility relate to each other with a specific stock, you also can identify powerful ways with which to trade the options.

The following table is a typical guide to how to trade the relationship between Implied and Historical Volatility, but I urge you to exercise caution here. Typical does *not* necessarily mean it's right! The key is what the relationship has been like in the past and whether the present is significantly different. Volatility swings are often likened to the "rubber band effect" where if the rubber band is stretched too tight in one direction or too loose in the other, it will generally revert back to its most natural position most of the time. Therefore, if Implied Volatility is generally around 70% for a stock, but for a period of time it plummets to, say 30%, could it be possible that the options prices might be good value? Or, using the same example, say Implied Volatility rockets up to 110%, could the options perhaps be overvalued? This is how the rubber band effect is best illustrated. Over the medium to long term, Implied Volatility does tend to veer toward the Historical Volatility figure, but this will depend upon how consistent the Historical Volatility of the underlying asset is.

Look for	Typical interpretation (not necessarily the right interpretation)
Implied > Historical	Options prices could be overvalued as a result of higher implied volatility; therefore, look to sell options premiums.
Historical > Implied	Options prices could be undervalued, indicating good buying opportunities, particularly if you anticipate underlying asset price movement.

Diagram 6.4.1 ● Implied Volatility and the rubber band effect.

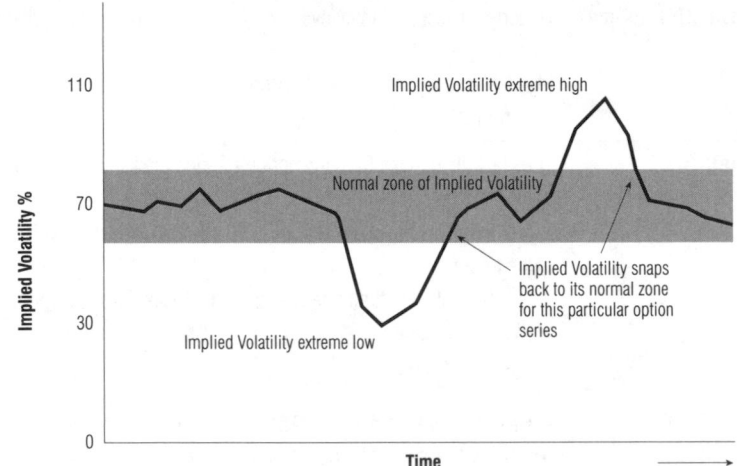

So in simplistic terms, some traders look to buy options with low Implied Volatility (because the option premium will be low) compared with the Historical Volatility of the underlying stock. In this way, the perception is that the options are cheap or undervalued; therefore, they must represent a good trade.

As stated earlier, this is a dangerous assumption to make. For a start, option premiums often have Implied Volatilities consistently inconsistent with the Historical Volatility of the underlying stock. Secondly, just because an option is cheap today, doesn't mean it'll be expensive tomorrow. So the rationale for that tactic is flawed. Of far more relevance would be to look at the history of Implied Volatility and see if current options prices are trading away from their own averages.

Similarly, some traders look to sell options with premiums reflecting high Implied Volatility (because the option premium will be high) compared with the Historical Volatility of the stock. Again, this is a flawed methodology in the real world of trading, even if the logic initially looks plausible.

Vega Characteristics

Vega is identical and positive for (long) calls and puts. This reflects the fact that higher volatility increases the option's premium. When vega is positive, it generally suggests that increasing volatility is helping our position. When vega is negative, it generally suggests that increasing volatility is hurting our position.

Example 6.4.2

Staying with our Microsoft example where the stock price is $69, let's look at the January 2002 $70 strike calls and puts respectively.

Chart 6.4.1 ● Long Call vega profile.

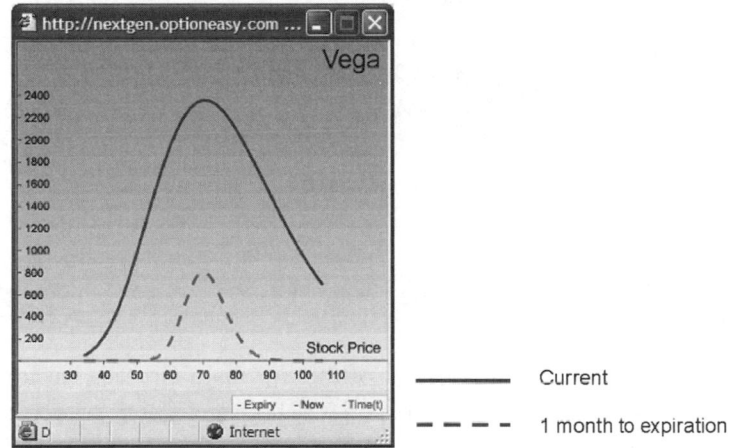

———— Current

– – – – 1 month to expiration

Chart 6.4.2 ● Long Put vega profile.

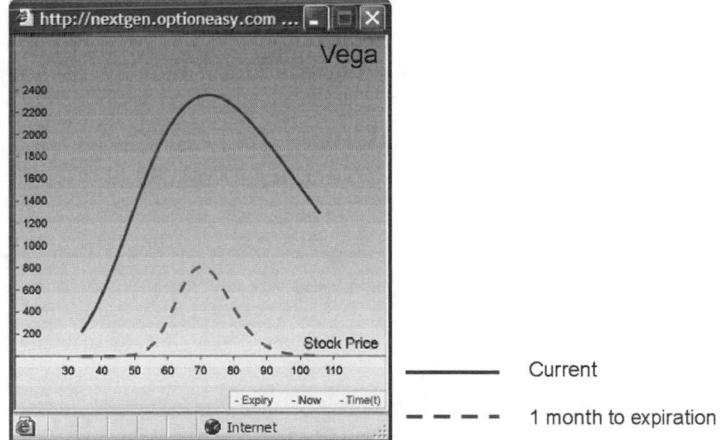

———— Current

– – – – 1 month to expiration

As you can see, vega is identical for both calls and puts. Notice how it increases around the money (strike price) and also how vega is vastly reduced where there is less time to expiration. This is because there is less time for increased volatility to make an impact on the Time Value component of the option's value.

Diagram 6.4.3 ● Vega summary.

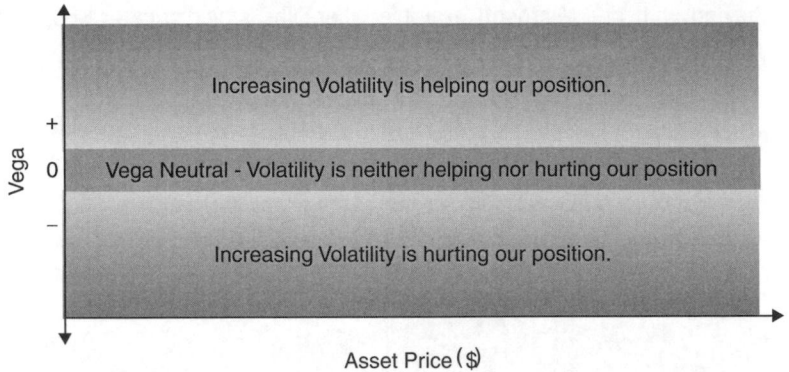

Rho P

Rho is arguably the least significant of the five main Greeks (sensitivities), and as such we'll only spend a little time on it. Rho is positive for stock call options and negative for some other assets such as call options on futures. This means that for call stock options, a higher risk-free interest rate translates to higher call pricing. The sensitivity is not nearly as pronounced as with the other Greeks and, as such, rho is not overly significant for our purposes.

Call rho is always positive, signifying that higher interest rates will improve a call's value. Put rho is always negative, signifying that higher interest rates will hurt a put's value.

Chart 6.5.1 ● Long Call rho profile.

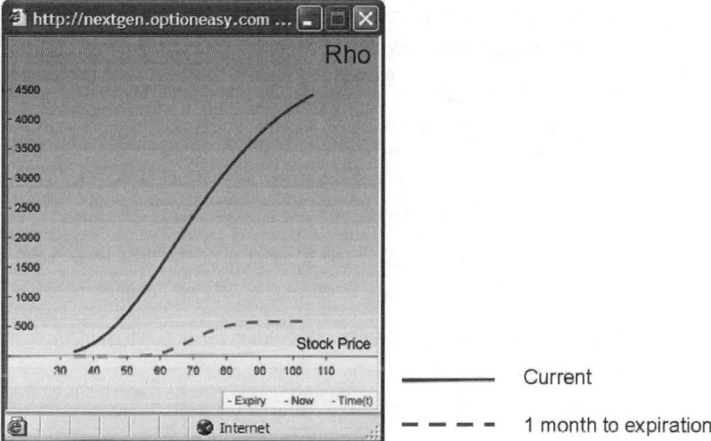

Current

1 month to expiration

Chart 6.5.2 ● Long Put rho profile.

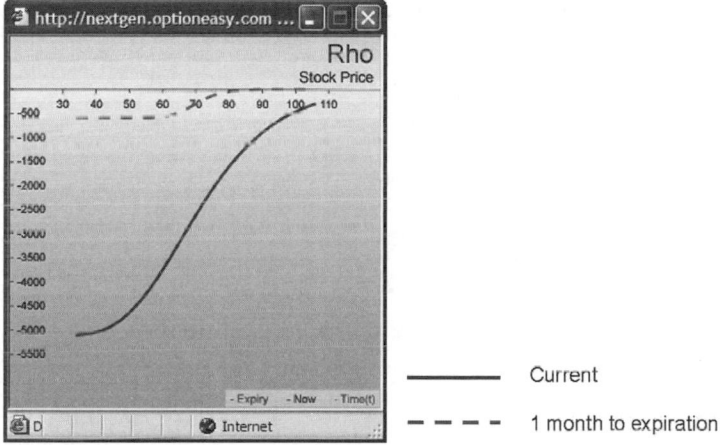

Current

1 month to expiration

Chapter 6 Major Learning Points

In this chapter we've learned the basics of the Greeks and understand that they are purely sensitivities of options to the various factors that form part of the various options pricing models.

Greek	Quick definition
Delta	The speed of the option price over the speed of the underlying asset price. Can also be viewed as the probability of an option expiring In the Money.
Gamma	Sensitivity of delta relative to the underlying asset price movement. Can also be viewed as the odds of a change in delta.
Theta	Option price sensitivity to Time Decay. When theta is positive, Time Decay is helping the position. When theta is negative, Time Decay is hurting the position.
Vega	Option price sensitivity to the underlying stock price volatility. When vega is positive, volatility is helping the position. When vega is negative, volatility is hurting the position.
Rho	Option price sensitivity to *interest rates*. When rho is positive, increasing interest rates are helping the position. When rho is negative, increasing interest rates are hurting the position.

Now that we know what factors affect the pricing of options, we can start to devise specific strategies to mitigate the impact of the important sensitivities, particularly delta and theta decay…

Bull Call Spreads and Bull Put Spreads

Most people think you can only trade the markets when they are going up. This is not so. You shouldn't really care in a predictive sense. Because whichever direction it's heading, I'll attempt to follow the trend and then analyze potential turning points and profit objectives. That's where advanced Fibonacci analysis comes in. Bearish strategies can be just as profitable as bullish strategies. But for now, we'll just concentrate on being bullish.

The question, "Where is the market heading?" cannot be asked or answered with any real sense of purpose without including the context of time frame. A five-minute chart may indicate strong upward movement, while the daily charts suggest either a downtrend or consolidation. As you become more experienced, you'll decide for yourself what time frame you're best suited to trade, but whatever the case, you should get into the habit of looking at multiple time frames. For example, if you're looking to trade the five-minute chart, do at least be aware of what the hourly and daily charts are doing. This will ensure that you're aware of a potentially more powerful trend or direction. If you're looking to trade intraday, then I would suggest you require Direct Access facilities to ensure you get fast fills.

We've spent a lot of time so far talking about maximum risk, maximum reward, and breakeven points. This is because these three numbers are the most important figures you need to be aware of in any kind of business or any kind of investment. At all times, we want to explore the possibilities of:

- reducing our risk,
- maximizing our reward, and

● minimizing our breakeven.

This is a simple concept, but one that requires us to understand what our risk profile is in the first place! This is why I put so much emphasis on this area.

The two strategies we're going to discuss in this chapter are

● Bull Call spread and

● Bull Put spread.

As you can imagine, the prerequisite for success in both strategies is that the market direction goes up (or at least not down) and that one uses calls and the other uses puts. And while both strategies appear to have the same risk profiles because the shapes are the same, they are fundamentally different strategies, requiring different criteria and different time frames. Both do share in common, however, the characteristics of reducing the risk and breakeven points of a bullish trade, while also providing attractive levels of maximum reward.

Bull Call Spreads

The Bull Call spread is a bullish strategy that involves the following steps:

Step 1   Buy lower strike calls.

Step 2   Sell same number of higher strike calls with the same expiration date.

The lower strike calls will be more expensive than the higher strike calls, so this will be a NET DEBIT transaction, that is, you will pay for the trade from funds out of your trading account.

Diagram 7.1 ● Bull Call spread.

Buy lower strike calls   Sell higher strike calls   Bull Call spread

The Bull Call spread is a lower-risk alternative to buying a straight call. Let's compare the risk profiles of these two strategies:

	Long call	Bull Call spread
Maximum risk	Call premium paid	Net debit of the spread (for example, what you pay)
Maximum reward	Unlimited	Limited to the difference in strike prices less the net debit paid
Breakeven	Strike price **plus** call premium paid	Lower strike price **plus** net debit paid

Here it's easy to see that while the long call has potentially unlimited reward, the breakeven and risk will be higher. A simple graphical representation demonstrates this:

Chart 7.1 ● Bull Call spread versus long call.

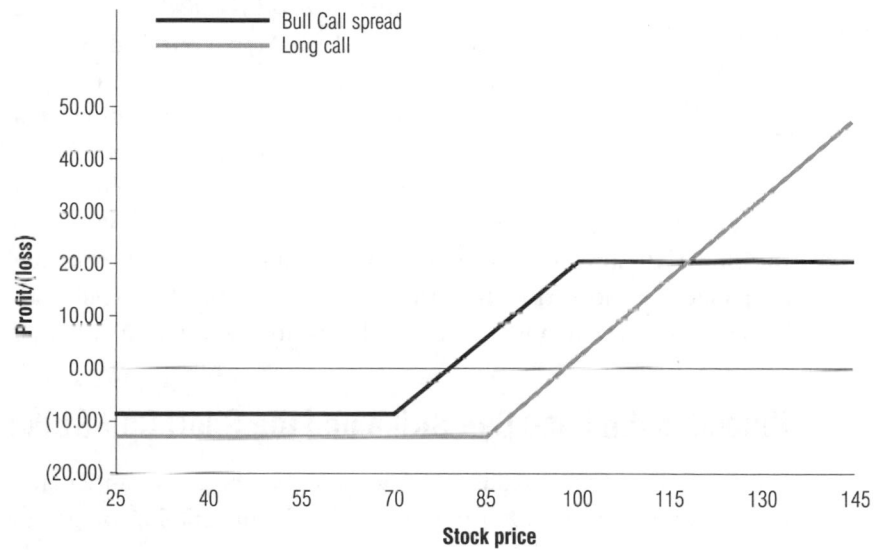

Example 7.1

XYZ stock is priced at $70. You are considering one of the following alternative strategies:

(a) Long Call — Buy Jan 2002 $70 strike call @ $13.00

(b) Bull Call spread — Buy Jan 2002 $70 strike call @ $13.00 and sell Jan 2002 $100 strike call @ $5.00 (net debit $8.00)

The respective risk profiles of (a) and (b) are as follows:

	Long call (a)	Bull Call spread (b)
You pay (net debit)	$13.00	$8.00
Max risk	$13.00	$8.00
Max reward	Unlimited	$22.00 (275% on risk)
Breakeven	$83.00	$78.00
Max risk on net debit	100%	100%

So we can clearly see that the Bull Call spread is less risky in terms of lower risk and breakeven points, but it also offers us a limited (albeit still attractive) potential reward. Note that the *maximum percentage loss on your net debit* is 100% in both cases. So if you spent more dollars on your Bull Call spread, you could still lose every one of those dollars if the stock closes lower than $70 at expiration. This is a vital point and one that is constantly overlooked.

You trade Bull Call spreads in circumstances where you anticipate the underlying asset price to rise.

You may have noticed that the Bull Call spread has the same shape as a Collar. The major difference in terms of risk profile is that the Bull Call spread offers more leverage and maximum potential return in exchange for more risk. In terms of structure, the Bull Call and Collar are completely different and are designed for entirely different risk objectives.

Selecting the Long Call Strike and the Short Call Strike

You trade Bull Call spreads in circumstances where you anticipate the underlying asset price to rise. For the Bull Call to be profitable, you generally require the asset price to rise. As you can see, maximum profit occurs at the higher strike price, and maximum loss occurs at the lower strike price.

The question is: Which options do you select for the long side and the short side?

● Generally you'll select the lower strike price (for the option you're buying) to be Near the Money (that is, close to the underlying asset price).

● The short side of the Bull Call spread involves you selling the higher strike call option against the one you've just bought. You want to select a strike price that is

- high enough to create a decent upside and

- low enough so that the premium you're selling does impact favorably upon your net debit and therefore your risk and breakeven points. Generally look to at least be able to double your amount of maximum risk for any spread trade that you do. Personally, I look for spreads that offer me at least 250% maximum return on maximum risk if the stock moves up toward the upper strike price.

Selling the higher strike call against the lower strike bought call creates three major effects:

1. It lowers your cost and therefore your risk and therefore your breakeven.

2. It caps your upside.

    The capping of the upside is not too hard to take if you manage to create a spread that is capable of more than doubling your money over the course of the trade if the market behaves in the way you expect it to.

3. Delta is hedged to an extent.

The option you sell will hedge the Delta of the overall trade and the effect is that the fluctuations of your position will be slowed down, but without harming your long-term (for example, at expiration) gearing effect. You may ask yourself why you want to slow down the possible fluctuations of your position. The reason is what happens if you're wrong on the direction? If you buy a simple ATM Call option and you get the direction wrong, your position will be decimated very quickly. With a Bull Call spread, the effect will be slower, which could give you the opportunity to exit the trade before more serious damage is done.

Safest Time Period to Trade the Bull Call Spread

Time Decay is detrimental to your position here, so you'll be safest to treat the Bull Call spread as a *long-term* strategy spanning at least six months to expiration, preferably more. I usually trade this strategy with at least a year left to expiration. Remember, as an option buyer you want to have as much time as possible to be right.

Example 7.2

Let's have a look at the January 2002 call options chain for MSFT ($68.49), taken from May 3, 2001, and see if we can construct an attractive Bull Call spread. Please note that this is not a trade that I am looking at trading myself; it's purely for illustration purposes only, taking advantage of a well-known name. For this reason, let's assume we've taken a decision that we're bullish about MSFT and we're looking for an appropriate trade.

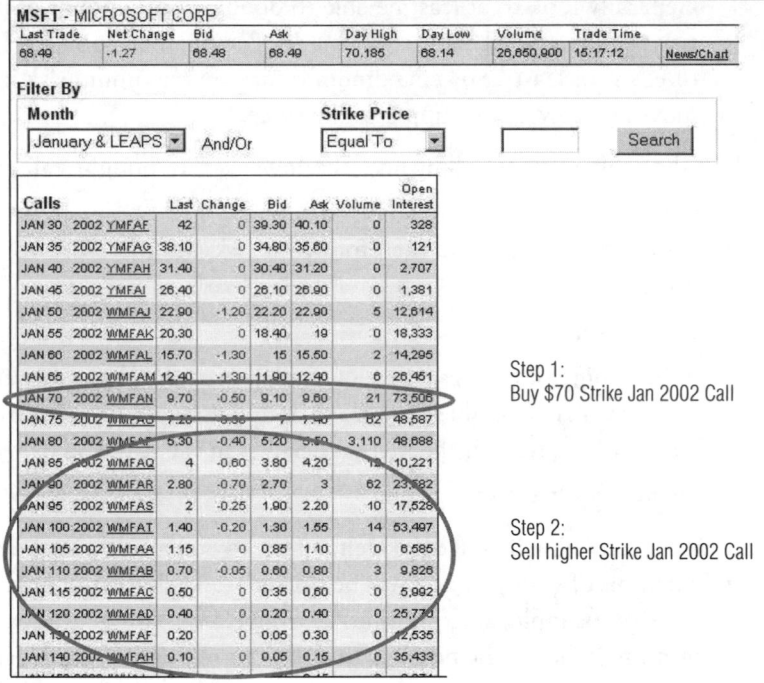

Step 1:
Buy $70 Strike Jan 2002 Call

Step 2:
Sell higher Strike Jan 2002 Call

Let's look at the choices of Bull Call spreads here:

Step 1	Long call	Buy $70 strike Jan 2002 call @ $9.60
Step 2	(i) Short call	Sell $75 strike Jan 2002 call @ $7.00
Or	(ii) Short call	Sell $80 strike Jan 2002 call @ $5.20
Or	(iii) Short call	Sell $85 strike Jan 2002 call @ $3.80
Or	(iv) Short call	Sell $90 strike Jan 2002 call @ $2.70
Or	(v) Short call	Sell $95 strike Jan 2002 call @ $1.90
Or	(vi) Short call	Sell $100 strike Jan 2002 call @ $1.30
Or	(vii) Short call	Sell $105 strike Jan 2002 call @ $0.85
Or	(viii) Short call	Sell $110 strike Jan 2002 call @ $0.60
Or	(ix) Short call	Sell $115 strike Jan 2002 call @ $0.35
Or	(x) Short call	Sell $120 strike Jan 2002 call @ $0.20

Let's look at the Risk Profiles for each alternative:

Step 1	Long call				
	Buy $70 strike Jan 2002 call @ $9.60				
Step 2	**Short call**	**Risk**	**Reward**	**Breakeven**	**Max ROI**
(i)	Sell $75 strike Jan 2002 call @ $7.00	$2.60	$2.40	$72.60	92.31%
✓ (ii)	Sell $80 strike Jan 2002 call @ $5.20	$4.40	$5.60	$74.40	127.27%
✓ (iii)	Sell $85 strike Jan 2002 call @ $3.80	$5.80	$9.20	$75.80	158.62%
✓ (iv)	Sell $90 strike Jan 2002 call @ $2.70	$6.90	$13.10	$76.90	189.86%
✓ (v)	Sell $95 strike Jan 2002 call @ $1.90	$7.70	$17.30	$77.70	224.68%
(vi)	Sell $100 strike Jan 2002 call @ $1.30	$8.30	$21.70	$78.30	261.45%
(vii)	Sell $105 strike Jan 2002 call @ $0.85	$8.75	$26.25	$78.75	300.00%
(viii)	Sell $110 strike Jan 2002 call @ $0.60	$9.00	$31.00	$79.00	344.44%
(ix)	Sell $115 strike Jan 2002 call @ $0.35	$9.25	$35.75	$79.25	386.49%
(x)	Sell $120 strike Jan 2002 call @ $0.20	$9.40	$40.60	$79.40	431.91%

Which one would you choose?
Out of all the above possibilities, the most attractive to me would be (iv) or (v). The reasons being that the risk and breakeven points are being materially lowered while the maximum reward and maximum Return on Investment are high enough to be attractive.

Profiles (ii) and (iii) are also attractive in terms of vastly reduced risk and breakeven, and for a relatively small increase in MSFT's stock price (16.8% and 24.1% respectively), the potential maximum returns of 127.27% and 158.62% represent significant leverage.

Bull Call Spreads and the Greeks

Delta	Delta peaks in between the two strike prices showing us that at these levels smaller movements in the stock price will be enough to generate large swings in the Bull Call spread value. With Bull Calls, Delta is more sensitive the shorter the time there is to expiration (see Chart 7.2).
Gamma	Gamma is positive while the spread is OTM (below the lower strike price) but becomes negative (showing the deceleration of the position Delta) as the asset price rises above the lower strike price.
Theta	Theta becomes positive as the position moves upward beyond the breakeven point. This

shows us that Time Decay is working against us when the Bull Call is OTM and unprofitable and for us when it is ITM. In practical terms, once we are ITM our profitability improves with the passage of time because our profit becomes purely the difference in the strike prices less what we paid for it, with the Time Value differential between the strikes becoming less and less of a factor (see Chart 7.3).

Vega   Vega moves from positive to negative as the position moves upward beyond breakeven point. This shows us that increased volatility is helpful while the position is not making money and unhelpful when we are actually in a profitable position in the trade. This makes perfect sense since if you're OTM, then increased volatility could improve your chances of moving into a profitable position. On the other hand, when you're already in a profitable position, increased volatility may shake the underlying asset price back down to an unprofitable position. Vega becomes less sensitive with the passage of time, particularly the last month since there is less time for fluctuations in volatility to impact the position.

Rho   Rho's impact is enhanced the longer there is left to expiration. Rho increases up to and around the strike prices and then tails off into negative territory, as the position becomes Deep ITM. Rho becomes less sensitive with the passage of time because the impact of interest rates reduces when there is less time for rates to have an effect.

Chart 7.2 ● $70–$90 strike Bull Call spread Delta profile.

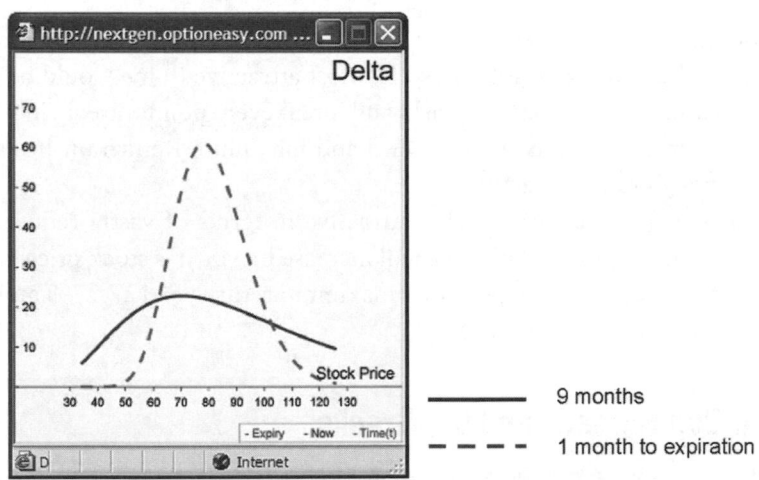

9 months

1 month to expiration

Chart 7.3 ● Bull Call spread Theta profile.

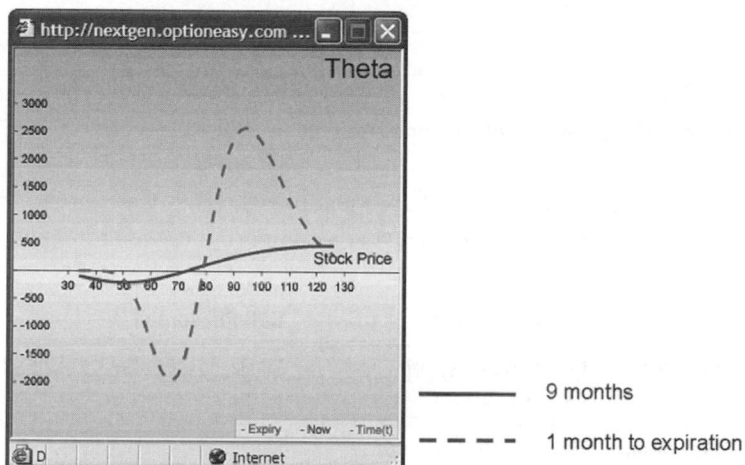

─────── 9 months

- - - - - 1 month to expiration

Bull Put Spreads

The Bull Put spread is a bullish strategy that involves the following steps:

Step 1   Buy lower strike put.

Step 2   Sell higher strike put with the same expiration date.

The lower strike puts will be cheaper than the higher strike puts because they are further OTM, so this will be a *net credit* transaction, that is, you will receive funds into your account for placing this trade, but your broker will require sufficient funds in your account (margin) to cover the risk exposure of the trade.

As a net credit transaction, the Bull Put spread can be looked upon as an *income strategy* on a monthly basis. You also can use a Bull Put spread in the same way that you use a Bull Call spread, for example, over the long term. The only problem with this approach is that you'll normally find that call options tend to have higher volatilities and therefore create better spreads in terms of risk, reward, and breakeven. Therefore, we will look at the Bull Put spread purely as a *short-term income strategy*. Conversely, the Bull Call spread is a net debit spread, meaning it cannot be used as an income strategy.

Memory Tip

Bull spreads
● *Buy low strike.*
● *Sell high strike.*

Bear spreads
● *Buy high strike.*
● *Sell low strike.*

Diagram 7.2 ● Bull Put spread.

| Buy lower strike puts | Sell higher strike puts | Bull Put spread |

The Bull Put spread looks (in shape) just like the Bull Call spread, but it has a number of distinguishing qualities. Let's compare the two strategies:

	Bull Call spread	**Bull Put spread**
Maximum risk	Net debit of the spread (i.e. what you pay)	Limited to the difference of the strike prices less the net credit received
Maximum reward	Limited to the difference in strike prices *less* the net debit paid	Limited to the net credit received
Breakeven	Lower strike price *plus* net debit paid	Higher strike price *less* net credit received
Maximum risk on net debit or net credit	100% risk on net debit	Can be greater than 100% risk on net credit

Example 7.3

It is May 4, 2001. MU is priced at $41.48. You are considering one of the following alternative bullish strategies:

(a) Bull Call spread	Buy Jan 2002* $40 strike call @ $11.90 and sell Jan 2002 $60 strike call @ $4.90 (net debit $7.00)
(b) Bull Put spread	Buy June 2001 $35 strike put @ $2.20 and sell June 2001 $40 strike put @ $3.80 (net credit $1.60)

* Note the vastly different time frames here. We're selecting a Bull Call spread that expires in January 2002 while comparing it with a Bull Put spread that expires in June 2001. This will have a material difference on your yields so we will compare yields on a monthly basis.

The respective risk profiles of (a) and (b) are as follows:

	Bull Call spread (a)	Bull Put spread (b)
You pay	$7.00 net debit	($1.60) net credit
Maximum risk	$7.00	$3.40
Maximum reward	$13.00 (185.71% on risk)	$1.60 (47.06% on risk)
Maximum monthly yield	13.12%	32.22%
Breakeven	$47.00	$38.40
Maximum risk on net debit (credit)	100% risk on net debit	212.5% risk on net credit

As you can see, the comparison between the two strategies isn't really fair because, despite the appearance of the risk profiles, these really are fundamentally different strategies in this context.[1] Notice here how the maximum monthly yield is much higher for the Bull Put spread and also how the breakeven is so much lower. In fact, because we selected strike prices below the current share price, it means that for the Bull Put spread to be profitable we only need the stock to either stay where it is or at least not drop below $38.40 from its current level of $41.48. In other words, we have $3.08 points or 7.42% cushion.

---

[1] If we had selected the same strike prices and expiration dates for both strategies then, with actual prices, the Bull Call spread would yield a maximum of 185.71% as above, and the Bull Put spread would yield a maximum of just 166.67%, thus demonstrating why the Bull Put spread is better employed as an income strategy in the market context of strong support and a short-term bullish outlook.

(a) Bull Call spread	Buy Jan 2002 $40 strike call @ $11.90 and Sell Jan 2002 $60 strike call @ $4.90 (net debit $7.00)
(c) Bull Put spread	Buy Jan 2002 $40 strike put @ $9.10 and Sell Jan 2002 $60 strike put @ $21.60 (net credit $12.50)

	Bull Call spread (a)	Bull Put spread (c)
You pay	$7.00 *net debit*	($12.50) *net credit*
Maximum risk	$7.00	$7.50
Maximum reward	$13.00 (185.71% on risk)	$12.50 (166.67% on risk)
Maximum monthly yield	13.12%	12.21%
Breakeven	$47.00	$47.50
Maximum risk on net debit (credit)	100% risk on net debit	60% risk on net credit

See how in this context the Bull Call spread is superior in just about every way. There are fewer dollars at risk, the maximum yield is higher, and the breakeven is lower. Now you can see why we look at the Bull Put spread as a short-term income strategy, making use of the net credit, and why we don't generally use it as a longer-term strategy because the Bull Call spread is a better alternative. I emphasize that the above comparison is shown to illustrate that we do **not** do credit spreads that are In the Money. Therefore, the Bull Put spread in this example is something we would never even consider.

Chart 7.4 ● Bull Put spread (b) versus Bull Call spread (a).

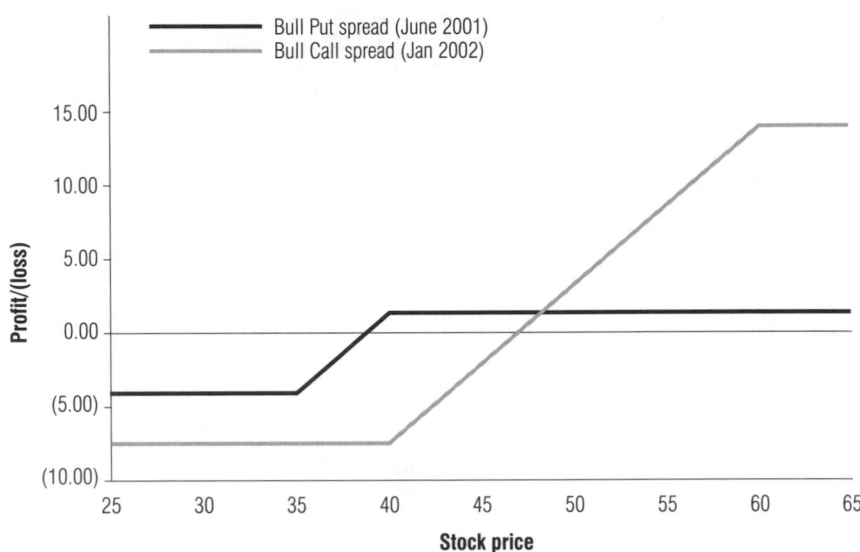

From the chart, you can easily see how the Bull Put breakeven is much lower than that of the Bull Call. At the same time, both the maximum risk and reward of the Bull Put are substantially lower than the Bull Call.

Selecting the Long Put Strike and the Short Put Strike

You trade a Bull Put spread in circumstances where you anticipate the underlying asset price to either rise or at least not fall below the level of the higher strike price selected. In other words, you are looking for very strong support such as a confirmed Double Bottom with moving averages or Fibonacci numbers backing you up. As you can see, maximum profit occurs at the higher strike price, and maximum loss occurs at and below the lower strike price.

The question is: Which strike prices do you select for the long side and the short side?

For a Bull Put spread to work as a short-term income trade, you generally want to select both strike prices to be below the current stock price. Unlike the Bull Call (debit) spread, here you want a tighter spread and one that requires your selected stock to do very little (if nothing at all) in order for you to make money from it. In most cases for US stocks, the best Bull Put spreads are to be found with strike prices just five points apart.

> You trade a Bull Put spread in circumstances where you anticipate the underlying asset price to either rise or at least not fall below the level of the higher strike price selected.

● Generally you'll select the higher strike price (for the option you're selling) to be well below the Money (that is, below the current stock price) and at a strong support level. This will depend on the maximum percentage return you can get for your spread, but in general I look for a very minimum of $0.50 from a $5 spread (for example, 11%) and preferably $1.00 from a $5 spread (for example, 25%). In an ideal world, you'll also be looking for this higher put strike price to be around 20% below the current stock price and at a strong support level.

● The strike price you buy (the lower strike) will preferably be just $5 below the higher strike that you choose to sell. You'll need to make sure that the net credit between the options you sell and the options you buy is going to yield you 11% at a bare minimum. The following table shows the yields and respective strike spreads:

Spread between strike prices	Bull Put net credit	Maximum yield (%)
	$0.25	5.26%
	$0.50	**11.11%**
	$0.75	17.65%
	$1.00	**25%**
$5	$1.25	33.33%
	$1.50	42.86%
	$1.75	53.85%
	$2.00	66.67%
	$2.25	81.82%
	$2.50	100%
	$0.50	5.26%
	$1.00	**11.11%**
	$1.50	17.65%
	$2.00	**25%**
$10	$2.50	33.33%
	$3.00	42.86%
	$3.50	53.85%
	$4.00	66.67%
	$4.50	81.82%
	$5.00	100%

Safest Time Period to Trade the Bull Put Spread

Time Decay is helpful to your position here, so you'll be safest to treat the Bull Put spread as a *short-term* income strategy, spanning just one month to expiration. Because in this strategy you are a *net seller* of options premium, you want to give the party on the other side of this trade as little time to be right as possible. Remember, when you buy options premium, you want as much time as possible to be right. With Bull Puts you are a net seller of premium (hence the net credit), so it's logical to give the person on the opposite side of the trade as little time as possible to be right.

Example 7.4

Let's have a look at the June 2001 put options chain for INTC ($29.95), taken from May 4, 2001, and see if we can construct an attractive Bull Put spread. Please note that this is *not* a trade that I am looking at trading myself; it's purely for illustration purposes only, taking advantage of a well-known name. For this reason let's assume we've taken a decision that we're bullish (or at least not bearish) about INTC and we're looking for an appropriate trade.

INTC - INTEL CORP

Last Trade	Net Change	Bid	Ask	Day High	Day Low	Volume	Trade Time	
29.95	-0.4502	29.95	29.96	30.53	29.30	16,694,300	11:33:24	News/Chart

Filter By

Month: June And/Or Strike Price: Equal To [   ] Search

Puts			Last	Change	Bid	Ask	Volume	Open Interest	
JUN	5	2001 NQRA	0	0	0	0.10	0	0	
JUN	10	2001 NQRB	0	0	0	0.10	0	0	
JUN	12.5	2001 NQRV	0	0	0	0.10	0	0	
JUN	15	2001 NQRC	0.10	0	0	0.10	0	10	
JUN	17.5	2001 NQRN	0.15	0	0.10	0.20	0	48	Step 1:
JUN	20	2001 NQRD	0.20	0	0.15	0.25	0	205	Buy lower Strike June 2001 Put
JUN	22.5	2001 NQRQ	0.45	+0.05	0.40	0.50	1	1,110	
JUN	25	2001 INQRE	0.65	0	0.70	0.80	0	3,786	
JUN	27.5	2001 INQRY	1.30	0	1.30	1.45	0	5,921	Step 2:
JUN	30	2001 INQRF	2.20	0	2.30	2.45	0	12,113	Sell $30 Strike June 2001 Put
JUN	32.5	2001 INQRZ	3.40	0	3.70	3.90	0	300	
JUN	35	2001 INQRG	5	0	5.40	5.70	0	450	
JUN	37.5	2001 INQRU	6.50	0	7.50	7.90	0	176	
JUN	37.5	2001 NQRU	0.05	0	0	0.10	10	0	
JUN	40	2001 INQRH	11.30	0	9.90	10.20	0	10	
JUN	42.5	2001 INQRV	0	0	12.40	12.70	0	0	
JUN	45	2001 INQRI	0	0	14.90	15.20	0	0	
JUN	47.5	2001 INQRW	0	0	17.40	17.70	0	0	
JUN	50	2001 INQRJ	20.20	0	20	20.30	0	0	

To select which would be the best Bull Put spread, let's take a look at a few of the alternatives:

Step 1	(i)	**Long put**	Buy $27.50 strike June 2001 put @ $1.45
Or	(ii)	**Long put**	Buy $25 strike June 2001 put @ $0.80
Or	(iii)	**Long put**	Buy $22.50 strike June 2001 put @ $0.50
Or	(iv)	**Long put**	Buy $20 strike June 2001 put @ $0.25
Step 2		**Short put**	Sell $30 strike June 2001 put @ $2.30

Let's look at the risk profiles for each alternative:

			Bull Put spread risk profile (both legs included)			
Step 1	**Long put**		Risk	Reward	B/E	Max ROI
(i)	**Buy $27.50 strike June 2001 put @ $1.45**	$1.65	$0.85	$29.15	51.52%
✓ (ii)	**Buy $25 strike June 2001 put @ $0.80**	$3.50	$1.50	$28.50	42.86%
(iii)	**Buy $22.50 strike June 2001 put @ $0.50**	$5.70	$1.80	$28.20	31.58%
(iv)	**Buy $20 strike June 2001 put @ $0.25**	$7.95	$2.05	$27.95	25.79%
Step 2	**Short put**					
	Sell $30 strike June 2001 put @ $2.30					

Which one would you choose?

For this strategy, I'd prefer to choose strike prices further below the current stock price, but from the alternatives, (ii) is probably the best of the options simply because the ROI is high and there isn't much difference between the breakevens between (ii) and (iii).

Chart 7.5 ● INTC $25–$30 strike June 2001 Bull Put spread.

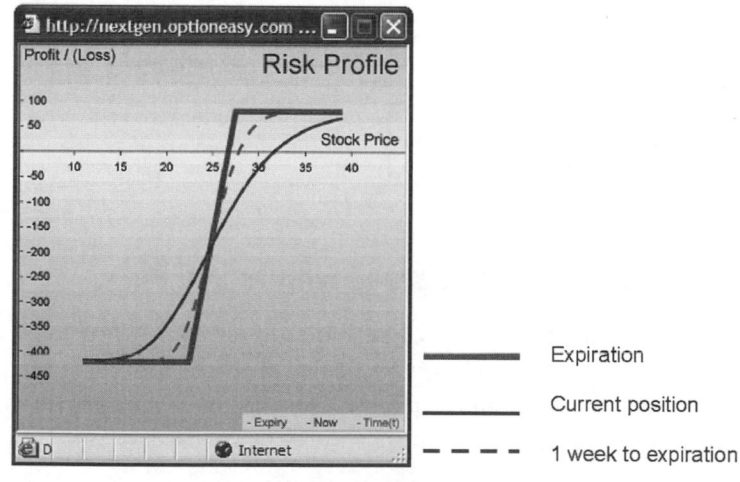

In an ideal world we prefer to select the short side (higher strike put) well below the current stock price. In this example we could, for instance, look at the $22.50–$27.50 strike June 2001 Bull Put spread:

Step 1	Long put	Bull Put spread risk profile (both legs included)			
	Buy $22.50 strike June 2001 put @ $0.50				
Step 2	**Short put**	**Risk**	**Reward**	**B/E**	**Max ROI**
	Sell $27.50 strike June 2001 put @ $1.30	$4.20	$0.80	$26.70	19.05%

Here, the maximum ROI is significantly less than what we were looking at before but look at how low our breakeven point is now. We have more than three points (10.85%) of cushion (remember the stock price is at $29.95) and the monthly return is over 13%. This particular trade offers lower risk in that the breakeven is that much lower than in the previous example.

Chart 7.6 ● INTC $22.50–$27.50 strike June 2001 Bull Put spread.

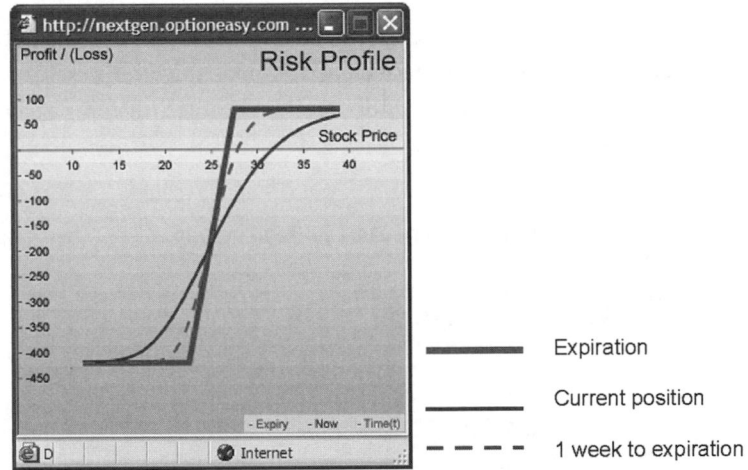

Comparison of Bull Put Spread with Naked Put

Many traders like to use the Naked Put strategy to sell premium on a stock they'd quite like to buy at a lower level. The problem with this strategy is that it comes at the price of unlimited potential risk as the stock goes down to zero if the stock were to plummet.

	Naked Put	**Bull Put spread**
Maximum risk	Exercise Price less Put Premium received	Limited to the difference of the strike prices less the net credit received
Maximum reward	Limited to the net credit received for the put	Limited to the net credit received
Breakeven	Exercise price less put premium received	Higher strike price less net credit received
Maximum risk credit on net credit	Can be **substantially** greater than 100% risk on **net credit** received	Can be greater than 100% risk on **net**
Margin required	Typically 25% of the stock price at inception of the trade (as required by your broker)	Limited to the risk of the Bull Put spread trade

Let's just compare a Naked Put with our preferred example above:

Example 7.5

It is May 4, 2001. XYZ is priced at $30. You are considering one of the following alternative bullish strategies:

(a) Naked Put	Sell June 2001 $27.50 strike put @ $1.30
(b) Bull Put spread	Buy June 2001 $25 strike put @ $0.80 and
	Sell June 2001 $30 strike put @ $2.30 (net credit $1.50)

	Naked Put (a)	**Bull Put spread (b)**
You receive	**$1.30 net credit**	**$1.50 net credit**
Maximum risk	$26.20	$3.50
Maximum reward	$1.30 (4.76% on max risk)	$1.50 (42.86% on max risk)
Maximum monthly yield	3.43%	29.47%
Breakeven	$26.20	$28.50
Maximum risk on net credit	2,015.38%	233.33%
Margin required	25% of the stock value = $7.50	$3.50 (i.e. max risk on the Bull Put trade)

The main advantage that the Naked Put holds over the Bull Put spread in this example is that the breakeven is more than two points lower. However, if we've concluded that major support for the stock (purely for illustrative purposes—this is not necessarily my view) is around $30, then we should have enough conviction about our trade to be happy with the Bull Put spread. I personally do not like the risk profile and associated dangers of Naked Puts (or Naked Calls for that matter).

Chart 7.7 ● $25–$30 June 2001 Bull Put spread (b) versus $27.50 June 2001 Naked Put (a)

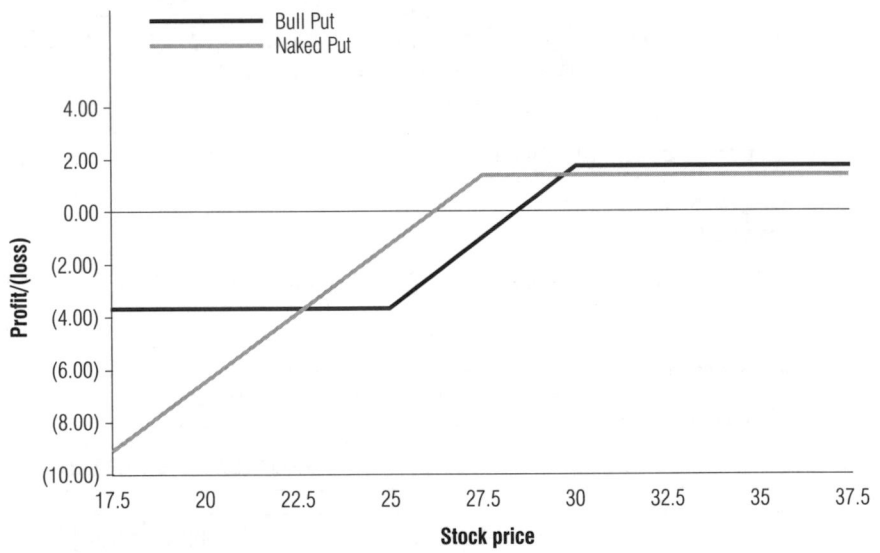

Bull Put Spreads and the Greeks

Delta	Delta peaks in between the two strike prices (i.e. near the money)—notice the difference between the one-month Delta profile and the one-week delta profile. This shows us that small movements in the underlying stock price at these levels will have a more dramatic impact on the value of the Bull Put position. Delta becomes much more sensitive as time decays. This means that the Bull Put risk profile itself becomes much more sensitive as time decays. This is because Time Value is depleting to negligible levels, and so the stock movement is being followed almost exclusively by Intrinsic Value at these levels. Notice that as the stock price veers away from the money (on both sides), Delta is hardly sensitive at all and that the most sensitive Delta action is occurring close to the two strike prices.

Gamma	The acceleration and deceleration of Delta is reflected in the Gamma values. As you would expect, Gamma peaks in positive territory where the stock is just below the lower strike price and troughs into negative territory where the stock is just above the higher strike price.
Theta	Theta moves from negative territory below the lower strike price to positive territory above the higher strike price. This tells us that time decay is working against us until we're in the money. Once we're moving above the breakeven point, Theta decay helps us because it means if the options expire, we're in profit, so it suits us for them to expire sooner rather than later. If the stock price is below the lower strike price, this is loss-making territory, so it doesn't suit us for the options to be expiring; therefore, Theta is negative. Remember with Theta, if it is positive, then time decay is helping us, and if it is negative, then time decay is hurting our position.
Vega	Vega is positive when we're below the lower strike price and turns negative as the stock rises to above our breakeven figures. This means that the Bull Put position is more positively sensitive to volatility when the stock price is below the lower strike price. This makes perfect sense given that if we're below the money, increased volatility would be helpful to our position since it would increase the chances of the stock price moving, hopefully in an upward direction, thus putting us into profit. Once we're in profit and above the higher strike price, we don't want increased volatility because it increases our chances of moving the stock price, potentially in a downward direction, which is detrimental to our position.
Rho	Rho's impact is enhanced the longer there is left to expiration. Rho increases up to and around the strike prices and then tails off into negative territory, as the position becomes Deep In the Money. Rho becomes less sensitive with the passage of time, since the impact of interest rates reduces when there is less time for rates to have an effect. This, of course, is utterly logical.

Chart 7.8 ● Bull Put spread Delta profile.

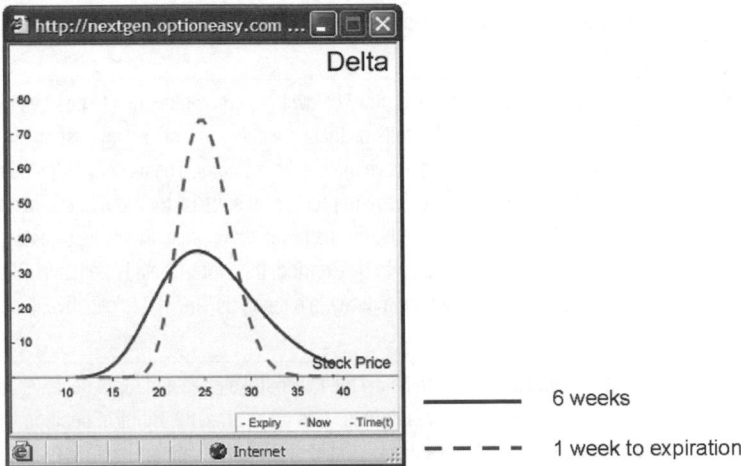

—————— 6 weeks

– – – – 1 week to expiration

Chart 7.9 ● Bull Put spread Theta profile.

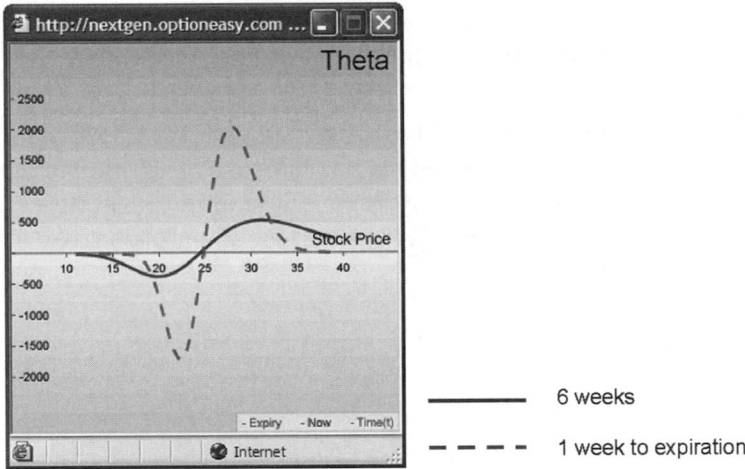

—————— 6 weeks

– – – – 1 week to expiration

Placement of the Short (Higher) Strike and the Importance of Strong Support

This is such a critical factor that it bears repeating as a summary. Here are the criteria for sound Bull Put spreads:

1. Choose strong stocks that are in up trends on a daily chart basis. Do not use the Bull Put spread as a reversal strategy where the stock has been falling.

   - Avoid low priced stocks of under $20 where possible (at the time of writing this may be quite a challenge).

   - Avoid stocks with less than 500,000 Average Daily Volume (ADV). Illiquidity in a stock price means that prices can jump violently both up and down. We want to employ the Bull Put spread on solid stocks where support is both strong and clearly identifiable. Low ADV is not conducive to solid price support.

   - You need to find stocks with high enough volatility in order to create a large enough credit between the two strike prices, the higher of which is well below the current stock price. At the same time you want to avoid excessive volatility or sectors where volatility is so unpredictable that you can't sleep at night.

   - Avoid stocks that are just about to announce earnings reports or similar. You don't want to be exposed to a sudden reversal in sentiment. The Bull Put spread is supposed to be a consistent strategy you can use every month (although during 2000–2001 this would have been difficult) for between 11% and 25% monthly returns where the breakeven point of your trade is significantly below the current stock price.

   - Look for strong price support, for example:

     - 61.8%, 38.2% and 50% confirmed retracement support levels (Fibonacci Analysis);

     - confirmed price support at a double or triple bottom;

     - confirmed price support on a moving average. Some people use 20-day exponential moving averages, and some use 25-period displaced moving averages. There is no right or wrong here in general terms. Just make sure that the moving average you're using has proved to be effective in the past with the stock you're thinking about using this strategy with.

2. Choose strike prices that are deep Out of the Money (for example here, lower than the current stock price). The lower the strike prices you select for your Bull Put spread, the greater the probability of a successful trade because the breakeven hurdle is that much lower.

Advantages of Spreads — A Summary

Spreads are far preferable than simple buying or selling single leg options. We've already seen how we can improve our risk and breakeven profiles without damaging our maximum profit potential. Here is a summary of why we like to use spreads for our options trading:

- Lower cost of trade—the sold option offsets the cost of the bought option.
- Lower overall risk of the trade.
- Lower breakeven of the (bullish spread) trade.
- Day to day fluctuations of the spread position are slowed down because of Delta hedging properties of creating the spread.
- Can be used for different time periods (Bull Calls for the long term and Bull Puts for the short term).

The *disadvantages* of spreads are less significant but worth bearing in mind:

- Higher commissions (because you are placing more trades *per se*).
- Profit potential capped.
- Day to day fluctuations slowed down— this can be disadvantageous if price action of the underlying asset goes your way from the beginning. Generally, however, Delta hedging is a major advantage and will help your trading psychology as much as anything else. There is nothing more damaging to trading psychology than experiencing fast, devastating losses or whipsaws. Delta hedging, as we've described in the last two chapters, is one way of minimizing the possibilities of either scenario occurring.

Chapter 7 Major Learning Points

In this chapter, we've learned how to create two popular bullish strategies, the Bull Call and the Bull Put spread, safely and responsibly. We've also compared and contrasted the two strategies not only to each other, but also to other basic strategies such as the Long Call and the Naked Put.

Furthermore, we've discussed how the Greeks work with these strategies and which sensitivities we need to hedge to minimize our risk while not compromising our maximum reward too much.

You can now understand which strategies you'll use in different circumstances and how Time Decay will affect your positions. You also can decide whether you want to use a long-term investment strategy (Bull Call) or a short-term income trading strategy (Bull Put). In either case you can now start to develop succinct and definable filters for selecting the appropriate stocks for each strategy.

We're now going to continue with more strategies and identify two more that we can use profitably when we expect higher volatility in terms of price action, but where we're not quite sure about the direction. These are known as Volatility Strategies, and some traders out there swear by them...

Two Basic Volatility Strategies

What if you're not sure about the direction of a stock, but you do feel sure that it's going to move significantly in one direction or another? Trading options gives you the ability to make low risk-high reward without even having to get the direction right! The two strategies we'll discuss in this chapter are Straddles and Strangles, which are both direction-neutral strategies.

Straddles

The Straddle involves the following steps:

Step 1   buying ATM strike puts and

Step 2   buying ATM strike calls with the same expiration date.

This will be a net debit transaction because you are paying for equal numbers of calls and puts. As such, the Straddle is an expensive strategy in terms of a cash requirement. However, if you play the strategy correctly, it needn't be a high-risk strategy even if the anticipated volatile price action doesn't materialize.

Diagram 8.1 ● Straddle.

Buy put **Buy call** **Straddle**

The risk profile of a Straddle is as follows:

	Straddle
Maximum risk	Net debit of the spread (that is, what you pay)
Maximum reward	Unlimited
Breakeven on the downside	Strike price *less* net debit
Breakeven on the upside	Strike price *plus* net debit
Maximum risk on net debit or net credit	100% risk on net debit

Can you see that this strategy has two breakeven points, one below and one above the strike price? Remember that the call and put share the same strike price, which should be as near to the money (that is to say, as close to the current stock price) as possible.

How to Find a Good Straddle Opportunity and How to Play It

Key criteria:

● Implied Volatility and Historical Volatility

● Price Consolidation Chart Pattern

● Stock Prices

● Timing

Let's look at each criterion in isolation and then piece them together so we can define a coherent strategy and filtering technique for finding and executing Straddle plays.

(i) Implied Volatility and Historical Volatility

Ideally we need a situation where the current Implied Volatility for the stock is low compared with its average Implied Volatility over the medium term, say, anything from three months to one year. (Remember, Implied Volatility is a figure derived from matching the current option price with the Options Pricing Model.)

In theory we also want a situation where Implied Volatility is lower than Historical

Volatility over a one-month, two-month, and three-month period. (Remember, Historical Volatility relates solely to the stock price itself.) Some stock option chains contain price series, which consistently reflect Implied Volatility being far greater than Historical Volatility or vice versa. This is why comparing Implied Volatility to itself (rather than to Historical Volatility) over different time frames is a more sound way to assess if Implied Volatility is too high or low.

You need to be able to see this dynamic before executing a good Straddle play. A stock may appear to have very high Implied Volatility as compared with Historical Volatility, but that is only part of the story.

Other signs to look for include looking at the wider market and the sector of the stock to assess whether the stock, sector, or market is poised for higher volatility. How can you tell whether this might be the case? First, you can look at the Market Volatility Index (VIX). The VIX is a volatility index as measured from the S&P 100 index. Generally the VIX will be low as prices rise and high (denoting high volatility) when prices are falling. This reflects the fact that prices tend to fall faster than they rise, hence the greater degree of volatility. Secondly, you should examine the price charts to see if there are any signs of consolidation in the price pattern.

(ii) Price Consolidation

In Chapter 4, "The Basics of Technical Analysis," we discussed consolidation patterns like Triangles and Pennants. These price patterns are clear indications of declining Historical Volatility, and by implication we would look to see that Implied Volatility was also declining. Furthermore, consolidation patterns generally precede a breakout of some sort, which is precisely what we want to happen shortly after placing our Straddle trade. Remember, with Straddles we're not overly concerned with direction; we're interested in explosive price movement and lots of it once we've placed the trade.

Consolidations occur as a result of highs and lows of individual price bars getting closer and closer together in terms of the length of each bar.

Diagram 8.2 ● Consolidation price patterns for Straddles.

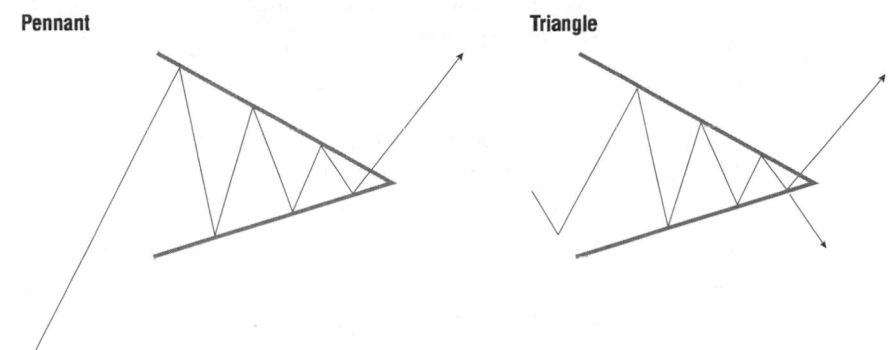

Pennant   Triangle

Chart 8.1.0 ● MNMD (May–June 1999).

Chart created on TradeStation®, the flagship product of TradeStation Technologies Inc.

You can see from this example that the Triangle price pattern lasted for more than a month before the price broke out at the end of May 1999. The longer the consolidation period and the more defined the pattern is (that is, the higher the wedge), generally speaking the greater the anticipated breakout will be.

Looking at the preceding example we can see that MNMD moved up around

20 points from $30 at the end of May 1999 to almost $50 by the end of August 1999. This is a move of around 67% and certainly qualifies as a decent (although not spectacular) Straddle example.

(i) Stock Price

Generally you want to avoid stocks below $15 for playing Straddles, though I've played them successfully on stocks under $10 where I was absolutely sure of a breakout. Remember that you're looking for anticipated explosive price action, which could go in either direction. This means that you need enough room on the downside to have a profitable trade if there is a savage downward movement (thus increasing the value of the put option).

(ii) Timing

The timing of a Straddle play is critical in terms of entry, time to expiration, and exit.

Entry

After you have identified a consolidating stock, look to see if there is any news anticipated on that stock, for example earnings reports. Other anticipated news items also can be highly relevant like government reports (CPI, PPI, GDP, Employment Report). The key is to place the trade *before* announcements are made, given that they may be the catalyst for the explosive move you're looking for. Ideally, aim to place your Straddle trade a week or two before earnings because often Implied Volatility starts to rise as earnings season approaches.

The timing of a Straddle play is critical in terms of entry, time to expiration, and exit.

Time to Expiration

You must give yourself enough time to be right but not so much time that the options premiums are so prohibitively high that it's difficult to make a profit.

Ideally you trade Straddles with expirations about three months out. Why? Because Time Value decays at its fastest one month before expiration and you'll want to exit your position (regardless of any price moves) with at least one month to expiration *at the latest*. The idea here is to minimize your risk. With Straddles, the greatest risk is that of time decay. If the stock price doesn't move much after you place the trade, you generally won't be risking too much, provided you don't leave it too long. The exception to that is if Implied Volatility suddenly plummets through the floor, dragging down options premiums at the same time.

If you're playing a Straddle in anticipation of a news event, such as earnings or a company announcement, you should exit fast if there are no surprises. This way you'll minimize your risk exposure considerably, particularly if you were anticipating a surprise in the first place.

In conclusion, the time to expiration for a Straddle can be anywhere from two to four months, but whatever happens, you should always exit the trade (if there's been no movement) with more than a month left to expiration.

Exit

There are a number of scenarios regarding the exit of a Straddle play. Let's take each one in turn:

(i) After a news announcement where there was no surprise and no price movement:

Look to exit within a couple of days where the lack of price movement confirms the lack of surprise.

(ii) After a news announcement where there was a surprise and requisite price movement:

You can play this scenario in any number of ways. If you have already set short-term realistic price targets (say, using Fibonacci), then you can define your own exit strategy according to a prescribed set of rules defined within those techniques.

You can sell the profitable side after a price move and keep the unprofitable side in anticipation of a price retracement the other way, whereupon you sell that side too. For example, if a stock rises after a news announcement, you may want to take profits by selling the profitable call options. The puts at that point won't be worth very much, but will increase again if the stock price retraces downward. Having retained the put option, you could then sell the puts once the retracement has occurred (provided there is still at least one month to expiration).

(iii) Never leave an open position on either side with less than one month left to expiration:

This rule takes precedence over all others.

(iv) Preset profit targets:

For example, you reach a 50% profit objective and exit the trade regardless of what you think will happen with the stock price. The danger with preset profit targets is that some traders hold out too long waiting for the profit target to get hit, and if it doesn't get hit, the profits will inevitably start to slip away into a loss-making position.

Straddles and the Greeks

Delta	The speed of a Straddle's position accelerates dramatically Near the Money. Delta is negative when the stock price is very low and accelerates into a positive value when the stock price is nearer and above the strike price. This shows us that when the stock price is lower than the strike price, further down movement is profitable, and when the stock price is higher than the strike price, continued up movement is required from the stock to make the Straddle profitable. Delta's profile is somewhat '"S"' shaped. Delta will generally be less than one (for one contract) when the stock price is ATM. This signifies that at that point, the value of the Straddle will vary with the stock price, but at a reduced speed.
Gamma	Gamma is always positive with a long Straddle and peaks where delta is rising at its steepest angle. This invariably occurs Near the Money, indicating that the Straddle is very sensitive to swings in the stock price at these levels.
Theta	Time decay affects the Straddle detrimentally. Theta assumes a "V" shape and is almost entirely negative, forming its trough At the Money. This makes total sense because with a long Straddle you are buying two options premiums and are heavily exposed to time decay. Where the stock price is far lower than the Straddle strike price, theta can have a fractional positive value.
Vega	Vega is entirely positive and forms a mountain-top shape, peaking At the Money. With the vega value peaking ATM this indicates to us that a small increase in volatility is going to increase the value of our Straddle position markedly.
Rho	Rho's impact is enhanced the longer there is left to expiration. Rho's profile is very much like delta's, forming an '"S"' shape by starting from a negative value when the asset price is low, to accelerating at its greatest degree around the Money and tailing off as the stock price rises well beyond the Straddle strike price.

Example 8.1 KOSP Straddle

Chart 8.1.1 ● KOSP price chart (May 2001).

Chart created on TradeStation®, the flagship product of TradeStation Technologies Inc.

In this example we're looking to go long the KOSP $25 strike August 2001 Straddle with the current stock price at $26.50 on May 30, 2001. Looking at the Asks for each option, the calls are costing $4.00 and the puts $2.15.

(a)Long Straddle	Buy August 2001 $25 strike call @ $4.00.
	Buy August 2001 $25 strike put @ $2.15.

The risk profile is as follows:

	Straddle (a)
You pay (net debit)	$6.15
Maximum risk	$6.15
Maximum risk with 1 month to expiration	c. $2.71 (44% of the trade)
Maximum reward	Unlimited on both sides
Breakeven (downside)	$18.85
Breakeven (upside)	$31.15
Maximum risk on net debit	100%
Call Implied Volatility	61.89%
Put Implied Volatility	62.97%
90-day Historical Volatility High	84.21%
90-day Historical Volatility Low	40.55%

Is this a good trade? Well, only time will tell.[1] Implied Volatility on the stock is not overtly high compared with its average Historical Volatility (around 61.89% for the call and 62.97% for the put) for the previous three months, but on the other hand it isn't all that low either. The consolidation pattern has also been a little on the short side.

The key is to look at the risk profile and evaluate your likely position with one month left to expiration (the middle line on the risk profile chart here). The maximum risk at that point in time would be around only $2.71 given that you still have the benefit of Time Value even if the stock hasn't moved at all. The breakeven points are also slightly friendlier at that point in time, being as they are a little closer to the central strike price.

One school of thought suggests that you can take the low of the last 60 trading days from the 60 trading-day high, divide that figure by two, and only make the trade if the cost of the (3-month) Straddle is less. Here, the 60 trading-day high is $28.87,

---

[1] By June 8, 2001, KOSP had reached $36.00, and this Straddle was worth around $12, almost a 100% return in just over one week. At this point I'd be tempted to sell the profitable call and keep the almost worthless put in anticipation of downward retracement.

and the 60 trading-day low is $14.31. The difference is $14.56, halved is $7.28 and the cost of our Straddle here ($6.15) is less, which therefore qualifies as being acceptable. If you're going to adopt this technique, then make sure that you're obeying the other rules, that is to say, an impending news event and a consolidating chart pattern.

Chart 8.1.2 ● KOSP Straddle risk profile.

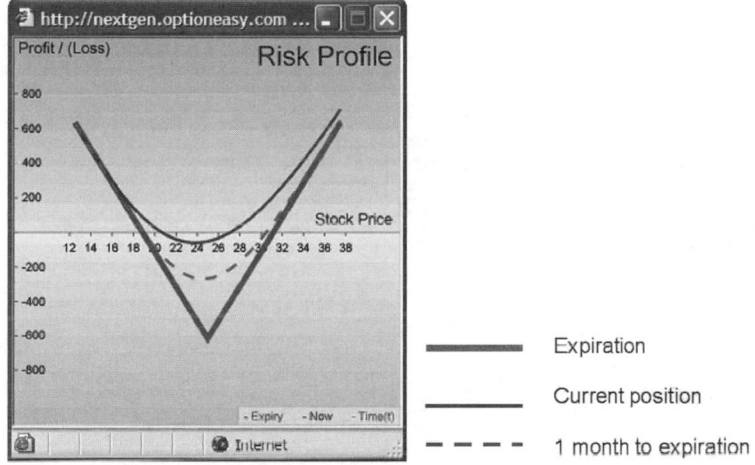

Expiration

Current position

1 month to expiration

Chart 8.1.3 ● KOSP Straddle delta profile.

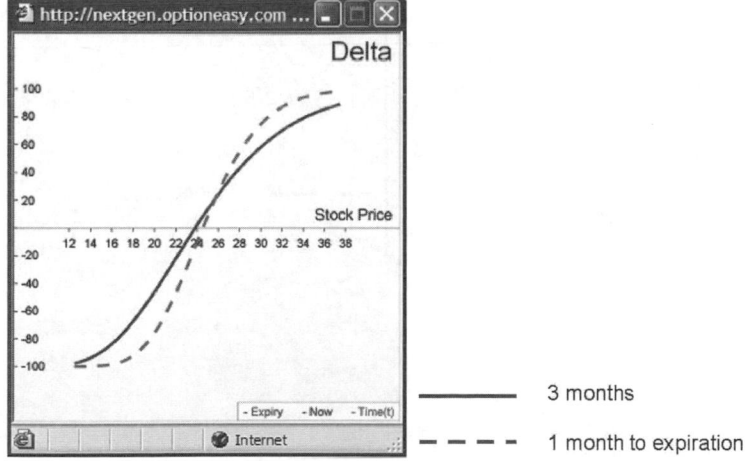

3 months

1 month to expiration

Chart 8.1.4 ● KOSP Straddle gamma profile.

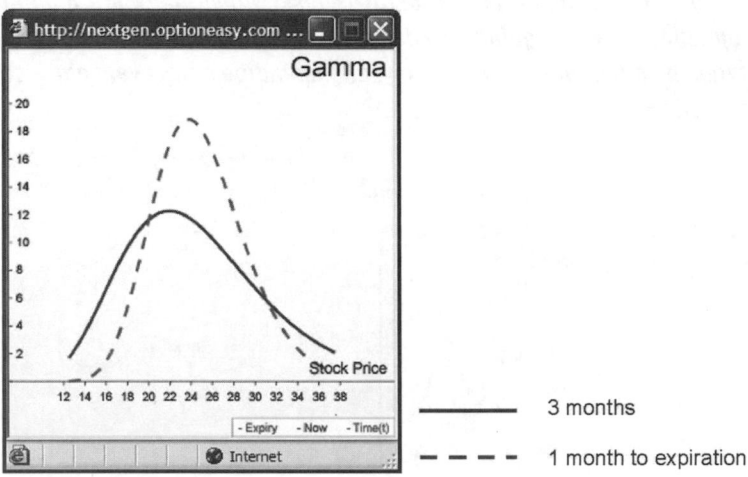

———————— 3 months

- - - - - 1 month to expiration

Chart 8.1.5 ● KOSP Straddle theta profile.

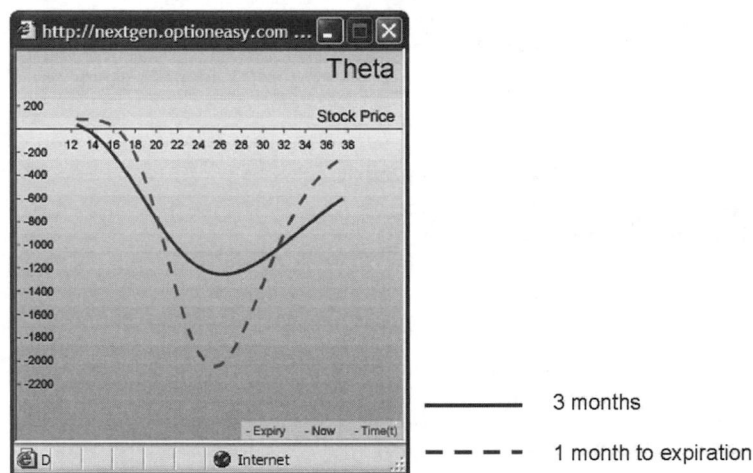

———————— 3 months

- - - - - 1 month to expiration

Chart 8.1.6 ● KOSP Straddle vega profile.

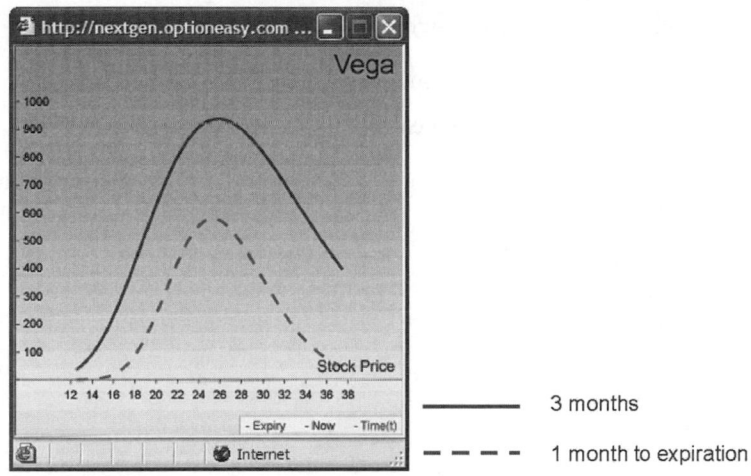

——— 3 months

– – – – 1 month to expiration

Chart 8.1.7 ● KOSP Straddle rho profile.

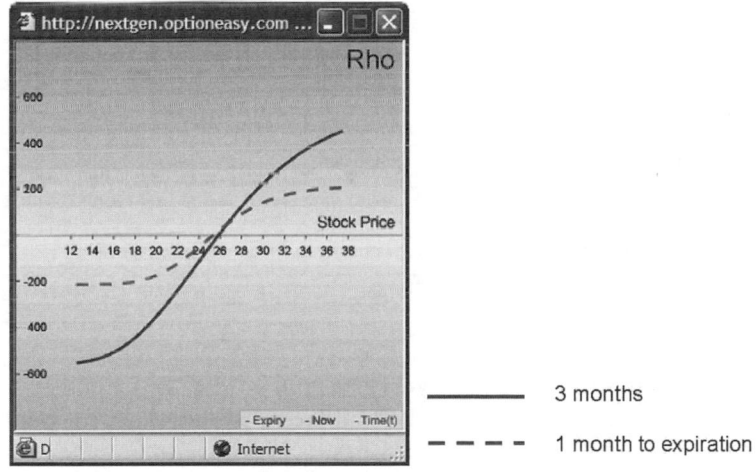

——— 3 months

– – – – 1 month to expiration

Strangles

The Strangle involves the following steps:

Step 1   buying OTM strike puts and

Step 2   buying OTM strike calls with the same expiration date.

This will be a net debit transaction given that you are paying for equal numbers of calls and puts. Because you are buying OTM options where there is no Intrinsic Value, the Strangle is a cheaper alternative to the Straddle. However, it also has a slightly different risk profile, although the basic rules are almost identical.

Strangle

Buy OTM put   **Buy OTM call**   **Strangle**

The risk profile of a Strangle is as follows:

	Strangle
Maximum risk	Net debit of the spread (that is, what you pay)
Maximum reward	Unlimited
Breakeven on the downside	Lower (put) strike price *less* net debit
Breakeven on the upside	Higher (call) strike price *plus* net debit
Maximum risk on net debit	100% risk on **net debit**

Again, this strategy has two breakeven points, one below and one above the strike price. The call and the put have different strike prices; the put strike price is below the current asset price, and the call strike price is above the current stock price. Because of the way calls and puts work, both strikes are OTM. In selecting your strike prices for the Strangle, you should make them as close to equidistant from the current stock price as possible.

Example 8.2.1 **KOSP Strangle**

We're looking to buy the KOSP $20 strike August 2001 put and buy the KOSP $30 strike call with the current stock price at $26.50. Looking at the Asks for each option, the calls are costing $1.85 and the puts $0.60. We'll also compare it to our Straddle just noted where we bought the $25 strike calls for $4.00 and the $25 strike puts for $2.15.

(b) Long Strangle*	Buy August 2001 $20 strike put @ $0.60 and
	Buy August 2001 $30 strike call @ $1.85

* By June 8, 2001, KOSP had reached $36.00, and this Strangle was worth more than $7.00, almost a 300% return in just more than one week. Because of the sharp rise, the Strangle has been even more successful than the Straddle because of its very low initial cost.

	Straddle (a)	Strangle (b)
You pay (net debit)	$6.15	$2.45
Maximum risk	$6.15	$2.45
Maximum risk with one month until expiration (estimated)	c. $2.71 (44% of the trade)	c. $1.91 (78% of the trade)

	Straddle (a)	Strangle (b)
Maximum reward	Unlimited on both sides	Unlimited on both sides
Breakeven (downside)	$18.85	$17.55
Breakeven (upside)	$31.15	$32.65
Maximum risk on net debit	100%	100%
Call Implied Volatility	61.89%	61.26%
Put Implied Volatility	62.97%	64.77%
90-day Historical Volatility high	84.21%	84.21%
90-day Historical Volatility low	40.55%	40.55%

Chart 8.2.1 ● KOSP Strangle risk profile.

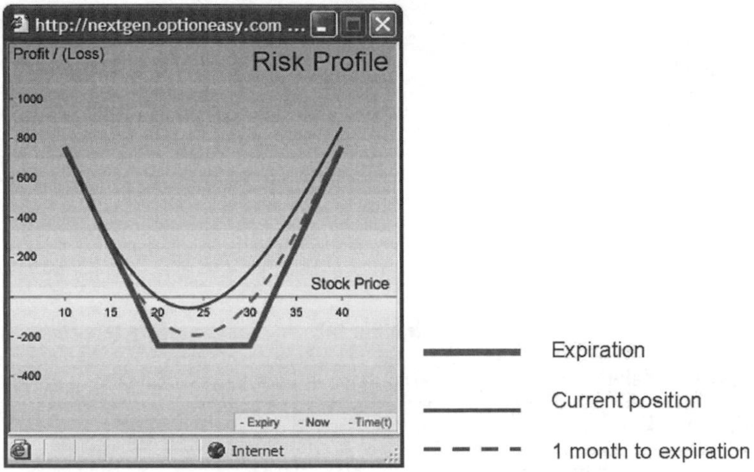

Comparison Between the Strangle and the Straddle

● With a Strangle we've exchanged wider breakeven points for lower risk, as compared with the Straddle. This means our breakevens will be a little more difficult to reach, but at least we're paying far less to achieve that.

● The net debit and maximum risk are far lower for the Strangle.

● The estimated maximum risk of the Strangle with one month left until expiration forms a higher percentage of the total maximum risk of the trade. However, the total maximum risk of the Strangle is far less than that of the Straddle.

● Both strategies offer an unlimited maximum reward, but the Straddle's risk profile is much steeper than the Strangle's. If KOSP's stock price were to reach either $10 on the downside or $40 on the upside, the Straddle's profit at expiration would be $8.85, while the Strangle's would only be $7.55. The Strangle, however, would show a greater percentage return because of its lower cost basis.

● For both strategies our maximum risk is 100% of our net debit of the trade.

Psychology of Volatility Strategies

Although straddles and strangles are exciting strategies to trade, it's important to understand that they also can be very challenging from a psychological point of view. The best way of illustrating this is by describing a couple of other experiences I've had.

In March 2003 I had found a great Straddle opportunity on Expedia (EXPE), which was trading at around $34.00 and about to announce earnings the following week. The stock had recently split, and the second Gulf War was imminent. The stock was forming a consolidation pattern, and with the threat of war, my judgment was that travel stocks would suffer. So, having conducted all the necessary analysis and calculations, I put on the July $35 strike Straddle at a cost of $8.20. The April expiration date was too close so I decided to go for the more conservative July expiration, yet at the same time I was expecting to exit this trade within two weeks. I had also calculated that there was strong Fibonacci support around three points lower. The other thing I should mention is that I was due to travel on business two days after putting the trade on.

The day after I placed the trade, EXPE plummeted down to the Fibonacci support level. My trading plan was to remain in the trade until after earnings were announced. But within 24 hours of placing the trade, I could see that I could already exit with a 10% profit and go on my travels in peace. So that's precisely what I did. I exited the position with the stock price precisely on the Fibonacci support level, and as the stock rose I congratulated myself on my sheer genius!

The following week, Expedia announced earnings, which were better than expected. It was also announced that there had been an offer for the entire company, which resulted in the stock price rising by more than $20 in the following days. How clever do you think I felt now? My Straddle would have been worth at least $24 including Time Value, almost 300% what I had paid for it! I had disobeyed my trading plan and therefore forewent a massive profit. Even though I'd made a profitable trade, the consequences of disobeying my trading plan made it a bitter disappointment.

The opposite of this trade was another one I did on HOV, which I had been stalking in May 2004. The stock was perfectly set up, so I put on the August expiration Straddle. Not only were earnings due to be announced, but also the Fed was announcing an interest rate rise during the same week. I was therefore convinced that having passed all the tests, HOV was due a big move.

Earnings were way ahead of expectations, and the stock rose $4.00 before retracing—not enough to make me swimming in profit yet, but not a bad start. The Fed announcement was in line with expectations, so now I was expecting

HOV to steeple upward. To be fair, it did try! But every time it tried to break out, back down it came. Having learned from my EXPE experience, my trading plan was to be more patient this time and wait the maximum amount of time (that is, until one month before expiration). Needless to say, this wait was agonizing until at last HOV plunged downward in early July, allowing me to exit with a modest profit and considerably less hair!

Do you see how the EXPE and HOV trades differed and how challenging they were from a psychological point of view? With EXPE, I made a small but quick profit in advance of a travel engagement. With HOV I had to wait and wait. In both instances there were serious temptations to stray from the trading plan. In the case of EXPE, there was no excuse. In the case of HOV, I should have exited after there was no serious movement following both news announcements. You can now see how strictly you must adhere to the trading plan straightjacket when you're trading this kind of strategy.

Chapter 8 Major Learning Points

In this chapter we've learned the basic rudiments of how to play an anticipated surge in volatility. The Straddle is a bread and butter strategy, simple to execute and well documented, while the Strangle is also a sound strategy for playing volatility.

The Straddle has, on balance, more advantages provided you play the strategy according to the rules outlined here. The rules are designed to minimize your risk while allowing you to maintain your chances of a high potential reward. Ultimately, the more we minimize the cost of entry, the steeper the Straddle profile will be and the faster you'll emerge into a profitable position as the stock starts to move in either direction away from the Exercise Price. By exiting the position with at least a month left to expiration, we're not over-exposing ourselves to time decay. Yes, we may encounter the odd loss here and there if the stock doesn't move at all, but we're not risking the bulk of our trade if we adhere to this rule with strict discipline.

The Straddle is, in this context, a low-risk and high-reward strategy, which many options traders select as their one and only strategy. You'll need to devise a filtering system and back test it so that you can increase your chances of selecting consolidating stocks efficiently and reliably. The filter you build should include the following components:

● Optionable.

● Consolidating chart pattern—that is, smaller spreads between price bar highs and lows on any time period from one week to three months.

- Implied Volatility lower now than the 90-day average (if you have the tools to make this filter).

- Implied Volatility lower than Historical Volatility of the previous 90 days.

- Sixty trading-day rule (this can act as an approximation of the previous two points).

Now we can look at two strategies, which will make us profits if the share price remains range-bound for a period of time—if you like the antithesis of Straddles and Strangles!

chapter 9

Two Basic Sideways Strategies

What if a stock has run out of steam and we're anticipating a period of consolidation or lower volatility for a period of time? What if we have identified a range-bound stock and we want to take advantage of this price pattern behavior? We can achieve this by trading low-risk, high-reward options strategies! The two strategies we'll discuss in this chapter are the Butterfly and the Condor, both of which produce profits provided the price remains within a certain price range, determined by the Exercise prices we select.

Butterflies

The Butterfly involves the following steps (you can use all calls *or* all puts with the Butterfly—you cannot mix the two):

Butterfly with Calls

Step 1	Buy 1 lower strike (ITM) call	There are two key points here:
Step 2	Sell 2 middle strike ATM calls	**1** The ratio between buying the ITM call, selling the ATM calls, and buying the OTM call is 1:2:1.
Step 3	Buy 1 higher strike (OTM) call	**2** The distance between the three adjacent strikes must be equal, with the middle strike being ATM or as close to ATM as possible.

Or:

Butterfly with Puts

Step 1	Buy 1 lower strike (OTM) put	There are two key points here:
Step 2	Sell 2 middle strike ATM puts	**1** The ratio between buying the OTM put, selling the ATM puts and buying the ITM put is 1:2:1.
Step 3	Buy 1 higher strike (ITM) put	**2** The distance between the three adjacent strikes must be equal, with the middle strike being ATM or as close to ATM as possible.

The Butterfly will be a net debit transaction given that the ITM and OTM options you buy will be more expensive than the two ATM options you are selling to create the strategy spread. Remember in the real world you'll be buying near the Ask and selling near the Bid, and even where you set a Limit Order (which you should do), you won't have much chance of being filled by being over ambitious on the price of entry. Therefore, find an overall price that you'd be happy to make the trade at, having calculated and considered your Risk, Reward, and Breakeven scenarios.

Long Call Butterfly

Buy lower strike call + Sell 2 ATM calls + Buy higher strike call = Long Call Butterfly

Long Put Butterfly

Buy lower strike put + Sell 2 ATM puts + Buy higher strike put = Long Put Butterfly

The Risk Profile of a Butterfly is as follows, regardless of whether you use all calls or all puts:

	Long Butterfly
Maximum risk	Limited to the net debit of the spread (what you pay)
Maximum reward	Limited to the difference between the adjacent strike prices less the net debit paid.
Breakeven on the downside	Lowest strike price *plus* net debit paid.
Breakeven on the upside	Highest strike price *less* net debit paid.
Maximum risk on net debit	100% risk on **net debit**.

As with Straddles and Strangles, the Butterfly has two breakeven scenarios, one to the downside and one to the upside. There the shared characteristics stop. The Butterfly can only yield a limited profit, and that can only occur at the middle Exercise price, the one nearest to the Money.

How To Find a Good Long Butterfly Opportunity and How To Play It

Key criteria:

- Rangebound stock pattern

- Implied Volatility and Historical Volatility

- Stock price

- Timing

Again, we'll look at each factor in isolation and then build a coherent methodology of finding and filtering for Long Butterfly trades.

(i) Rangebound Price Chart Pattern

We would like to find price patterns where we can identify clear lines of support and resistance to such a degree that we feel comfortable that the price will remain within those bounds. There is never a guarantee of such events materializing or not materializing, but ultimately we're simply looking to reduce our risk wherever possible. Fortunately the Butterfly is an innately low-risk strategy in the first place, but we want to now increase our probability of success.

Wide Butterfly

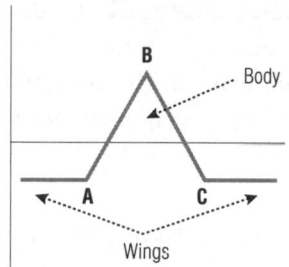

Narrow Butterfly

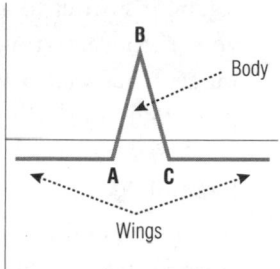

Wide Butterfly characteristics:

1 Strikes A and C are wider apart. B is equidistant from them both.
2 Greater Maximum Risk than with Narrow Butterfly.
3 Lower Maximum Reward (as evidenced by height of B).
4 Higher probability of profit (because a wider span above breakeven).

Narrow Butterfly characteristics:

1 Strikes A and C are closer together. B is still equidistant from them both.
2 Lower Maximum Risk than with Wide Butterfly.
3 Higher Maximum Reward (but less chance of achieving it).
4 Lower probability of profit (because of the narrow span above breakeven).

So Step 1 is to find a price pattern with clear and distinguishable support and resistance. The wider the Butterfly, the less risky your trade will be in terms of probability of success, but the more risky it will be in terms of the net debit to pay for it.

(ii) Implied Volatility and Historical Volatility

In a perfect Long Butterfly world, you'll be looking for stocks that have experienced higher than their average Implied Volatility levels but where you expect the price action to calm down, leading to lower volatility levels for the duration of your trade.

This is easier said than done because even lowering volatility levels doesn't necessarily help us with regard to the *direction* of price action, and the success of a Long Butterfly is dependent on price action remaining range-bound (and, depending on where you currently are within that range, price direction could be a vital factor). So be aware that before you start looking at volatility levels in this way, you must ensure you're dealing with a price series with distinctive and strong support and resistance lines. Therefore, you should be looking at trades where the stock price is right in the middle of those support and resistance levels, equidistant from both. When this is the case, your lowest strike will be at or just below support, the highest strike price will be at or just above resistance, and the middle strike will be equidistant from them both and as close to ATM as possible.

(iii) Stock Price

Again, it's better to avoid the really low priced stocks (under $20) even though you're concentrating here on price action keeping within a specific trading range. You want a wide enough wingspan on the Butterfly to improve your probability of profit, even if you'll end up paying a bit more for it.

(iv) Timing

As with all options trades, timing is crucial for Long Butterflies. Here are some rules for trading this strategy:

Entry

After you've identified your Long Butterfly stock, you need to make sure that there is *no* news coming soon. Ideally, all the news relating to that particular stock will have just passed, that is, earnings reports and any announcements concerning the stock or its sector. Furthermore, it's best if some of the major government announcements, such as the CPI, PPI, GDP, Inflation Report have been made recently too. The idea here is that you do *not* want any surprises that might disturb the rangebound pattern of the stock.

Time to Expiration

The optimum timing for selecting expirations for your Long Butterfly is all about balance. Time Decay works in your favor because the longer you leave it, the more chance the price has of breaching one of your Long Butterfly's wings. This leaves two potential dilemmas:

- If you choose an expiration date that is too close (under one month), you'll be faced with a large net debit and hence risk because the only option of any real value will be the deep ITM option which you buy (either calls or puts).

- If you choose an expiration date that is too far away (more than two months), you're increasing the probability that the price will breach one of the wings of the Butterfly and put you into a loss-making position.

I've found that the answer is to choose between one and two months for the optimal time frame for Long Butterflies. The reason is that it gives the ATM options (that you are selling as part of the spread) enough time to be of *some* value to reduce your net debit—and hence risk. At the same time, you're not giving the position too much time to breach the wings of the Butterfly.

Exit

As time progresses toward expiration, then so your maximum potential profit increases. So it makes sense to let the Long Butterfly run on as close as you can to expiration without risking the underlying price pattern breaching the wings. If you have to exit before expiration, you simply unravel the spread by selling the options you bought and buying the options you sold.

Make sure you're paying attention to likely timing of any relevant news items and their possible content. Anything untoward could lead to an explosion of volatility, which could then harm your position. You don't want to be in a Long Butterfly position at the outset of any major news about your stock, the appropriate sector, or industry.

Butterflies and the Greeks

Delta	Delta is positive, peaking at the lower strike price when the stock price is below the middle strike price. This means that a positive move upward from the lower strike price will be beneficial to our Butterfly position.
	Delta is neutral (zero) when the stock price is equal to the middle strike price. At this point we require no movement in the stock price to reach maximum profitability at expiration.
	Delta is negative, reaching its trough at the higher strike price. This means that at this level, we require the stock price to fall for our Butterfly position to move into profit.
	The Greek profiles for the Call Butterfly are identical to those of the Put Butterfly.
Gamma	Gamma troughs when the stock hits the middle Exercise price, thus demonstrating that movements away from this area would be detrimental to the Butterfly position. Gamma peaks at or below the lower strike price and at or above the higher strike price.
Theta	Theta looks like an inverted Gamma on the Greek Profile Charts, peaking at the middle strike price and troughing at or below the lower strike and at or above the higher strike. Can you now see the logic of why this is so?
Vega	Vega resembles Gamma with Butterflies, troughing at the middle Exercise Price and peaking at or below the lower Exercise Price and at or above the higher Exercise Price. Again, can you now see the logic of this?
Rho	Rho is positive, peaking at the lower strike price when the stock price is below the middle strike price.
	Rho is neutral (zero) when the stock price is equal to the middle strike price.
	Rho is negative, reaching its trough at the higher strike price when the stock price is above the middle strike price.

Example 9.1.1 FRE Butterfly (June 2001)

I've highlighted this stock as an example because at the time of writing, it is showing strong support and resistance lines. I don't trade Butterflies personally, but let's take a look at this nevertheless. Remember, with Butterflies you can do either all calls or all puts but never mix them up. For illustration purposes we'll do both so we can compare. We'll also compare a Narrow Butterfly (a) with a Wide Butterfly (b) and assess which one we prefer.

We are going to compare a 60-65-70 (narrow) strike Butterfly with a 55-65-75 (wide) strike Butterfly using all calls and all puts for each one, thus giving us four examples.

Chart 9.1.1 ● RE price chart (June 2001).

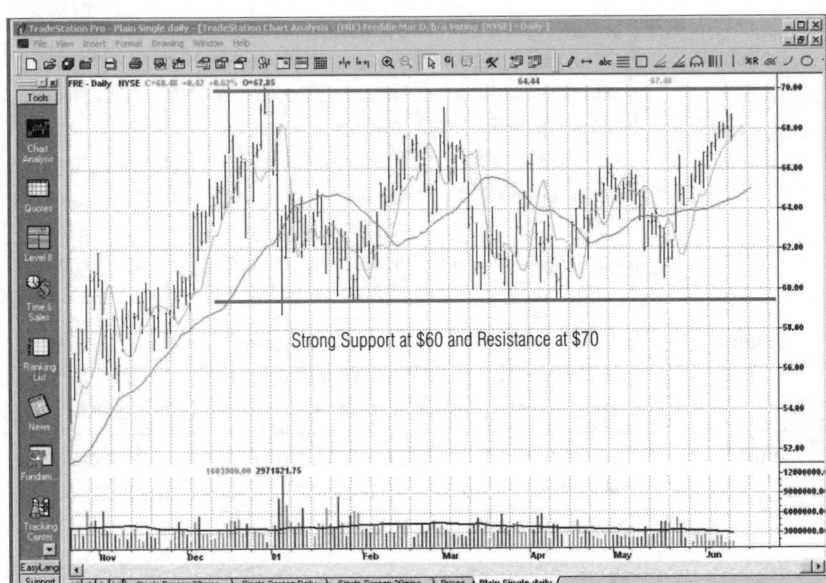

Chart created on TradeStation®, the flagship product of TradeStation Technologies Inc.

(a) Narrow Butterfly: strikes of $60, $65 and $70

FRE - FREDDIE MAC

Last Trade	Net Change	Bid	Ask	Day High	Day Low	Volume	Trade Time	
68.48	+0.42	0	0	68.70	67.40	1,604,100	16:01:00	News/Chart

Filter By

Month				Strike Price			
All	▼	And/Or		Equal To ▼			Search

Calls	Last	Change	Bid	Ask	Volume	Open Interest	Puts	Last	Change	Bid	Ask	Volume	Open Interest
JUN 50 2001 FREFJ	15.30	0	18.20	18.70	0	8	JUN 50 2001 FRERJ	0.35	0	0	0.15	0	20
JUN 55 2001 FREFK	12.30	0	13.20	13.70	0	0	JUN 55 2001 FRERK	0.25	0	0	0.15	0	145
JUN 60 2001 FREFL	7.70	0	8.30	8.70	0	682	JUN 60 2001 FRERL	0.05	0	0	0.15	0	1,008
JUN 65 2001 FREFM	3.20	-0.20	3.40	3.70	18	3,529	JUN 65 2001 FRERM	0.15	+0.10	0	0.15	19	1,089
JUN 70 2001 FREFN	0.25	0	0.10	0.25	0	1,413	JUN 70 2001 FRERN	1.90	0	1.60	1.80	0	177
JUN 75 2001 FREFO	0.25	0	0	0.15	0	718	JUN 75 2001 FRERO	7.10	0	6.30	0.70	0	78
JUN 80 2001 FREFP	0.10	0	0	0.15	0	600	JUN 80 2001 FRERP	0	0	11.30	11.80	0	0
JUL 50 2001 FREGJ	15.80	0	18.40	18.90	0	520	JUL 50 2001 FRESJ	0.40	0	0	0.15	0	662
JUL 55 2001 FREGK	13.20	0	13.50	14	0	113	JUL 55 2001 FRESK	0.20	0	0	0.15	0	801
JUL 60 2001 FREGL	8.70	0	8.70	9.10	0	008	JUL 60 2001 FRESL	0.25	0	0.10	0.25	0	1,957
JUL 65 2001 FREGM	4.10	+0.10	4.50	4.80	10	5,737	JUL 65 2001 FRESM	1	+0.10	0.80	0.95	5	3,428
JUL 70 2001 FREGN	1.55	0	1.55	1.75	0	3,967	JUL 70 2001 FRESN	3.20	0	2.75	3	0	396
JUL 75 2001 FREGO	0.40	0	0.30	0.45	0	1,846	JUL 75 2001 FRESO	9.50	0	6.50	6.90	0	75
OCT 50 2001 FREJJ	15.80	0	19	19.50	0	44	OCT 50 2001 FREVJ	0.30	0	0.25	0.40	0	372
OCT 55 2001 FREJK	12.20	0	14.40	14.90	0	77	OCT 55 2001 FREVK	0.80	0	0.50	0.65	0	373

As you can see, there's very little difference between the call Butterflies and the equivalent put Butterflies. In reality we would place the entire trade as a single limit order anyway.

	Narrow Call Butterfly	Narrow Put Butterfly
Buy $60 strike option (ask)	$9.10	$0.25
Sell 2 × $65 strike options (bid)	$4.50 × 2 = $9.00	$0.80 × 2 = $1.60
Buy $70 strike option (ask)	$1.75	$3.00
Net debit	$1.85	$1.65
Maximum risk	$1.85	$1.65
Maximum reward	$3.15	$3.35
Maximum Return on Investment	170.27%	203.03%
Breakeven (downside)	$61.85	$61.65
Breakeven (upside)	$68.15	$68.35
Maximum risk on net debit	100%	100%

With the Wide Butterfly example the Risk, Reward, Breakeven analysis is identical with calls and puts:

(b) Wide Butterfly: strikes of $55, $65 and $75

FRE - FREDDIE MAC

Last Trade	Net Change	Bid	Ask	Day High	Day Low	Volume	Trade Time
68.48	+0.42	0	0	68.70	67.40	1,604,100	16:01:00 News/Chart

Filter By

Month [All ▼] And/Or   Strike Price [Equal To ▼] [ ]   [Search]

Calls	Last	Change	Bid	Ask	Volume	Open Interest	Puts	Last	Change	Bid	Ask	Volume	Open Interest
JUN 50 2001 FREFJ	15.30	0	18.20	18.70	0	8	JUN 50 2001 FRERJ	0.35	0	0	0.15	0	20
JUN 55 2001 FREFK	12.30	0	13.20	13.70	0	0	JUN 55 2001 FRERK	0.25	0	0	0.15	0	145
JUN 60 2001 FREFL	7.70	0	8.30	8.70	0	682	JUN 60 2001 FRERL	0.05	0	0	0.15	0	1,008
JUN 65 2001 FREFM	3.20	-0.20	3.40	3.70	18	3,529	JUN 65 2001 FRERM	0.15	+0.10	0	0.15	19	1,089
JUN 70 2001 FREFN	0.25	0	0.10	0.25	0	1,413	JUN 70 2001 FRERN	1.90	0	1.60	1.80	0	177
JUN 75 2001 FREFO	0.25	0	0	0.15	0	718	JUN 75 2001 FRERO	7.10	0	6.30	6.70	0	78
JUN 80 2001 FREFP	0.10	0	0	0.15	0	500	JUN 80 2001 FRERP	0	0	11.30	11.80	0	0
JUL 50 2001 FREGJ	15.80	0	18.40	18.90	0	520	JUL 50 2001 FRESJ	0.40	0	0	0.15	0	662
JUL 55 2001 FREGK	13.20	0	13.50	14	0	113	JUL 55 2001 FRESK	0.20	0	0	0.15	0	801
JUL 60 2001 FREGL	8.70	0	8.70	9.10	0	998	JUL 60 2001 FRESL	0.25	0	0.10	0.25	0	1,957
JUL 65 2001 FREGM	4.10	+0.10	4.50	4.80	10	5,737	JUL 65 2001 FRESM	1	+0.10	0.80	0.95	5	3,428
JUL 70 2001 FREGN	1.55	0	1.55	1.75	0	3,957	JUL 70 2001 FRESN	3.20	0	2.75	3	0	396
JUL 75 2001 FREGO	0.40	0	0.30	0.45	0	1,846	JUL 75 2001 FRESO	9.50	0	6.50	6.90	0	75
OCT 50 2001 FREJJ	15.80	0	19	19.50	0	44	OCT 50 2001 FREVJ	0.30	0	0.25	0.40	0	372
OCT 55 2001 FREJK	12.20	0	14.40	14.90	0	77	OCT 55 2001 FREVK	0.80	0	0.50	0.65	0	373

	Wide Call Butterfly	Wide Put Butterfly
Buy $55 strike option (ask)	$14.00	$0.15
Sell 2 × $65 strike options (bid)	$4.50 × 2= $9.00	$0.80 × 2 = $1.60
Buy $75 strike option (ask)	$0.45	$6.90
Net debit	$5.45	$5.45
Maximum risk	$5.45	$5.45
Maximum reward	$4.55	$4.55
Maximum Return on Investment	83.49%	83.49%
Breakeven (downside)	$60.45	$60.45
Breakeven (upside)	$69.55	$69.55
Maximum risk on net debit	100%	100%

The main comparison to make, therefore, is whether to choose the Narrow Butterfly or the Wide Butterfly. The Wide Butterfly has a greater probability of success but has a far lower maximum reward.

Chart 9.1.2a ● **FRE Long Call Butterfly risk profile (narrow).**

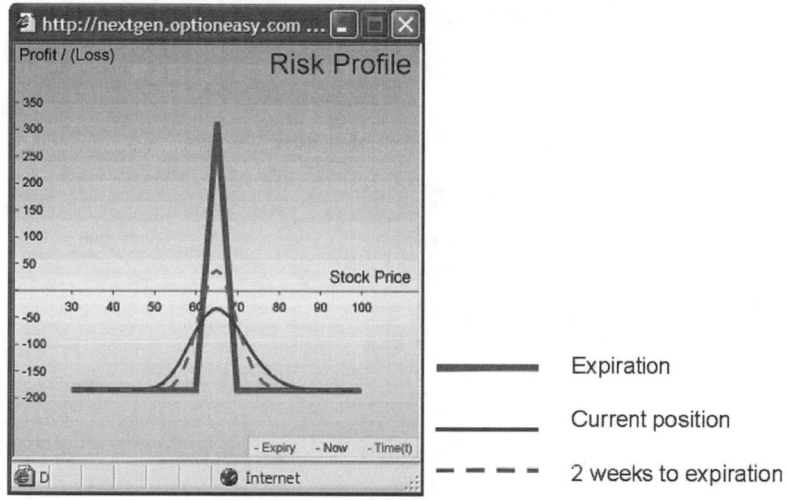

Expiration

Current position

2 weeks to expiration

Chart 9.1.2b ● **FRE Long Call Butterfly risk profile (wide).**

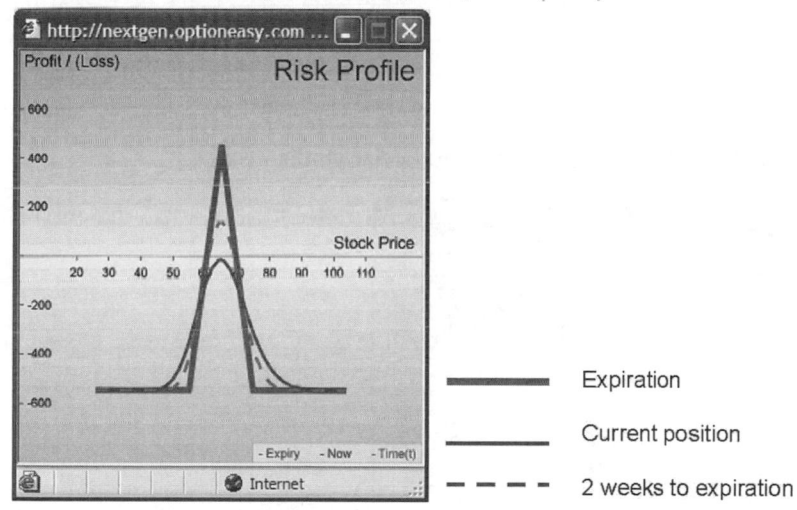

Expiration

Current position

2 weeks to expiration

See how the Wide Butterfly has a wider span—the price scale should give you a clue, since this one is in increments of ten and the Narrow Butterfly price scale is in increments of just five.

Chart 9.1.3a ● **FRE Long Put Butterfly risk profile (narrow).**

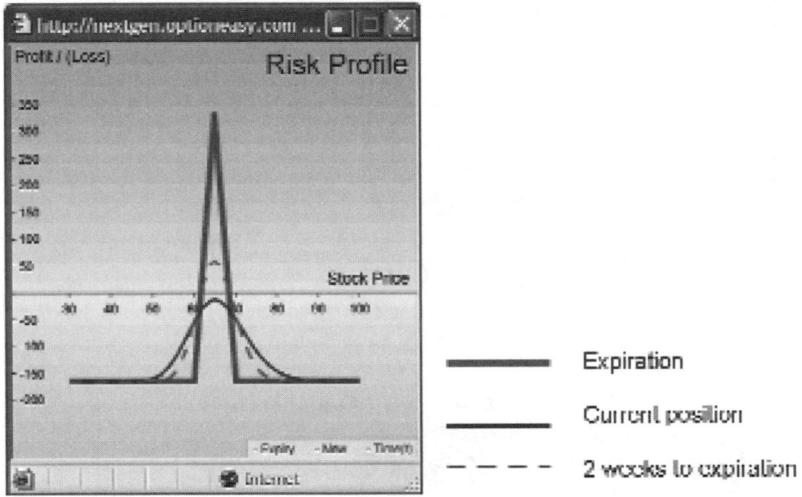

Chart 9.1.3b ● **FRE Long Put Butterfly risk profile (wide).**

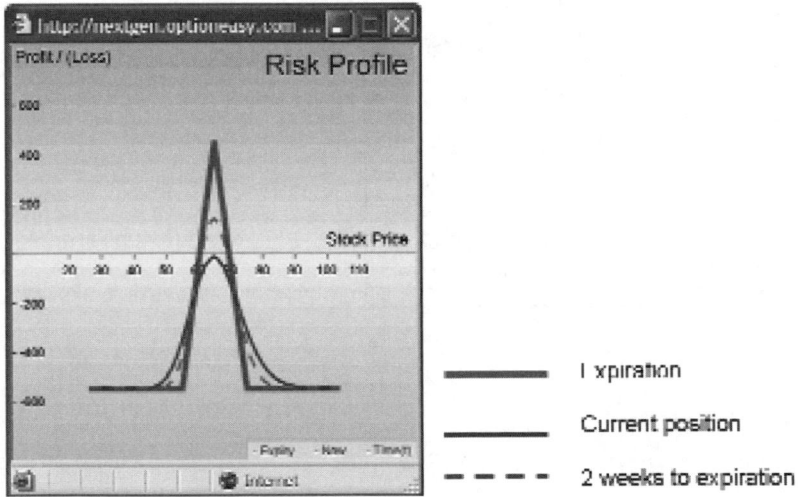

Risk Profiles of All Butterflies*

	Narrow Call Butterfly	Wide Call Butterfly	Narrow Put Butterfly	Wide Put Butterfly
Buy $55 strike option (ask)		$14.00		$0.15
Buy $60 strike option (ask)	$9.10		$0.25	
Sell 2 × $65 strike options (bid)	$4.50 × 2 = $9.00	$4.50 × 2 = $9.00	$0.80 × 2 = $1.60	$0.80 × 2 = $1.60
Buy $70 strike option (ask)	$1.75		$3.00	
Buy $75 strike option (ask)		$0.45		$6.90
Net debit	$-.85	$5.45	$1.65	$5.45
Maximum risk	$1.85	$5.45	**$1.65**	$5.45
Maximum reward	$3.15	$4.55	$3.35	$4.55
Maximum Return on Investment	170.27%	83.49%	**203.03%**	83.49%
Breakeven (downside)	$61.85	$60.45	$61.65	$60.45
Breakeven (upside)	$68.15	$69.55	$68.35	$69.55
Maximum risk on net debit	100%	100%	100%	100%
Probability of profit	**35.33%**	**45.06%**	**36.70%**	**45.06%**

*The July 2001 options expired on Friday, July 20, 2001, at which time FRE closed at $67.56. On the basis of having traded the narrow Put Butterfly at a risk of $1.65, your position at Expiration was worth $2.44, in other words, a 48% profit on this trade. The bought $30 strike put would have expired worthless, thus you lose the $0.25 you paid for it; the sold $65 strike puts would have expired worthless, thus you would keep the entire $1.60 premium that you received; and the $70 strike put you bought for $3.00 was worth only $2.44 at expiration, thus losing $0.56. Subtracting $0.25 and $0.56 from $1.60, you therefore made a total of $0.79 (48%) *profit* in just six weeks on your original stake of $1.65, not bad for an unseen example of a strategy I don't trade!

The narrow Put Butterfly in this example (Chart 9.1.3a) seems to be the best choice in terms of maximum reward and minimum risk. But in saying that, it's still possible to lose 100% of what you paid. And given the low probability of success (just 36.70%) and the narrow breakeven bands (which partly cause that low probability), I would be more comfortable with a wider spread. However, a wider Butterfly here means significantly reduced maximum profit, and there is still the possibility of a 100% loss. On balance, I wouldn't do this trade even if the support and resistance lines were compelling in themselves alone.

Chart 9.1.4a ● FRE Butterfly delta profile (narrow).

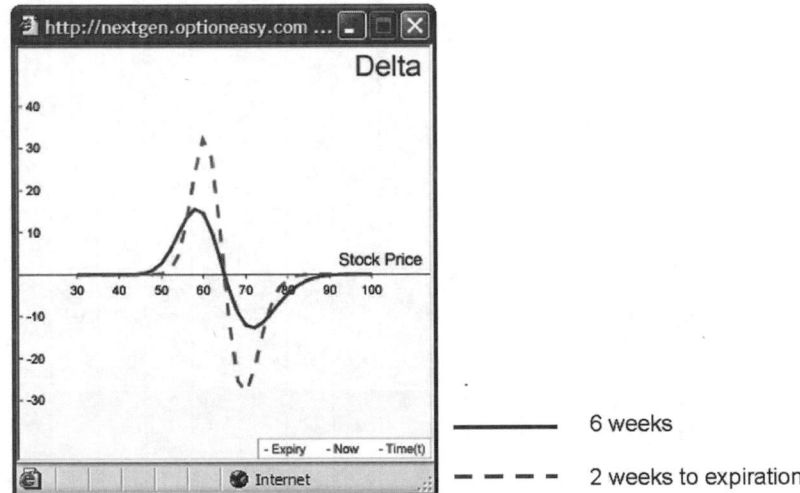

Chart 9.1.4b ● FRE Butterfly delta profile (wide).

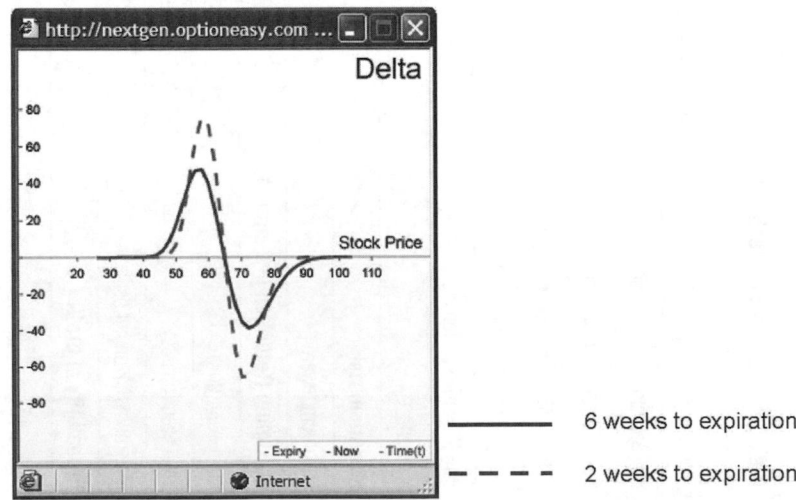

Chart 9.1.5a ● **FRE Butterfly gamma profile (narrow).**

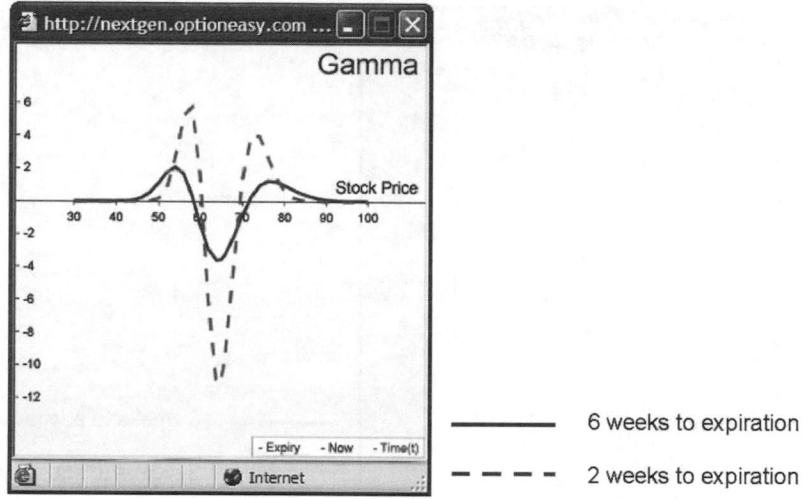

6 weeks to expiration

2 weeks to expiration

Chart 9.1.5b ● **FRE Butterfly gamma profile (wide).**

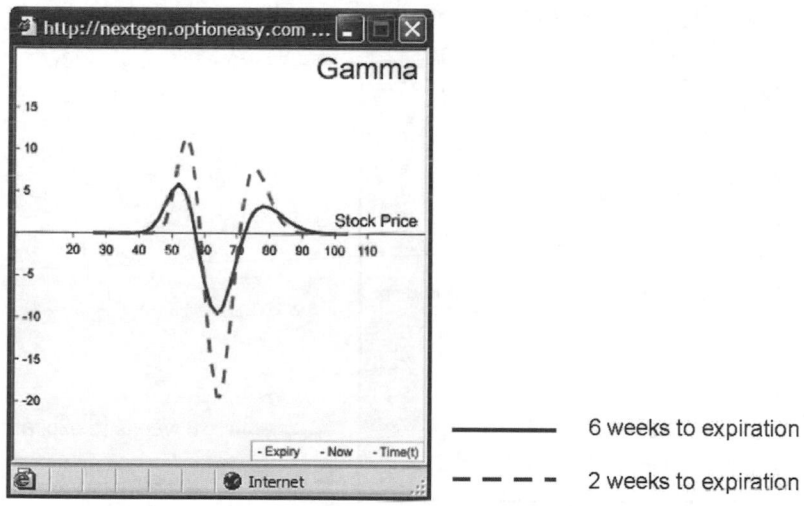

6 weeks to expiration

2 weeks to expiration

Chart 9.1.6a ● **FRE Butterfly theta profile (narrow).**

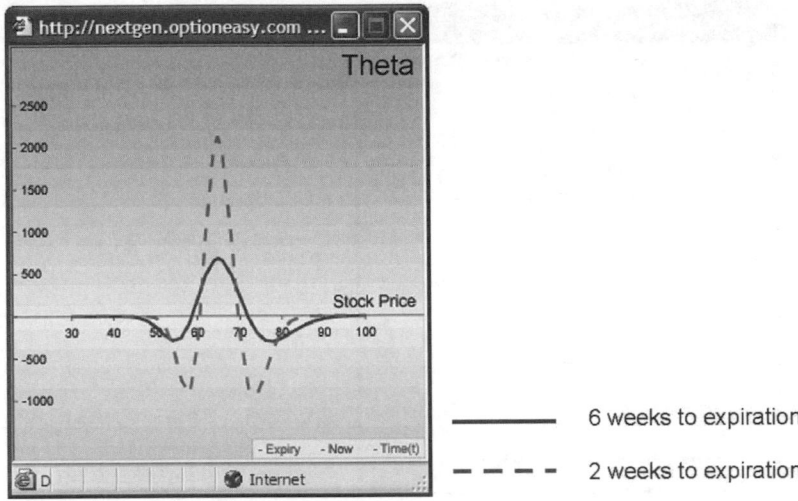

———————— 6 weeks to expiration

– – – – – 2 weeks to expiration

Chart 9.1.6b ● **FRE Butterfly theta profile (wide).**

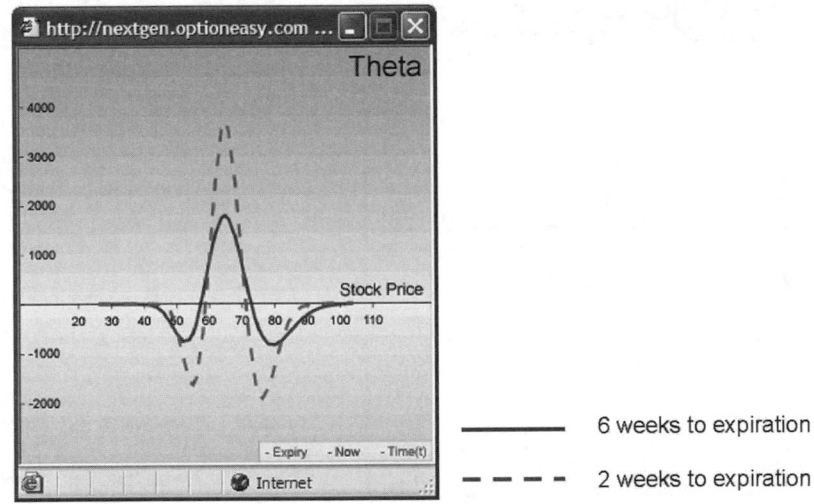

———————— 6 weeks to expiration

– – – – – 2 weeks to expiration

Chart 9.1.7a ● FRE Butterfly vega profile (narrow).

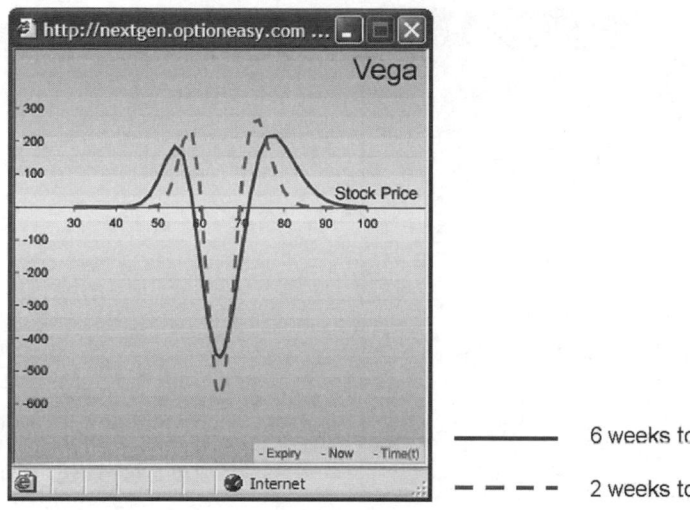

—————— 6 weeks to expiration

– – – – 2 weeks to expiration

Chart 9.1.7b ● FRE Butterfly vega profile (wide).

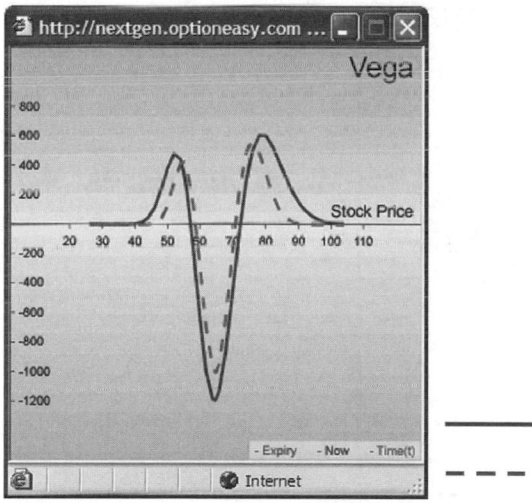

—————— 6 weeks to expiration

– – – – 2 weeks to expiration

Chart 9.1.8a ● FRE Butterfly rho profile (narrow).

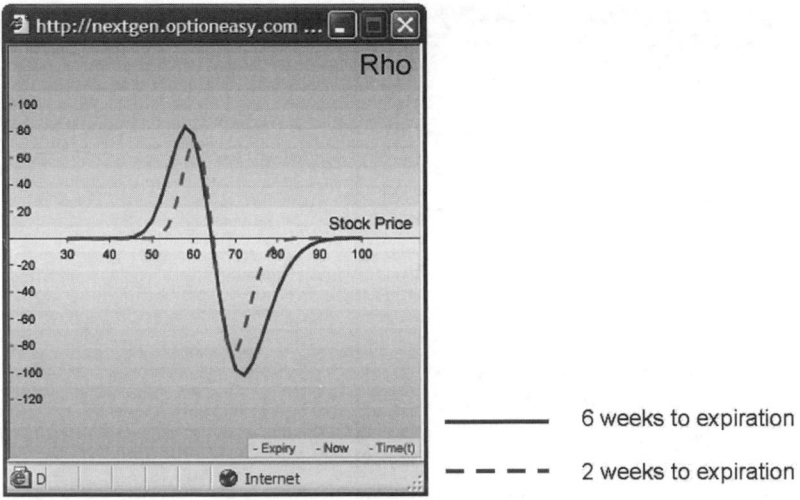

6 weeks to expiration

2 weeks to expiration

Chart 9.1.8b ● FRE Butterfly rho profile (wide).

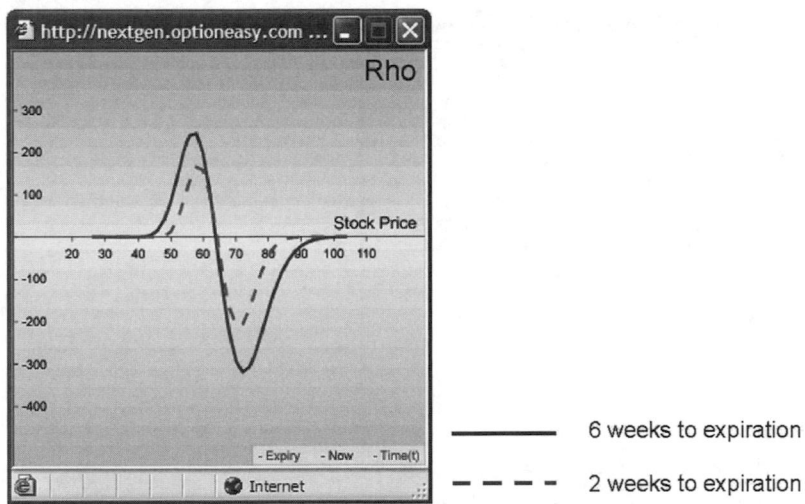

6 weeks to expiration

2 weeks to expiration

Condors

Condors work in a similar way to Butterflies except that there is an extra middle leg involved, which therefore widens the spread and flattens out the top portion of the risk profile. The Condor involves the following steps (as with Butterflies, you can use all calls *or* all puts with the Condor—you cannot mix the two):

Condor with Calls

Step 1	Buy 1 lower strike (ITM) call	There are two key points here:
Step 2	Sell 1 lower middle strike (ITM) call	**1** You trade the same number of contracts for each leg of the Condor.
Step 3	Sell 1 higher middle strike (OTM) call	**2** The distance between the four adjacent strikes should be equal, with the stock price being somewhere between the two middle strike prices.*
Step 1	Buy 1 higher strike (OTM) call	

* Although this is the strict definition of a Condor, it is also fine to create a Condor where the distance between the two extreme strikes and their respective neighboring middle strikes is the same.

Or:

Condor with Puts

Step 1	Buy 1 lower strike (OTM) put	There are two key points here:
Step 2	Sell 1 lower middle strike (OTM) put	**1** You trade the same number of contracts for each leg of the Condor.
Step 3	Sell 1 higher middle strike (ITM) put	**2** The distance between the four adjacent strikes should be equal, with the stock price being somewhere between the two middle strike prices.*
Step 4	Buy 1 higher strike (ITM) put	

* Although this is the strict definition of a Condor, it is also fine to create a Condor where the distance between the two extreme strikes and their respective neighbouring middle strikes is the same.

We can create the same Condor risk profile shapes by using all calls (call-call-call-call) or all puts (put-put-put-put) for each of the four Condor legs.

The Condor will be a net debit transaction because the ITM and OTM options that you buy will be more expensive than the two nearer the money (middle) options that you are selling to create the strategy spread. Remember, don't be over ambitious with your Limit Order, but do make sure that you place this trade as a Limit Order!

Long Call Condor

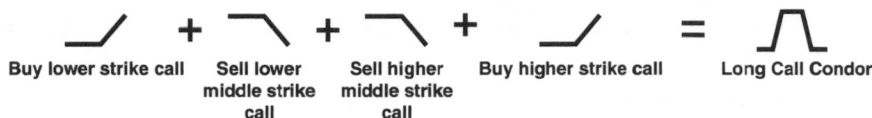

Buy lower strike call | Sell lower middle strike call | Sell higher middle strike call | Buy higher strike call | Long Call Condor

Long Put Condor

Buy lower strike put | Sell lower middle strike put | Sell higher middle strike put | Buy higher strike put | Long Put Condor

The risk profile of a Condor is as follows, regardless of whether you use all calls or all puts:

	Long Condor
Maximum risk	Limited to the net debit of the spread (what you pay).
Maximum reward	Limited to the difference between adjacent strike prices less the net debit paid.
Breakeven on the downside	Lowest strike price *plus* net debit paid.
Breakeven on the upside	Highest strike price *less* net debit paid.
Maximum risk on net debit	100% risk on **net debit**.

Again, there are two breakeven scenarios with condors and, as you can see, it is a similar strategy to the Butterfly. The Condor can only yield a limited profit, but this time it is achievable between the two middle strike prices.

Example 9.2.1 FRE Condor (June 2001)

With FRE we want to capture the $60 to $70 range within our maximum profit profile. Because there is no $80 strike we cannot do the $50–$60–$70–$80 Condor. Instead we'll try the $55–$60–$65–$70 Condor. Remember, you can use all calls or all puts. Both are highlighted, but the net debit (and therefore risk) is cheaper with puts here, so we'll use puts.

Step 1	Buy 1 July 2001 $55 put	(OTM)
Step 2	Sell 1 July 2001 $60 put	(OTM)
Step 3	Sell 1 July 2001 $65 put*	(OTM)
Step 4	Buy 1 July 2001 $70 put	(ITM)

*Notice that this third leg put's strike price is below the current stock price ($68.48). Ideally, we want the stock price to be in between the Step 2 and Step 3 strikes. We'll now see if this shortcoming is going to cause us problems in constructing a good trade.

Chart 9.2.1 ● FRE price chart (June 2001).

Chart created on TradeStation®, the flagship product of TradeStation Technologies Inc.

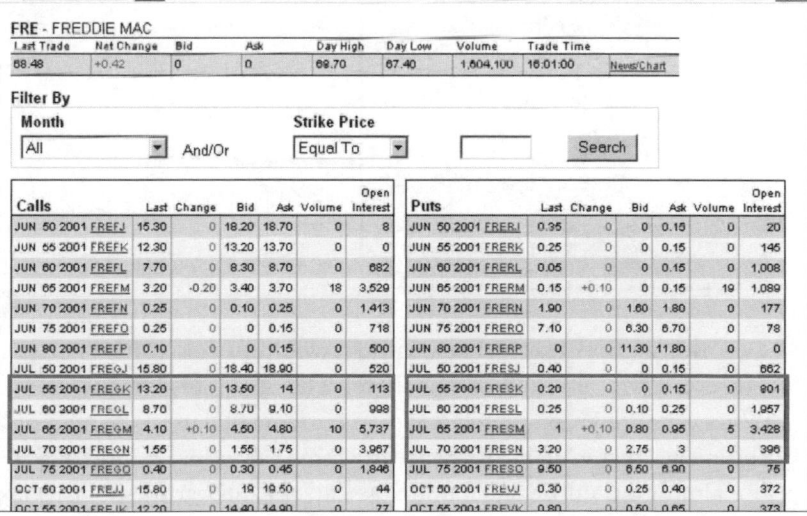

FRE - FREDDIE MAC

Last Trade	Net Change	Bid	Ask	Day High	Day Low	Volume	Trade Time	
68.48	+0.42	0	0	69.70	67.40	1,604,100	16:01:00	News/Chart

Filter By

Month: All ▼ And/Or Strike Price: Equal To ▼ [ ] Search

Calls	Last	Change	Bid	Ask	Volume	Open Interest
JUN 50 2001 FREFJ	15.30	0	18.20	18.70	0	8
JUN 55 2001 FREFK	12.30	0	13.20	13.70	0	0
JUN 60 2001 FREFL	7.70	0	8.30	8.70	0	682
JUN 65 2001 FREFM	3.20	-0.20	3.40	3.70	18	3,529
JUN 70 2001 FREFN	0.25	0	0.10	0.25	0	1,413
JUN 75 2001 FREFO	0.25	0	0	0.15	0	718
JUN 80 2001 FREFP	0.10	0	0	0.15	0	500
JUL 50 2001 FREGJ	15.80	0	18.40	18.90	0	520
JUL 55 2001 FREGK	13.20	0	13.50	14	0	113
JUL 60 2001 FREGL	8.70	0	8.70	9.10	0	998
JUL 65 2001 FREGM	4.10	+0.10	4.50	4.80	10	5,737
JUL 70 2001 FREGN	1.55	0	1.55	1.75	0	3,967
JUL 75 2001 FREGO	0.40	0	0.30	0.45	0	1,846
OCT 50 2001 FREJJ	15.80	0	19	19.50	0	44
OCT 55 2001 FREJK	12.20	0	14.40	14.90	0	77

Puts	Last	Change	Bid	Ask	Volume	Open Interest
JUN 50 2001 FRERJ	0.35	0	0	0.15	0	20
JUN 55 2001 FRERK	0.25	0	0	0.15	0	145
JUN 60 2001 FRERL	0.05	0	0	0.15	0	1,008
JUN 65 2001 FRERM	0.15	+0.10	0	0.15	19	1,089
JUN 70 2001 FRERN	1.90	0	1.60	1.80	0	177
JUN 75 2001 FRERO	7.10	0	6.30	6.70	0	78
JUN 80 2001 FRERP	0	0	11.30	11.80	0	0
JUL 50 2001 FRESJ	0.40	0	0	0.15	0	662
JUL 55 2001 FRESK	0.20	0	0	0.15	0	901
JUL 60 2001 FRESL	0.25	0	0.10	0.25	0	1,957
JUL 65 2001 FRESM	1	+0.10	0.80	0.95	5	3,428
JUL 70 2001 FRESN	3.20	0	2.75	3	0	396
JUL 75 2001 FRESO	9.50	0	6.50	6.90	0	75
OCT 50 2001 FREVJ	0.30	0	0.25	0.40	0	372
OCT 55 2001 FREVK	0.80	0	0.50	0.65	0	373

Long Condor with puts (a)	
Buy $55 strike option (ask)	$0.15
Sell $60 strike options (bid)	$0.10
Sell $65 strike option (bid)	$0.80
Buy $70 strike option (ask)	$3.00
Net debit	**$2.25**
Maximum risk	**$2.25**
Maximum reward	**$2.75**
Maximum Return on Investment	**122.22%**
Breakeven (downside)	**$57.25**
Breakeven (upside)	**$67.75**
Maximum risk on net debit	**100%**

Chart 9.2.2 ● FRE Long Put Condor risk profile chart.

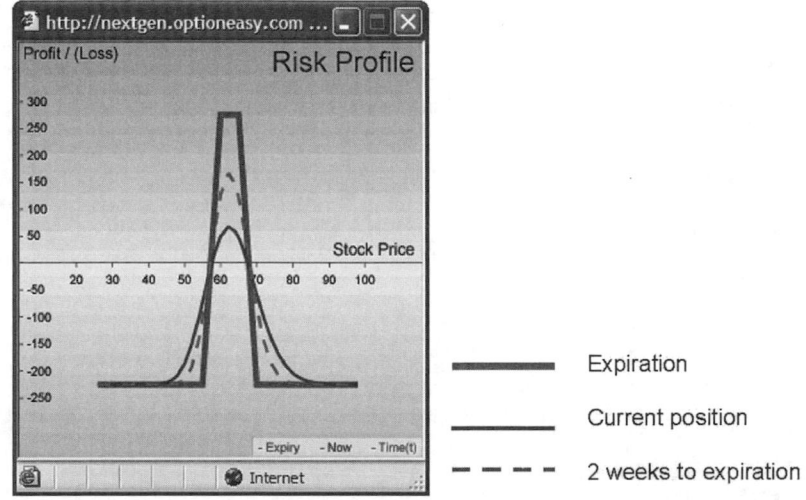

Is this a good trade? Personally, I wouldn't touch it! There's not enough return for the amount of risk here. The main problem with it is that the breakevens don't completely envelop our consolidation channel of $60 to $70. This means that even if FRE remains within our upper bound of $70 we can still lose almost our entire stake if it closes at, say, $69 at the options' expiration.

The solution is, in theory to trade an "adjusted" Condor with strikes at $55–$60–$70–$75. Notice that the "body" is wider. The only problem with this solution is that although our breakevens would be $59.20 and $70.80, the maximum reward is only 19.05%, which is hardly worth the risk.

Looking at both risk profiles, we can see another problem, namely that we have to wait until expiration for any significant maximum upside. This significantly reduces our flexibility in the event of a price breakout beyond the breakeven bands.

	Long "adjusted" Condor with puts (b)*	Long "adjusted" Condor with calls (c)*
Buy $55 strike option (ask)	$0.15	$14.00
Sell $60 strike options (bid)	$0.10	$8.70
Sell $70 strike option (bid)	$2.75	$1.55
Buy $75 strike option (ask)	$6.90	$0.45
Net debit	**$4.20**	**$4.20**
Maximum risk	**$4.20**	**$4.20**
Maximum reward	**$0.80**	**$0.80**
Maximum Return on Investment	**19.05%**	**19.05%**
Breakeven on (downside)	**$59.20**	**$59.20**
Breakeven on (upside)	**$70.80**	**$70.80**
Maximum risk on net debit	**100%**	**100%**

*The risk profile chart for calls and puts is identical in this instance because the net debits are the same.

Chart 9.2.3 ● FRE long "'adjusted"' Condor risk profile chart*.

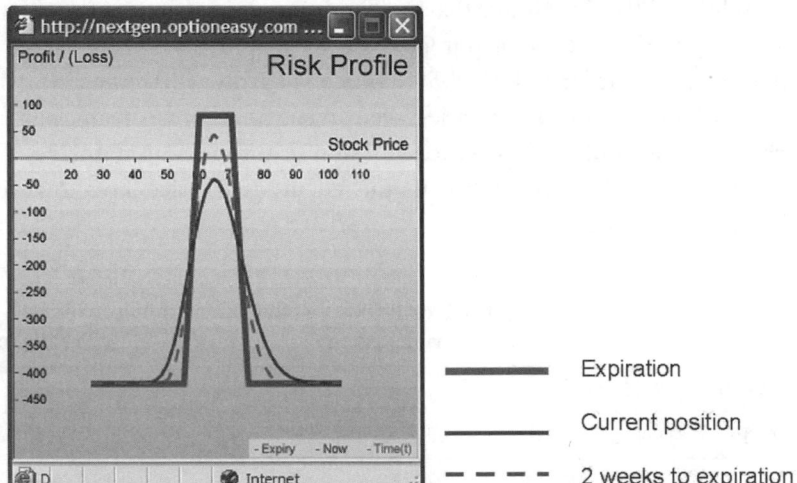

* The risk profile chart for calls and puts is identical in this instance because the net debits are the same.

In conclusion, I wouldn't be doing any of these Condors in this particular instance with FRE.

Comparison Between the Butterfly and the Condor

● With a Condor we have a greater target for our maximum return, spanning the two middle strike prices; whereas the Butterfly's maximum return occurs only if the stock lands on the single middle strike price at expiration.

● The Condor can incur a greater net debit because, typically, your first leg (with calls) or last leg (with puts) involves buying a Deep In the Money option, which is expensive.

● Both strategies offer the investor "limited" maximum risk and limited maximum upside. Take note, however, that the maximum risk with these strategies is still 100% of what you spend on them.

Chapter 9 Major Learning Points

In this chapter we've learned how a Butterfly and a Condor can be used to trade stocks that are caught in a horizontal price channel. Because we've taken a real life example without the benefit of hindsight, we've been able to analyze and explore a trade that we simply wouldn't do (that is, the Condor here). By the time you read this, you'll see what the net result would have been at the July expiration date (July 20, 2001).

Ideally, you're looking for consolidating or rolling stock patterns with clearly defined lines of support and resistance. The Butterfly is an easier trade to place because it involves just three legs and is therefore easier to place the spread centrally around the current stock price. The Condor can run into problems because it is typically more expensive than the nearest equivalent Butterfly and, as happened in our example here, you may not be able to find the optimum strike prices to construct the trade.

Provided the stock price doesn't move beyond (or too close to) the breakeven bounds, you can sell the spread at expiration to capture the optimum return. The problem with these two strategies is that you typically have to wait until expiration to obtain anything near the maximum return. The longer you have to wait, the more chance you give the stock to breach your breakevens.

Remember, with Butterflies and Condors your outer wing strike prices should be outside your identified levels of support and resistance. In other words, your lowest strike should be below support, and your highest strike should be above resistance. This is so that you can be in profit if the stock remains within those bands of support and resistance.

chapter 10

Trading and Investing Psychology

What kind of investor are you, or are you more of a trader? Are you in this for excitement or for cold-blooded profit? Are you mechanical in your style, or do you shoot from the hip? Do you like to build systems, or are you more motivated by making profits?

These are important questions for you to consider and answer with 100% honesty. You can save yourself a lot of time, money, and energy by not trying to be something you're not! What you say to yourself is far more important than what you say to others, although that, too, is important! If you've tried to hit a homerun and it went wrong, admit it to yourself, take responsibility, and then you can set about resolving the problem. Many newcomers constantly try to hit homeruns or five-baggers and wonder why they have no trading capital left!

Consider the *Myths and Realities* and *Tips and Good Habits* we've listed here for you.

Myths and Realities

Myth	Reality
"The stock can't go any lower."	A stock can go down to zero—if it does so and you're long in the stock, you could face a 100% loss unless you use a Stop Loss.
"The stock can't go any higher."	This statement is just as farcical as the one above. Furthermore, it doesn't actually mean anything. In theory, a stock can continue to go up forever, although nothing lasts forever, as we all know. Stocks can continue to appreciate

Myth	Reality
	year in year out, during good times and bad. The markets, being somewhat irrational, do go overboard, and many securities do get over or under valued at some point in time. If they didn't, there would never be any opportunities for us to invest or trade in the first place. These excesses, which are caused by mass greed, fear, and hype in the marketplace, give us our opportunities on a daily basis.
"The stock has doubled every year for the last five years, so it'll double again this year."	We all know that stocks have personalities, but this is taking personalities too far. I've witnessed so-called gurus express this type of simplification in their seminars, and it's highly misleading. Whatever has happened in the past is no guarantee of what will happen in the future. The past may well give us some clues as to how a security may behave, but a stock doubling every year is an over-generalization. Please stay away from over-simplified solutions and glib comments. They're great for making the exponents rich and wasting the customers' time. If it sounds too good to be true, then it generally is. Trading and investing is a serious business and should be treated with respect. Sure you can do it—that's what this book is all about—but you'll definitely have to devote time to it and make it your passion. During the great Bull run of the 1990s, this sort of ridiculous comment was rife. Do avoid making and listening to sweeping statements and predictions. Start to look at price movements as opportunities and be prepared to admit defeat sooner rather than later if the price violates a Stop Loss or some other predefined parameter you have set.
"Shorting stocks is too risky..."	Shorting a stock is no more risky than buying a stock, provided that you use sound rules about Stop Losses and money management. In fact, most of the time stocks will fall far faster than they rise, so by definition, shorting can't be as risky. (Please do not confuse shorting a stock with selling an option naked. Selling an option naked is highly risky, and I don't advocate it to anyone other than advanced traders.) Where people get worked up about shorting stocks is in three areas. First, the mechanics of the trade. Shorting involves selling something you don't actually own. For this to be accomplished, you effectively have to borrow the stock from your broker and then sell It. To close the position, you'll have to buy the stock back, hopefully at a lower price (so that you'll have made a profit!). Second, the "Uptick Rule" states that you

Myth	Reality
	can only short a stock on an uptick. For Direct Access daytraders who rattle through hundreds of tickets per day, this can be a valid point given that every tick is meaningful, but for other traders and investors it's not a major factor when weighed against the benefits. The third complaint with shorting is that you'll have to effectively pay the dividend to the actual owner of the stock. So just make sure you're not shorting dividend-paying stocks at the appropriate record date.
	As a trader, you won't actually see the mechanics, and, frankly, aside from the dividend payment, what difference does it make anyway? Secondly, there is the technical risk of unlimited loss. But this is only true if the stock literally goes ballistic (upward) in a flash. As we've discussed, it's far more likely for a stock to halve in value overnight than double in value overnight. To add in a tier of safety, some of you may want to avoid shorting immediately prior to major announcements like earnings. For that matter, you may want to avoid any kind of trade (except Straddles) immediately prior to a major announcement. Picking your direction for a stock is an entire process in itself, but, for me, it's far more risky to see securities as instruments that can only go up. This is a blinkered view that naturally biases a predominantly Bullish outlook. Far better to see both upward and downward price movement as opportunities, and then you'll not end up looking for signs that simply aren't there.
	From a psychological point of view, accepting that you can make money from a stock falling changes the entire trading and investment mindset. For a start it becomes more of a business decision-making process. Rather than looking for stocks that are going up only, you're now looking for profitable opportunities in either direction. This is a far more healthy approach since you start from a position of neutral bias, not purely Bullish.
"The cheaper an option is, the better, even if it means it's closer to expiration. I can't lose much if it's only a dollar."	WRONG! WRONG! WRONG! I've seen people consistently do this and literally lose 100% of their trade (not to mention their accounts) in a matter of days. When you buy an option, give yourself enough time to be right. Don't be cheap. 100% is 100% even if you only paid 1 cent per option. If you really want high leverage and insist on a short-term option, then you'll need to hedge against Time Decay, and that means buying Deep in the Money options. These will be more expensive in terms of cost, but far better value because you won't be losing as much Time Value as the expiration date looms.
	Remember, a cheap short-term option can end up being extremely expensive.

Tips and Good Habits

Get yourself into a relaxed, confident, and controlled state of mind before you make any kind of trade or even analysis.	We'll cover more on this under the heading "Your Optimal Mindset" later in this chapter. A well-known statistic makes the claim that 80% of trading success is down to psychology, and 20% down to technical ability. I don't know how they calculated that, but the point is well made. Whatever your technical capabilities or knowledge, your state of mind is absolutely vital to the success of your business, and you must be in a good frame of mind to do yourself justice.
Create your Trading or Investment Plan and write it down in specific and precise language before you trade.	Don't confuse trading rules with a black-box system. Your trading plan should be a set of Rules, which you follow implicitly time and again. Sure, you can build in some flexibility, combinations and permutations to these Rules, but write them down and understand them. Also keep them handy, particularly when you're trading or making an investment decision. A mind map is the best way of achieving this in a succinct and visual way. A mind map is simply a drawing, like if you imagine a series of branches off a central tree, where you're using different colors and symbols to depict the rules, as opposed to simply writing them down in a list. Ideally, you should do both. We'll cover this area in more detail during the next chapter, but the Rules need to embrace when to enter, when to exit, when to use a specific options strategy, and when to activate your Stop Losses (which may change according to the strategy you're trading).
Only use Risk Capital that you can stand to lose.	This is another golden rule. Do not use capital that is essential for your food, rent, or mortgage. The stakes are already high enough without you increasing them by using capital that you simply can't afford to lose. Additionally, don't use capital that would cause problems between you and your partner if you were to proceed. If you're starting out on your trading career, believe it or not, you're a major success if you're still in the game after two years. If you're making profit at that point, then you're in the major leagues. The trading and investment world is littered with the corpses of former traders who either burned themselves or their capital out! Start with reasonable expectations and keep your Risk Capital low initially. As you make consistent progress you'll be able to steadily increase your Risk Capital with comfort. A rule of thumb is to never risk more than 5% of your trading capital on any one trade. For smaller accounts under $20,000, then 10% is fine.
Don't overtrade.	Only have as many trades on as you can handle without going nuts! If you can handle 20 trades on at once and be relaxed, confident and in

control, then that's fine. We're all different and we all have different styles of trading. Honestly discover for yourself what suits you, both in terms of portfolio and your preferred time frame. For longer-term investors, a larger portfolio may be more manageable. For shorter-term day traders, one or two live trades should be enough.

Stick to two to three strategies you like and that work!

Believe it or not the very best and most successful traders in the world only use a couple of trading strategies. There are many things to consider when making an investment decision, so why complicate the matter? There are really only three eventualities—the price will go up, down, or sideways. The only other parameter to consider is timescale, that is, how long is it going to take to go up or down or how long will it remain static or range-bound. This is enough to be thinking about without having to consider a whole myriad of strategies as well!

Different people like different strategies, and that's why there's a selection included in this book. When you understand what you feel comfortable with and you're being successful, stick with it and don't try to be too clever!

Do not fall in love with or hate a stock and don't get wedded to a position.

This is one of the big rules. A stock does not make you money. Your decision makes your position profitable, and you only bank that money when you exit that profitable position.

Similarly, a stock doesn't lose you money, so there's no point in trying to "even the score" on a stock where you lost money in the past! At the same time, just because you may have lost with a stock in the past doesn't mean you can't make money with it in the future, should the appropriate triggers be signaled according to your Rules. And, of course, just because you made money with a stock in the past, doesn't guarantee you success next time, although if you get to know a stock's personality, your chances of success can be enhanced, provided you're willing to see both directions, up and down, as profitable opportunities. If you find yourself saying something like, "I invest in XYZ Corp. It simply has to go up because of blah blah blah," then pinch yourself hard and think again. It may well go up, but make sure that you're making an impartial judgment and stick to your trading plan. Make absolutely no exceptions whatsoever. So many times I've heard the agonized wailings of "I just can't understand why the stock keeps going down!" Well, if it broke your Stop Loss or violated any of your Rules, then you should have exited the position anyway, so you can't get hurt more!

Stocks, commodities, and all securities in general are just instruments that you can buy and sell. Some people only trade one stock, index, future or commodity. This is fine because it's not the same as being wedded to a position; they're simply using that security as their preferred instrument to trade both up and down.

With options, make sure you understand your risk profile before executing any trade.	However simple the options strategy is, please ensure that you fully understand your risk, reward, and breakeven scenarios for the trade you're considering before you make the trade. These figures and their respective charts are your eyes on the trade. Trade with your eyes open and use the tools that help you achieve this.
Keep a trade journal.	Get yourself one of those big diaries and make it your habit to write down your stock picks (and reasons why) every day. You want to write down the stock symbol, the direction in which you surmise it's heading, the reason for this (that is, the Technical and Fundamental Analysis that is backing your judgment), and the appropriate time frame during which you anticipate the move to occur.
	When you make a trade, also record the time of the trade, the strategy, and any other relevant details you think might affect your decision-making performance. I know some highly successful traders who take a note of the weather, what they've eaten and drunk, and all manner of other details, which they subsequently use to analyze their record and make adjustments to their trading plan.
Visit an exchange.	Spend at least a day and see first-hand what happens at an exchange. For those of you who live in a major financial center, there's no excuse! It will help you see what actually has to occur for your order to be processed. An appreciation of the market mechanics is all I'm suggesting here, not an in-depth thesis.
	In the open-outcry system events are happening so fast you'll get to appreciate that the floor-traders (locals) aren't actually that bothered by your individual trade. Some day traders become paranoid that (somehow) the floor-traders are part of a conspiracy to hunt down their stops. Two solutions exist here. First, stop being paranoid; it's not the right frame of mind in which to trade anyway. And secondly, take care in where you set your stops…(read on).
Set stops (at least in your head).	Placement of stops is an art, but it is also very personal to the individual. Try to avoid the obvious place where everyone else is and place it slightly beyond that area, hopefully just out of reach of the savvy locals who will invariably gravitate to a congested area of stop orders.
	What we're trying to accomplish here is to avoid the gambling mentality where discipline is thrown out of the window. You can imagine the scenario where a husband comes back home from the casino to his long-suffering wife. He's promised her that if he gambles at all, he'll only put a total of $100 at stake. Yet he comes back home with his tail between his legs, sheepishly admitting that he's actually blown $1,000, only to then triumphantly announce, "But don't worry, dear, I'll win it all back tomorrow night!" This is the stuff of nightmares. Do not become a gambler; do be disciplined in all aspects of your trading, from analysis, to entry, management, and then exit.

Where possible, don't fight the market.	If you're making a directional trade, then make sure you're not at odds with the market. It's more powerful than any one stock! You should always bear in mind what's going on in the wider marketplace before entering your trade.
Loss of opportunity is preferable to loss of capital (Joe DiNapoli (1988)* Trading with DiNapoli Levels*).	Don't kick yourself over lost opportunities (the one that got away!) and definitely do not refer to them as times when you "lost $XXXXXX." All you lost was an opportunity; nothing actually happened to your bank balance. You neither spent money, lost money, nor made money, so there's no point in crying about it. If you spotted a great opportunity and didn't act on it, ask yourself why and at least give yourself credit for spotting it in the first place. The market provides opportunities on a daily basis. You'll find another one, and next time you'll remember that, provided it's consistent with your rules, you'll act on it with more certainty and with the benefit of past experience.
Avoid tips from friends, family, or friends of friends unless you play them as a Straddle, Strangle, or a Synthetic Call.	Virtually all of us have taken a stock tip, haven't we? And we've also been burned by them too, haven't we? Well, accepting the fact that we're all human and that we could be tempted to listen to a red-hot tip again, here's the way to play them: Only play a tip as a Straddle, Strangle, or as a Synthetic Call (where you buy the stock and a put option). So often, these red-hot pieces of information end up going in the opposite direction and fast too! By playing the Synthetic Call, you're at least buying some insurance when you buy the stock (see section "Synthetic Calls" in Chapter 5, "Two Popular Strategies and How to Improve Them"). And by playing the Straddle or Strangle, you're making the assessment that the tipped stock will move wildly in one direction—you're just not sure which way! (see section "Straddles and Strangles" in Chapter 8, "Two Basic Volatility Strategies").
Avoid penny stocks and illiquid securities.	Don't be fooled into thinking a cheap stock is necessarily good value. Also do make sure that whatever you buy you can sell too. Illiquidity generally leads to volatility in the stock price and a wide jump between the Bid and the Ask. Avoid these kinds of securities and stick to those stocks with at least 500,000 Average Daily Volume (ADV).
Avoid forecasting.	Even analysts, with their tremendous back-office and high-tech support, constantly get their forecasts on stock direction wrong. Notwithstanding a cynical viewpoint that analysts' main raison d'être is to attract corporate customers as opposed to correctly forecasting price movements, it's important that you don't get sucked into constantly making predictions about where the market is heading. Now, you may ask the question, "But isn't trading and investing predicated on making price forecasts in the first place?" Well, that's a good point, but your emphasis shouldn't be on forecasting so much as reacting quickly to the information supplied by the market, whether via Technical or Fundamental Analysis. It may be semantics, but by

getting entrenched into constantly making predictions for your buddies, you run the risk of altering your psychology and start to become wedded to your own predictions even if they turn out to be wrong. What we want to achieve here is a totally pragmatic approach to trading, treating it exclusively as a business enterprise and using high-probability trading techniques. As Jeff Yass (Schwager, 1992) of Susquehanna Investment Group puts it "...if you can give up your ego and listen to what the markets are telling you, you can have a huge source of information."

Take full responsibility for your actions.	Whatever the circumstances of a trade, always assume responsibility for it come rain or shine. Ultimately, it's your money, so you must be responsible for pressing the button, even it is your broker who's advising you. By taking responsibility, you give yourself control to either continue making good trades or correcting any bad decisions or strategies. This rule applies to life in general and not just trading! Those who continually blame other people or circumstances (we've all met this sort) are never able to resolve their problems or issues mainly because by doing that they absolve themselves from any ability to rectify their situation in the first place.

Taking responsibility is not the same as self-flagellating! You want to avoid the sort of self-defeating phrases such as "If only I'd done such and such ...I'm such an idiot!" Far healthier is to look back on your trade and ask yourself honestly whether you followed your Trading Plan and if not, how you will rectify that problem next time around. Could you make your plan more compelling, for instance? |
| ***Avoid message boards like the plague.*** | The vast majority of these are dangerous places where innocent newcomers get manipulated by "pumpers" and "dumpers" who have nothing better to do than spend all their time either hyping or slamming a stock. Emotions run high within Message Boards, and we know that wildly fluctuating emotions have no place in a serious investing or trading mindset. There is so much misinformation within the chatroom forums that my advice is for you to avoid them like the plague. At best, they are frequented by well meaning but highly emotional traders/investors; at worst they are fraudsters' playgrounds. Either way, you're best advised to stay away. Sure, there may be the odd decent one, but from what I've seen they can be extremely hazardous for the uninitiated and uninformed. |
| ***Do your homework on so-called gurus and teachers.*** | The problem isn't that there's not enough education in the field of trading. The problem is that there's too much but much of it is worthless! Please be careful of those advertisements that are selling you a dream, because that's precisely what they are selling you, except that it can turn out to be a nightmare! There simply needs to be some more integrity within this industry. Yes, you can master the knowledge and |

practical application to become a successful investor/trader. If you're new to all this then it's not going to happen overnight and you are going to have to make this your hobby. It's a fact of life, but part of discovering what's really good and useful is also finding what's dross along the way.

I've looked in on seminars where I was appalled at what I was hearing. It's astounding what people have been getting away with in this field and it's the ones who are selling 100% hype who are the most distasteful. I've seen conferences that were really little more than pumped-up jamborees of organized mass hysteria, crammed full of misrepresentation. I've also met the delegates of these conferences weeks later, totally confused and not knowing where to turn, particularly as they've just gone and blown their risk capital while they were still on a high.

Brash newcomers with no tangible experience are also dangerous. You should ask to see their credentials, such as do they have any financial experience whatsoever, either academic or commercial? I've seen people set up courses when not only did they have absolutely no financial background whatsoever, but they had (in their tiny investment experience of only a few months!) also lost their entire trading capital, hence setting up the course in order to generate income! Incredible but true.

Don't dismiss those with academic backgrounds, provided they have the communication skills to sustain your interest! Academics understand the theory and are generally less inclined to misinform about "amazing new discoveries." The trick is to find someone who not only understands the subject matter in depth, but can use and communicate this knowledge to practical effect in making profits on the markets.

Those with a purely commercial background are probably more likely to be the ones selling a fantasy. They might have a decent trading record (often on the back of a bull market), but you'd be surprised how many so-called gurus have a miserable trading record! I've actually witnessed well-known teachers trade first hand and I've seen some not very pretty sights! Swearing and screaming at the computer screen for a fill, thumping the desk in agitation as they incurred a drawdown! Not exactly great trading psychology, there! That's not to say that those who can't do can't teach. But my chief objection is to the misrepresentation that they actually practice what they preach, when in reality they don't and their own poor results bear that out. I've seen courses where the instructor admits he doesn't trade. That's fine, provided he admits it. Then it's up to you, the delegate, to try the taught material and then make up your own mind.

Ultimately, you want to get a reference of some sort about any guru or teacher you're looking to go and learn from. Try to find ex-delegates or those who've read their material and ask them:

- whether they learned anything useful;
- whether they implemented the lessons; and
- whether those teachings worked in practice (that is to say, results).

Black-box systems don't work forever...

For the sake of clarity, what we're talking about here is the type of system where you, the user, are required to do nothing whatsoever, but simply take the automated signals as your decision-making guide.

I'm not into black-box systems myself and I've tried dozens of them, all with great enthusiasm! They tend to work for a limited period of time, and then they stop. The problem is that they're by definition static in design and rigid in their construction, which is exactly what prevents them from automatically adapting to constantly changing market conditions. You'll save yourself much valuable time by staying away from things like "the answer to all your prayers!"

The real key to being successful with that sort of thing is to jump on it when it's actually working for that limited period of time. Then you can make a fortune provided you quit when it stops working! How are you going to get on board at the beginning and time it just right to get off just in time when it becomes ineffective? Well, that's the $64 million question! And most of the time the sell-by date will have already passed once you get to see it!

Remember, you should treat investing and trading as a business. Typically, this will require you to put in some effort. So steer clear of anything that claims you can make wild successes doing nothing. I'm not suggesting you have to become a rocket scientist to get the hang of this. Far from it. But you will have to put in the effort yourself, so be prepared. You can certainly do it, and the rewards will be all down to you.

Beware of advertorials that sound too good to be true!

There are many adverts and publications that claim unprecedented levels of successful results with headings such as "The Automatic Way to Unbeatable Profits!" I've seen such "systems," and invariably there's a catch. The most outrageous ones I've seen so far are that the so-called unbeatable systems haven't even been tried live but were simulated with an optimization function! A system that bases itself with the advantage of hindsight has no value whatsoever because as traders we don't have that advantage. Not only that, but look for the caveats in the small print that admit that the "results" of the system are based only on mid prices and take no account of the bid-ask spreads. That is no way to test any plausible system.

Paper trading is a valid research exercise for any system you may choose to adopt. However, you must paper trade as if you were trading. This means that you buy at the Ask and sell at the Bid, you add the correct amount of commissions, and you are completely honest with yourself. Paper trading is not the same as trading with real money at stake, so honesty with yourself becomes a vital ingredient for its usefulness and validity to you.

Hard work is one of the keys to your success here, and I'd be more inclined to investigate a methodology that advised me about hard work first.

Do get involved in physical activity.	Trading and investing typically involves being at a computer much of the time. It's imperative that you get out and about and get the blood flowing in a healthy way. I'm not suggesting running marathons, but you really should seek some fresh air and some form of physical exercise, even if it's walking the dog. If nothing else, it'll free the mind up. I know some traders who go fly-fishing. I tried it too, just to see what all the fuss was about, and discovered the secret. It was that when you're doing an activity such as fly-fishing, it's so absorbing and takes so much concentration that it's impossible to think about anything else. And that's extremely healthy for you. The last thing you want to be doing is thinking about trading (and the one that got away) all the time. Find an activity, any activity that you can escape to so that you can get away from work and strike some balance. As the saying goes, "Change your body, change your mind; change your mind, change your body." For me, it's swimming.
	Energy is a vital ingredient in this game, so you should also consider what you eat. I'm not advocating anything too specific here, but exercising some moderation is going to be a good thing! Personally I now avoid caffeine. Not because I don't like it, but because I can really feel the buzz it gives me and that's not something I find helpful for being calm. So I'll drink decaf instead! Whatever works for you is the right answer, but do ensure that it is working for you. What tastes fantastic isn't always working for you!

Your Optimal Mindset

Have you ever made a truly great decision when you were feeling bad, depressed, morose, or really uptight and tense? Well, guess how many people make trading and investment decisions when they're crippled with stress! Lots. And that includes gurus—I've witnessed it! So what is the optimal mindset and how can we get you there? Just read on here now.

This is arguably the most important part of the book. Without a sound, uncluttered frame of mind, trading won't be as smooth as it needs to be to make you money. It's not just a question of rule setting, although rule setting is an essential part of the process. The rules need to be compelling for a start, but even then you need to have the discipline and confidence to follow them.

Be Relaxed, Confident, and in Control

Your optimal mindset is one where you're feeling totally *relaxed*, *confident*, and in *control*. This applies to trading or for that matter any other activity where you're pursuing excellence. If your Trading Plan is robust, then you're more likely to be in the right frame of mind as you trade.

Be Relaxed

When you think about it, this makes perfect sense. When you're feeling relaxed, your body and mind can operate at their absolute optimum performance levels because they are unrestricted by the friction caused by tension, stress and bad, cluttered thought patterns. Being relaxed means you can physically and mentally operate smoothly. Don't confuse relaxation with lying on the couch, sleeping, or watching TV. That's not what we mean by the word "relax." What we mean is getting yourself into a state where your mind is alert, free, and uncluttered and where your muscles are soft and completely free of tension. If you press down on one of your shoulders and jump up in pain, this is a sign that you're not relaxed enough! If you press down and the muscles are soft and you experience no pain, then you are nearer the relaxed state you need to be in. With office-type occupations, tension tends to make itself obvious around your neck and shoulders area. You need to be free of that.

Get yourself into a state where your mind is alert, free, and uncluttered.

Be Confident

When you have a credible trading plan and have learned techniques that will enable you to trade and invest with greater probabilities of success, then you should start to feel more confident in your ability to make consistent and sustained profits over the short, medium and long term. I cannot impress upon you enough the importance of stacking the odds in your favor before you actually press the buy or sell button. Make sure you're comfortable with whatever technique you're using, having successfully paper traded it first. This will enable you to feel the calm confidence you need to have longevity in this business.

Stack the odds in your favor before you actually press the buy or sell button.

Be Controlled

By definition, if you're relaxed and you're confident, then you have more chance of being in control too. And if you're in control of your actions and emotions, then the virtuous cycle will ensue, and you'll become even more relaxed and confident as well. All the time, we're talking about a calm and smooth approach to trading and investing. You can be calm and yet still have the speed of thought, hunger, and confidence to make important decisions quickly, efficiently, and effectively.

Building the Resource State of Relaxation, Confidence, and Control

Ultimately whatever works for you is the answer, but here are a few pointers. To anyone who's even considering not reading this section, let me point out that Trading "Wizards" (Schwager, 1992) such as (the late) Robert Krausz and Charles Faulkner were and are great exponents of techniques such as Neuro Linguistic Programming (NLP) and hypnosis in order to achieve enhanced trading performance. As someone who's had plenty of exposure to both these areas (which aren't mutually exclusive anyway), I can vouch for their effectiveness in all sorts of scenarios.

Breathing

The first step in achieving a relaxed state is to get your breathing right. Take a long, slow, deep breath, filling all your stomach, and then allow yourself to breathe out as slowly as you possibly can. Do this for a few breaths, and I can guarantee you'll now begin to feel different and more relaxed. All too often we don't pay enough attention to the way in which we breathe, but it's a good habit to get into because in many cases we really do need to start breathing in a healthier manner. Think about it this way, how long can you go without food? How long can you go without water? How long can you go without oxygen? Do you get the picture? We need oxygen to stay alive, and that gives us a clue to the fact that we perform our tasks better when we employ our lungs to something nearer their capacity. Since we already know that deep, steady breathing will encourage a relaxed state, and we also know that we perform physical and mental tasks better when we're feeling relaxed, it also stands to reason that when you're breathing deeply and steadily you'll, by definition, perform better in this state.

Recreating the Resourceful State

Step two is where you start to generate feelings of great confidence for yourself. Remember, the most important thing is to have a robust trading plan. That is your trump card. All these other techniques are simply bonuses. Without a properly formed plan, they won't be that helpful.

Have you ever felt confident before? Even if your initial answer might be no, think again! We've all felt confident about *something* before! We're not talking about saving the world or anything like that! We could be talking about a time when you felt confident about a meal you were cooking, or a paper you were writing, a meeting you had, a sporting achievement or a piece of art you were creating. Some people even feel confident about having no confidence at all!

When you've decided upon what it was that you were feeling confident about, start to go back in your mind and recall in detail what you were seeing at the time, what you were hearing and how you were feeling at that time. Build the images you saw in your mind and notice the colors and the focus of the pictures, how far those images are in your mind, the size of the images, whether they're in 2D or 3D and whether they're still shots or motion pictures. Allow yourself to become fully and comfortably aware of the sounds and what you heard, paying attention to the richness of sound quality, the source of the noises, the depth, pitch and tonality of what you were hearing. And notice the way you're beginning to feel about it all, as you literally re-experience the feelings of confidence again. Now you can begin to amplify those feelings by playing with the images, making them bigger, brighter, more colorful, more dynamic, moving pictures. You can increase the richness of the sounds you were hearing, even adding a soundtrack to the pictures. We've all listened to wonderfully inspirational music that touches us, makes our spine tingle and makes us feel invigorated or just very calm and controlled. That's that kind of music that will assist your imagination and ultimately, the task in hand, like your trading. See yourself in the pictures within your imagination and bring the image of yourself in that confident state nearer and nearer until you can actually step into the image life size and be in it, applying it to your trading. Notice how you're feeling with the addition of the soundtrack—it should help to magnify the effects of your positive feelings. You can now start to apply that same soundtrack to your trading both now and in the future. Does it help you feel more confident in this scenario? You can actually play the real soundtrack out loud if you like and not just in your head. The effects should be tangible.[1]

---

[1] Remember that much of your confidence in trading should be predicated on the basis that you have a Trading Plan that you've back tested and seen work, provided you follow the rules. The sequence just described is detailed so that you can access the feelings of confidence more readily in the knowledge that you do have a sound Trading Plan already.

Anchoring the Resourceful State

Step three involves you creating a stimulus-response association between your Resource State and a subtle physical action....

At the peak of your feeling totally confident, your breathing rhythmically, steadily and feeling calm, relaxed and alert, and as all these good feelings are at their most intense, trigger a stimulus such as clicking your fingers in a distinct way, or pinching the back of your hand. The idea is that this will have the effect of linking that stimulus with the Resourceful State feelings you've just created (and amplified) so that in the future you'll be able to call upon the Resourceful State at will.

Your "soundtrack music" should be uplifting and can even be triumphant if you like, but do make sure that it doesn't make you overexcited. The music itself can also become a very powerful anchor for generating the Resourceful State of mind. It works even better when you combine the music with the physical anchor (say, of clicking your fingers) you just created. I know people who always listen to a section of their "anchor music" before embarking on any endeavor of real significance, whether it's an important meeting, a phone call, trading, or even going on a date! We want to feel confident yet focused and controlled at the same time. Sportsmen and sportswomen often equate this phenomenon as being "in the zone." They make references to feeling "10 feet tall" when they go onto the field of play with an overwhelming but calm sense of certainty about what it is they're about to achieve. In Eastern cultures and some martial arts, the feeling is likened to being totally centered, where you enhance your awareness of your own center of gravity, which is about two inches below your naval. You should feel "in the zone." You see yourself completely controlling your thoughts, emotions, and actions. It's almost cold-blooded, but it's very effective and ensures that you can maintain an aloof detachment from the mayhem of the markets yet be able to react to them profitably, mechanically, and unemotionally when you're required to take decisive actions. By controlling your breathing, you'll maintain control of your thoughts and actions, which in turn will help you to feel relaxed and confident, thus perpetuating this virtuous cycle.

For step four, you now need to test the anchor and ensure that it works. If by listening to the music and triggering the physical anchor (clicking your fingers) you begin to feel good sensations such as your breathing automatically slowing down, your spine tingling, a markedly increased sense of well-being and confidence, and so on, then it's working. If you feel no effects when you trigger the physical anchor, go through steps one through three again and amplify the sounds, pictures, and feelings, and if you haven't already done so, play your uplifting soundtrack out loud on your stereo while you create the anchor again.

For more detailed information on hypnosis for traders, look up Robert Krausz, and for any decent NLP material look up Richard Bandler's work or Charles Faulkner for NLP and trading specifically. I know plenty of would-be great traders who simply haven't spent the time or energy to create the optimal mindset for trading. As such, they remain average to poor in their results, and yet they have all the technical knowledge they require and more.

Money Management and Rule Making

Much has been written about money management in the field of trading and investment. Ultimately it boils down to trading in an emotional vacuum and sticking by your predetermined Rules. Remember that trading and investing are two separate and distinct activities requiring an overlapping of but not identical skills. In terms of mindset, there is definitely a full overlap. Having the right mindset will help you to stick to your Rules and apply your stops at the appropriate and preordained times.

Your Rules should embrace your entry, management, and exit decisions, and they need to be good enough to stick to.

It's common sense not to bet the farm on any single investment decision, and it's common sense to spread your risk around in a manageable way where you can track your dealings and act fast if necessary.

It's also common sense to take your profits according to your Rules and ensure that they allow you to do so. Your Rules should embrace your entry, management and exit decisions, and they need to be good enough to keep. One of the most common sentences in the trading world is, "I would have made a profit, but I keep breaking my rules!" Sound familiar? This is the most common statement I hear. The question therefore is this: Are your rules worth keeping in the first place? Because if they are, then you need to find a way of keeping them; and if they're not, then you need to find some better ones! Always look for a common sense approach and you shouldn't go too far wrong. If in doubt ask someone you respect.

A Real Life Example of Money Management

I wanted to trade a stock that I'd been tracking for some time. The stock was trading at more than $32 but had a critical support level at $20. At the time I didn't consider shorting it, but I wanted to track it until it hit my predetermined target price. I was already fully invested elsewhere, so I phoned my bank manager and explained the situation, asking him for a considerable loan if the correct circumstances arose. "If the stock hits $20, then I'm buying. If it breaks below $19.00, then I'll get out, pay back the loan, and take a small loss. In the meantime, I'll keep you informed as to its progress—it may never happen at all!" Over the next four weeks the stock kept falling, and each week I'd phone up my bank manager and tell him triumphantly that the stock was falling and to make sure the funds were ready when I needed them. Finally, after about a month, I was ready. The stock hit the target zone, and I phoned the bank and bought it! I'd had plenty of time to think about this and the psychological impact that surrounded this rather aggressive trade.

The Rule was set and most definitely so! The money wasn't even mine, but if I violated my Stop Loss rule, I'd have been in some trouble. Now I'm not suggesting that anyone try what I did, but just consider the psychology of it. There was no way that I was going to even consider violating my Stop Loss Rule here. Because the money wasn't technically mine, I took even more care than I would if it had been. That's an unusual approach to take, but I'd made a promise and I was going to stick to it, even in the most commercial of situations. I simply don't see a difference between promises made in business and those made personally. If I make a promise, I keep it and don't falsify details in the meantime. So, for me, this was a very powerful motivating factor to make me keep my Stop Loss Rule in this instance.

What I learned was that for me, it was a good idea to treat every investment as if it were that loan from the bank or someone who was depending on me. That way I'd always stick to my Stop Loss and other money management rules. As it happens, the stock doubled in less than six months, and I sold the whole lot at around $38.50. Everyone was happy, especially me! So now I always make that promise to obey my Stop Loss, and it works every time.

The fear of loss in such a public manner is enough to motivate me to plan my trade around a predetermined profit and Stop Loss target. If something seems to be going awry in the price action and I'm still in a profitable position, I'll take my profits early and move on. There's nothing so frustrating in watching a profitable position turn against you into a loss-making position. The fear of loss can be crippling to many traders who experience "freeze" which is a bit like the "yips" that some golfers suffer. By publicly stating what you're going to do, you can not only overcome the fear factor, but actually use it beneficially to stick to your Trading Plan. Having a trading buddy can help in this department; it just depends on what works for you.

Chapter 10 Major Learning Points

In this chapter we've learned the crucial role that psychology and good thinking play in trading and investing lifestyles. Many of the best known and most successful traders apply various mind techniques to enhance their working performance, just like professional sportsmen and women do.

Good thinking embraces your Trading Plan and your trading plan will be a by-product of good thinking. This will filter into your trading performance and ultimately into your lifestyle as well.

Putting It All Together— A Call to Action

So now that you're armed with all sorts of strategies and techniques that you can use to enhance your trading skills, we now need to put together a trading plan. It's always best to trade with high probability of success and well-defined parameters that you can stick to. Professional card players operate in this way. By counting the cards (a proven technique frowned upon by the casinos), the pros can identify periods of high and low probability for placing higher or lower bets. This is precisely the way I like to trade, stacking up the probabilities of success and sticking to the plan, come what may. While my own trading systems are discretionary in nature, they are loaded with rules so that there's little room for deviation.

Stack up the probabilities of success and stick to your plan.

Step 1—Choose Your Favored Strategies (Keep It Simple!)

I'll consider using the following strategies at various times:

Strategy	Minimum probability required
Buying or shorting the underlying asset	High
Straddles or Strangles (Volatility plays)	High
Collars	High
Covered Calls	High to very high
Deep in the Money calls or puts	Very high
Bull Call and Bull Put spreads	Very high
Bull Put spreads	Very high
Bear Put and Bear Call spreads	Very high

The probability table is just to give you an idea that if I don't think there's more than a reasonable chance of success, I won't place the trade in the first place. For options trades, I require high probability, and the higher the leverage of a trade (for example, Deep in the Money Calls or Puts), the more certainty I require. If I can't find an appropriate trade or if I'm not in the right frame of mind, I'll stay out. There's a lot of power in saying no to a trade for the right reasons, and it's a further indication that you're totally in control of your decision making. At the same time, however, we're not looking for inertia!

Step 2—Set Your Filters[1]

You can build sophisticated filters on even the most reasonably priced charting packages nowadays, such as TCNet (Telecharts 2000), which now comes with real time data.

---

[1] This won't be necessary if you choose to trade just one stock. For example, many traders simply trade the SPY, which is the stock derivative equivalent of the S&P 500 index. By and large the SPY mimics the movement of the S&P 500 and has its own options chain, so you can trade the options too. Personally, I'll trade the SPY but only on the high-probability scenarios. Remember, there's no shame in sitting on the sidelines if you're not sure or if your entry requirements are not met.

What Do You Filter For?

This depends on your personal preferences. I filter specifically for moving or "thrusting" stocks (DiNapoli, 1998)—for example, stocks that have moved up or down for more than ten periods (days or weeks) in a row. I always use the daily filters first and have so far never needed to use the weekly settings considering there are always plenty of opportunities whether the market is up, down, or even sideways. I also backdate the search so that I can see stocks that had been thrusting up to a week ago but may be turning now.

> I'm looking for stocks that look over-extended (in either direction) and are ready for a retracement of some sort.

Specifically, I'm looking for stocks that look over-extended (in either direction) and are ready for a retracement of some sort. I look for the 15% biggest gainers or losers in both the last 30 days and those that have continued to move the most since hitting a five-day high or low. I always filter for stocks of adequate Average Daily Volume of at least 500,000 shares.

Trading Stocks or an Index

Many traders only trade one index or one stock. This tactic has several advantages:

(i)   It avoids the need for filtering for stocks.

(ii)   It avoids the peculiarities of individual stocks.

(iii) Trading an index embraces the laws of mass human behavior, thereby confirming the validity of advanced Fibonacci analysis.

(iv)   The trader gets to intimately understand the "personality" of that one instrument which he/she trades. Some people say this can be dull; others maintain the reason for trading is not for excitement but for higher probability of success.

Filtering for individual stocks will expose the trader to potentially explosive moves, which may suit strategies such as straddles and strangles better. Furthermore, the trader must be alive to news events, which may occur specific to the stock. This means doing your homework and knowing when the earnings and other reports will be announced. For example, in general you don't want to be trading a Butterfly just prior to an earnings announcement!

A major advantage of trading a number of stocks (as opposed to just one) is that you can diversify your portfolio, a widely appreciated risk management tool in itself. However, as Warren Buffett says, most people who diversify don't actually understand the first thing about any of the stocks they're trading! So, there are powerful arguments both ways. The very best traders I know trade very few securities and know them intimately. Go to www.themarketmatrix.co.uk if you're interested in this style of trading.

Step 3—Designing Your Trading Plan for Each Entry and Exit

Stacking Up the Probabilities

Your trading plan should be designed to enhance your chances of success. If it doesn't, it's not going to be good enough to keep you to the discipline of the plan in the first place. The better your trading plan is, the more you'll feel compelled to stick with it—its record of success should be the acid test.

In Chapters 3 and 4 we covered just some of the Technical and Fundamental Analysis techniques, which can either be used as filters for finding stocks or as indicators for assessing trend or price direction. Different traders and investors have their own preferences, and there are many discretionary trading styles that can work. It's up to you and your own psychology. Some people can trade 300+ tickets per day successfully, others just ten every year. Ultimately you're the one who has to decide here. If your style of trading leans toward the former, then make sure you choose a day trading firm that will give you the necessary training, support and, more importantly, speed of execution.

> **The better your trading plan is, the more you'll feel compelled to stick with it—its record of success should be the acid test.**

After you have decided what security to trade and your preferred time frame, to increase the probability of success, your trading plan should include at least one of the following:

- A method of identifying support and resistance. I use seriously advanced Fibonacci for this. Go to www.themarketmatrix.co.uk for more information on the best Fibonacci techniques available.

- A method of identifying if a stock is overbought, oversold, or temporarily over-stretched. You can use Joe DiNapoli's Oscillator Predictor for this, as contained within his book, *Trading with DiNapoli Levels* (www.fibtrader.com) (DiNapoli, 1998). The Oscillator Predictor can be crudely approximated by using TC2000's Envelope Channel indicator with the settings at 5 Periods and Width 8, Simple.

- Oscillators such as MACD or Stochastics so you can identify if your stock is in a trend, rangebound, or potentially at a turning point.

- Stop losses and profit objectives—trading should be like running a business. Use your support and resistance levels to determine your entry and exit decisions.

- Keeping an eye out for key news events that might affect your chosen stock or the market as a whole—and ultimately your trade.

- Timing indicators, including Fibonacci or even lunar cycles. All these methods have been shown to work if you use the proper methods. Timing is the key to any success in the markets. For more information, again go to www.themarketmatrix.co.uk.

Settings for Stochastic and MACD

You can use the settings as recommended in Joe DiNapoli's book, *Trading with DiNapoli Levels* (www.fibtrader.com).

The idea is to use a weak stochastic setting in conjunction with a strong MACD setting. The MACD setting of 8.3896, 17.5185, 9.0503 is trend indicative, while the "Preferred" Stochastic setting of 8,3,3 is a weaker, more sensitive indicator. Where both the MACD and Stochastic are moving in the same direction (and haven't crossed over), then the trend is in place. If the Preferred Stochastic crosses over but the MACD trend is still intact, then the MACD signal holds sway, but you can take advantage of the short-term price movement as reflected by the Stochastic crossover. For example, in the case of an uptrend, if the MACD remains intact but the Preferred Stochastic crosses over downward, this may indicate a brief pullback. Traders can take advantage of the pullback by fading against the Stochastic signal and with the MACD signal, in other words, buying on the pullback. The level at which to do this will depend on your support and resistance analysis, where you'll be looking for a low risk entry point. If you can find a Fibonacci level combined with a distinct chart pattern, then you have a higher probability of the security making a turn in that price area.

Table 11.1 ● Sample Trading Plan (Once You Have Filtered for Your Stocks)*

Stock	Price	Date	Support/ resistance	Overbought/ Oversold	MACD	Stochastic	Chart patterns	News	Entry plan	Exit plan
KOSP	$26.00	May 30, 2001	S x R x		✓	x	Strong Pennant consolidation	Earnings on August 1, 2001	August 2001 $25 Straddle at $6.15	Sell calls with stock at $35.00; sell puts with stock at $19.00; or exit 1 month before Expiration
WLP	$105	July 17, 2001	S x R $106.62 Fibonacci Resistance Level	OB Oscillator Predictor	x Slowing	✓ Crossing	Double Top	Earnings on July 26, 2001	Sell short above $105	Buy Stop at $108. Otherwise take profits on strength below $100
FRE	$68.48	June 12, 2001	S $60 R $70		Turning down	✓	At strong resistance, channelling between $60 and $70	Earnings on July 18, 2001	60/65/70 July 2001 Butterfly	Exit on close above $70 or below $60; hold to Expiration**
UNH	$53	May 24, 2001	S $50.50 R x	OS Oscillator Predictor	x	Turning	Triple Bottom at $50.50	Earnings on July 27, 2001	Buy stock over $52	Stop loss below $50

* All stocks in the chart above were selected from my two "thrusting stocks" filters made on the actual dates given in the table.

** A weakness of the Butterfly is that if the stock prices move outside the outside strike prices, the trader can be left with a substantial loss position. While we can make adjustments to effectively shift the Butterfly position up or down, these adjustments are somewhat complex for our purposes, and we want to promote simplicity in our trading.

Chart 11.1 ● WLP (July 17, 2001) short rationale.

*Chart created on TradeStation®, the flagship product of TradeStation Technologies Inc.

①	**Chart pattern**	Double Top (or even triple top)	✓
②	**Fibonacci resistance**	Strong Fibonacci resistance at around $106.00	✓
③	**Oscillator Predictor**	Breached to the upside	✓
④	**MACD crossover**	MACD is slowing here, but not crossing yet	✗
⑤	**Stochastic crossover**	Stochastic is crossing downward	✓

Interpretation

According to these criteria, this is a solid short trade, one that might even justify a more leveraged approach, for example, buying $110 strike put options. An additional factor supporting the trade is that Volume is falling below its Average Daily Volume (see bottom indicator on the chart), demonstrating flagging demand for this stock at these price levels. Our Buy Stop is set if the stock closes above the November 1, 2000, high of $108.00. We would interpret a close above this level as a sign of strength in the stock moving to the upside.

Chart 11.2 ● UNH (24 May 2001) long rationale.

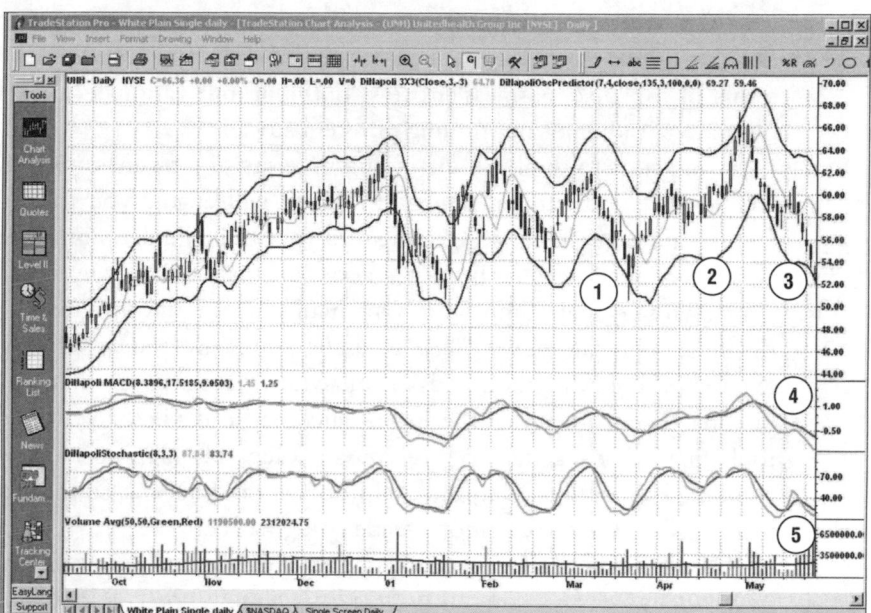

*Chart created on TradeStation®, the flagship product of TradeStation Technologies Inc.

①	**Chart pattern**	Triple Bottom at $50.50	✓
②	**Fibonacci support**	Fib support between $48 and $49	✗
③	**Oscillator Predictor**	Breached to the downside	✓
④	**MACD crossover**	Not yet turning	✗
⑤	**Stochastic crossover**	Clearly turning upwards but not yet crossed	✗

Interpretation

This is a more speculative trade, much of it resting on the Triple Bottom support and Oscillator Predictor breach criteria. Fibonacci support is under $50, which doesn't quite count as a tick mark when the stock is at $53.00. One way to play this is to wait until there is a sure sign of support holding in this area, which does indeed happen on May 29 and 30, 2001, by which time the Stochastic has crossed and the MACD is turning. On May 24, 2001, this is more of a stock trade, and you shouldn't be considering a highly leveraged options position until you have more tick marks in the boxes.*

---

*By all means consider adding more criteria to your own trading plan. For example, Volume Pattern would be a good addition to this.

Chapter 11 Major Learning Points

In this chapter we've learned how to start to structure our trading decisions in terms of a proper business process, outlining our rationale for selecting and ultimately trading or not trading different stocks.

If you start to think about trading in terms of a business process, you'll be able to take a structured approach, which will enable you to outline all the factors and criteria that are pertinent to your ultimate decision.

Discretionary trading plans are very personal. This is why you need to put your own personal stamp on it. One man's meat is another man's poison, but the most important rule is: *Keep it simple*. Too many traders spend all their time experimenting with thousands of analytical tools, never quite finding their nirvana. The truth is that there is no nirvana, so it's best to find a selection of tools that work together to give you an acceptably high probability of success combined with built-in buy and sell stop loss mechanisms, so that you don't get too badly hurt in the event of a trade going wrong.

There are four things that can happen to you as a trader or investor. *You can make a lot of money, you can make a little money, you can lose a lot of money, and you can lose a little money. Provided we can remove the "losing a lot of money" from the equation, you should do well at this.*

You can now build your own trading plan and start to implement a simple and sound template for all your investment and trading decisions. You can use your own parameters, you can follow my suggestions here, or you can mix the two. The details are up to you. This book covers the tools that have yielded consistently good results for people over a long period of time. I personally use the methods contained in the Market Matrix (www.themarketmatrix.co.uk) but have also benefited from the other techniques described.

The trick is in the implementation, and that is why you need a proper trading plan that's simple to interpret and easy to follow. This way you'll avoid being a gambler and instead become a real player, trading profitably with high probabilities on your side. And while we want to remain emotionally neutral in this activity, it's OK to allow yourself to feel some real excitement and anticipation about your success in consistently applying these principles.

chapter 12

Stock Futures and Options Strategies (Bonus Chapter)

It seems as if we're constantly entering into new eras of trading and investing with all the changes and innovations that are occurring as a result of the increasing pace of technology. One of the latest financial innovations, undertaken separately by LIFFE and the CBOE with the CME, has been the creation of "stock futures" whereby you can take a long position in a stock without actually having to put your cash into it. This is not the same as equity margin because the stock future itself is the instrument that you trade, not the stock itself.

Buying a (stock) future is similar to agreeing to buy shares at a future date but agreeing on the price at the time of the trade.

Obviously, the stock future's pricing is derived from the underlying stock, and you'll need to have the appropriate funds within your brokerage account to trade it. However, those funds will be earning you interest given that they are only required to cover your position according to your broker's requirements, not actually acquiring a security. In other words, the stock future is literally a futures contract. As such, it requires no cash investment from you, *per se*, unless you lose. This is quite different from using margin to buy an underlying stock for cash.

Buying a (stock) future is similar to agreeing to buy shares at a future date but agreeing on the price at the time of the trade. Selling a (stock) future is similar to agreeing to sell shares at a future date but agreeing on the price at the time of the trade. Unlike shorting a stock, selling a stock future does not compel the seller to "borrow" the shares to enter the agreement.

Each future has a "delivery month," and the prices of futures from different delivery months will not only be different from each other, but also different from the price of the underlying share.

Whereas an option confers on the buyer the right, not the obligation, to buy or sell an asset at a certain price by a predetermined date, a future simply confers the obligation on both parties. Both the buyer and the seller face the risk that the underlying share price changes before the delivery date. This risk can be hedged by the buying or selling of options or the underlying shares.

A future confers the obligation to buy or sell on both parties to the trade.

At this point in time, only a limited number of stocks are available as stock futures in the LIFFE portfolio of "Universal Stock Futures" (launched in January 2001). With the CBOE (OneChicago) single stock futures, one contract is an agreement to deliver 100 shares of a specific stock at the expiration date. By and large there are four expiration dates available for trading OneChicago single stock futures. For more information, go to www.onechicago.com.

Futures Pricing

In theory, the futures price should be equal to the cost of buying the shares and holding them until the delivery date when the futures expire. If the futures price is above this level, then you could make a guaranteed return by buying the underlying stock and selling the future. If the futures price is less than this level, then you could make a guaranteed return by buying the future and selling the stock. When a futures price moves away from the correct theoretical price, the markets will generally bring the prices back into line to prevent these "arbitrage" scenarios.[1]

The total cost of buying stock and holding it until the future's expiration is made up of the following factors:

1. the underlying stock price

2. time to delivery

3. interest rates

4. dividends payable on the stock prior to the delivery date

---

[1] Arbitrage is the process whereby traders can take advantage of short-term pricing anomalies to make guaranteed profits on a trade. The markets will normally ensure that such anomalies are extremely short-lived.

In simple terms, the theoretical stock futures price should be:

Theoretical futures price = current stock price + interest costs − dividends received

However, because futures are traded in the open market, their pricing also will be subject to the laws of supply and demand, plus the added factor of traders' different expectations of interest rates and dividends, which will lead to fluctuating prices toward and away from the Theoretical Fair Value Price.

Stock Futures and Options Strategies

Stock futures offer investors and traders a myriad of possibilities, not just for increased leverage, but also for more dynamic hedging possibilities using combinations between the underlying stock itself, the stock future, stock options and soon, options on the stock futures. In Chapter 5 we covered three strategies that used combinations of buying or selling the individual stock with buying or selling calls or puts. Those strategies were

● Synthetic Calls,

● Covered Calls, and

● Collars.

Remember the basic composition of these strategies with stocks:

Strategy	Leg 1	Leg 2	Leg 3	Your account
Synthetic Call	Buy stock	Buy put		Net debit
Covered Call	Buy stock	Sell call		Net debit
Collar	Buy stock	Buy put	Sell call	Net debit

With the advent of stock futures, there are significant implications for Leg 1 on all of these strategies. Because each strategy involves buying the stock itself, the strategy will be a net debit transaction, requiring sufficient funds in your account to facilitate the purchase of those shares. With stock futures, you won't actually have to buy the stock itself, so your net debits for all three strategies are going to be significantly reduced, and subject to pricing, you'll end up with the same or similar risk profiles as well.

With stock futures, the same strategies will generate slightly different implications for your account:

Strategy	Leg 1	Leg 2	Leg 3	Your account
Synthetic Call	Long Stock Future	Buy put		Net debit*
Covered Call	Long Stock Future	Sell call		Net credit
Collar	Long Stock Future	Buy Put	Sell Call	Net debit*

* Net debit is far lower than for the same strategies using stocks as opposed to stock futures.

While the Collar and Synthetic Call remain net debits (requiring you to pay cash up front to construct the strategies), with stock futures the Covered Call actually becomes a net credit trade because the second leg actually involves you pulling in options premium from selling the Call options—while the first leg involves you taking a long position in a futures contract as opposed to physically buying the underlying asset. The Collar and Synthetic Call net debits with stock futures are therefore massively reduced in comparison to the equivalent spreads with stocks. Note, however, that the risk profile of each strategy remains the same shape whether you're playing with stocks or stock futures.

Strategy Table

Strategy	Execution	Benefits	Disadvantages	Component Parts	Risk Profile
Long Call	Buy a call.	Capped risk; uncapped reward; better leverage than stock purchase.	Can lose entire stake if the call expires OTM (out of the money).		
Long Put	Buy a put.	Capped risk; uncapped reward; better leverage than straight stock shorting.	Can lose entire stake if the put expires OTM (out of the money).		
Short Call (naked)	Sell a call.	Short-term income strategy.	Uncapped risk and capped reward.		
Short Put (naked)	Sell a put.	Short-term income strategy.	Uncapped risk and capped reward.		
Covered Call	Buy stock and sell call.	Protected income strategy. Profit assured if stock remains static or rises. Calls can be sold on a monthly basis to generate income.	Uncapped risk and capped reward.		
Collar	Buy stock, buy ATM put, and sell OTM call.	Can be a riskless strategy if executed correctly with the right stock.	Net debit out of your account. Works best for long-term trades where you leave it alone.		

appendix I continued

Strategy	Execution	Benefits	Disadvantages	Component Parts	Risk Profile
Covered Put	Sell stock (short) and sell put.	Net credit into your account.	Uncapped risk and capped reward.		
Synthetic Call	Buy stock and buy put.	Capped risk and uncapped reward. Good insurance tactic.	Expensive strategy.		
Synthetic Put	Short stock and buy call.	Capped risk and uncapped reward.	More complex than simply buying puts.		
Covered Short Straddle	Buy stock and sell put and call with same strike and expiration date.	Enhanced income (compared with Covered Call).	Very high risk and capped reward. Not recommended.		
Covered Short Strangle	Buy stock and sell lower strike put and higher strike call with same expiration date.	Enhanced income (compared with Covered Call).	Very high risk and capped reward. Not recommended.		
Bull Call Spread	Buy lower strike calls and sell higher strike calls (same expiration).	Capped risk; lower breakeven point than simply buying a call.	Capped reward.		
Bull Put Spread	Buy lower strike puts and sell higher strike puts (same expiration).	Capped risk; lower breakeven point than simply buying a put; net credit into your account.	Capped reward.		

Strategy	Execution	Benefits	Disadvantages	Component Parts	Risk Profile
Bear Call Spread	Sell lower strike calls and buy higher strike calls (same expiration).	Capped risk; bearish income strategy.	Capped reward.		
Bear Put Spread	Sell lower strike puts and buy higher strike puts (same expiration).	Capped risk.	Capped reward.		
Bull Call Ladder	Buy lower strike calls, sell higher strike calls, and sell even higher strike calls (all same expiration).	Cheap strategy.	Uncapped risk if stock rises sharply; confusing as to whether this is a bullish or bearish strategy.		
Bull Put Ladder	Buy lower strike puts, buy higher strike puts, and sell even higher strike puts (all same expiration).	Uncapped reward as the stock falls.	Expensive; confusing as to whether this is a bullish or bearish strategy.		
Bear Call Ladder	Sell lower strike calls, buy higher strike calls, and buy even higher strike calls (all same expiration).	Uncapped reward as the stock rises.	Expensive; confusing as to whether this is a bullish or bearish strategy.		

appendix I continued

Strategy	Execution	Benefits	Disadvantages	Component Parts	Risk Profile
Bear Put Ladder	Sell lower strike puts, sell higher strike puts, and buy even higher strike puts (all same expiration).	Cheap strategy.	Uncapped risk as the stock falls; confusing as to whether this is a bullish or bearish strategy.		
Straddle	Buy puts and calls with same strike price and expiration.	Capped risk; profitable if stocks rises or falls significantly; uncapped reward.	Expensive; low volatility required for entry whereas high volatility required once you are in.		
Short Straddle	Sell puts and calls with same strike and expiration.	Net credit into your account; profitable if stock shows low volatility and does not move.	Uncapped risk on either side.		
Strangle	Buy lower strike puts and buy higher strike calls (same expiration).	Capped risk; profitable if stocks rises or falls significantly; uncapped reward.	Low volatility required for entry whereas high volatility required once you are in.		
Short Strangle	Sell lower strike puts and sell higher strike calls (same expiration).	Net credit into your account; profitable if stock shows low volatility and does not move.	Uncapped risk on either side.		

Strategy	Execution	Benefits	Disadvantages	Component Parts	Risk Profile
Strip	Buy 2 puts and 1 call with same strike and expiration.	Capped risk; profitable if stocks rises or falls significantly; uncapped reward.	Expensive; low volatility required for entry whereas high volatility required once you are in.		
Strap	Buy 1 put and 2 calls with same strike and expiration.	Capped risk; profitable if stocks rises or falls significantly; uncapped reward.	Expensive; low volatility required for entry whereas high volatility required once you are in.		
Long Call Butterfly	Buy 1 lower strike call, sell 2 middle strike calls, and buy 1 higher strike call. All strikes evenly apart.	Capped risk and a cheap strategy to enter; can be very profitable if stock shows low volatility after you are in.	Capped reward; awkward to adjust.		
Long Put Butterfly	Buy 1 lower strike put, sell 2 middle strike puts, and buy 1 higher strike put. All strikes evenly apart.	Capped risk and a cheap strategy to enter; can be very profitable if stock shows low volatility after you are in.	Capped reward; awkward to adjust		
Short Call Butterfly	Sell 1 lower strike call, buy 2 middle strike calls, and sell 1 higher strike call. All strikes evenly apart.	Capped risk; profitable if stock shows high volatility after you are in.	Capped reward; awkward to adjust.		

appendix I continued

Strategy	Execution	Benefits	Disadvantages	Component Parts	Risk Profile
Short Put Butterfly	Sell 1 lower strike put, buy 2 middle strike puts, and sell 1 higher strike put. All strikes evenly apart.	Capped risk; profitable if stock shows high volatility after you are in.	Capped reward; awkward to adjust.		
Modified Call Butterfly	Buy 1 lower strike call, sell 2 middle strike calls, and buy 1 higher strike call. Middle strike closer to higher strike than to lower strike.	Capped risk and a cheap strategy to enter; can be very profitable if stock shows low volatility or rises modestly after you are in.	Capped reward; awkward to adjust.		
Modified Put Butterfly	Buy 1 lower strike put, sell 2 middle strike puts, and buy 1 higher strike put. Middle strike closer to higher strike than to lower strike.	Capped risk and a cheap strategy to enter; can be very profitable if stock shows low volatility or rises modestly after you are in.	Capped reward; awkward to adjust.		
Call Ratio Backspread	Sell 1 or 2 lower strike calls and buy 2 or 3 higher strike calls. Buy greater number of higher strike calls in ratio of 0.67 or less.	Capped risk; uncapped and highly geared reward if stock rises significantly.	Lots of volatility required after entry and in the right direction (upward) for your trade to be profitable.		

Strategy	Execution	Benefits	Disadvantages	Component Parts	Risk Profile
Put Ratio Backspread	Buy 2 or 3 lower strike puts and sell 1 or 2 higher strike puts. Buy greater number of lower strike puts in ratio of 0.67 or less.	Capped risk; uncapped and highly geared reward if stock falls significantly.	Lots of volatility required after entry and in the right direction (downward) for your trade to be profitable.	*(diagram)*	*(diagram)*
Ratio Call Spread	Buy lower strike call and sell greater number of higher strike calls (ratio of 0.67 or less).		Uncapped risk; capped reward.	*(diagram)*	*(diagram)*
Ratio Put Spread	Buy higher strike put and sell greater number of lower strike puts (ratio of 0.67 or less).		Uncapped risk; capped reward.	*(diagram)*	*(diagram)*
Long Call Condor	Buy lower strike call, sell middle strike call, sell next middle strike call, and buy higher strike call. All strikes evenly apart.	Capped risk and a cheap strategy to enter; can be very profitable if stock remains rangebound after you are in.	Capped reward; awkward to adjust.	*(diagram)*	*(diagram)*

appendix I continued

Strategy	Execution	Benefits	Disadvantages	Component Parts	Risk Profile
Long Put Condor	Buy lower strike put, sell middle strike put, sell next middle strike put, and buy higher strike put. All strikes evenly apart.	Capped risk and a cheap strategy to enter; can be very profitable if stock remains rangebound after you are in.	Capped reward; awkward to adjust.		
Short Call Condor	Sell lower strike call, buy middle strike call, buy next middle strike call, and sell higher strike call. All strikes evenly apart.	Capped risk; profitable if stock shows high volatility after you are in.	Capped reward; awkward to adjust.		
Short Put Condor	Sell lower strike put, buy middle strike put, buy next middle strike put, and sell higher strike put. All strikes evenly apart.	Capped risk; profitable if stock shows high volatility after you are in.	Capped reward; awkward to adjust.		
Long Call Synthetic Straddle	Sell 1 stock and buy 2 ATM calls.	Capped risk; profitable if stock rises or falls significantly; uncapped reward; cheaper than doing a normal Straddle.	Low volatility required for entry whereas high volatility required once you are in.		

Strategy	Execution	Benefits	Disadvantages	Component Parts	Risk Profile
Long Put Synthetic Straddle	Buy 1 stock and 2 ATM puts.	Capped risk; profitable if stocks rises or falls significantly; uncapped reward.	Even more expensive than normal Straddle; low volatility required for entry, whereas high volatility required once you are in.		
Short Call Synthetic Straddle	Buy 1 stock and sell 2 ATM calls.	Profitable if stock shows low volatility and does not move.	Uncapped risk on either side; expensive because you are buying the stock.		
Short Put Synthetic Straddle	Sell 1 stock and 2 ATM puts.	Cheap strategy that brings in a net credit to your account; profitable if stock shows low volatility and does not move.	Uncapped risk on either side; large margin required.		
Long Iron Butterfly	Buy lower strike put, sell mid strike put, sell next mid strike call, and buy higher strike call. (Middle strikes can be the same.)	Cheap strategy that brings in a net credit to your account; capped risk; profitable if stock doesn't move much; capped risk.	Capped reward; margin required.		

appendix I continued

Strategy	Execution	Benefits	Disadvantages	Component Parts	Risk Profile
Short Iron Butterfly	Sell lower strike put, buy mid strike put, buy next mid strike call, and sell higher strike call. (Middle strikes can be the same.)	Capped risk.	Expensive strategy.		
Calendar Call	Buy long-term call and sell shorter-term call (same strikes).	Capped risk; can sell the shorter-term calls on a monthly basis in order to generate income.	Capped reward; can become loss-making if the underlying asset rises too much.		
Calendar Put	Buy long-term put and sell shorter-term put (same strikes).	Capped risk; can sell the shorter-term calls on a monthly basis in order to generate income.	Capped reward; can become loss-making if the underlying asset rises too much.		
Diagonal Call	Buy long-term lower strike call and sell shorter-term higher strike call.	Capped risk; can sell the shorter-term calls on a monthly basis in order to generate income.	Capped reward.		
Diagonal Put	Sell shorter-term lower strike put and buy longer-term higher strike put.	Capped risk; can sell the shorter-term calls on a monthly basis in order to generate income.	Capped reward.		

Strategy	Execution	Benefits	Disadvantages	Component Parts	Risk Profile
Guts	Buy lower strike calls and higher strike puts.	Capped risk; profitable if stocks rises or falls significantly; uncapped reward.	Expensive because you're buying ITM options.	(diagram)	(diagram)
Short Guts	Sell lower strike calls and higher strike puts.	Net credit into your account; profitable if stock shows low volatility and does not move.	Uncapped risk on either side.	(diagram)	(diagram)
Long Synthetic Future	Buy ATM call and sell ATM put.	Simulates going long on a stock with no or very little net debit or credit.	Same leverage as the underlying.	(diagram)	(diagram)
Short Synthetic Future	Sell ATM call and buy ATM put.	Simulates going short on a stock with no or very little net debit or credit.	Same leverage as the underlying.	(diagram)	(diagram)
Long Combo	Sell OTM (lower) put and buy OTM (higher) call.	Almost simulates going long on a stock with no or very little net debit or credit.	Same leverage as the underlying.	(diagram)	(diagram)
Short Combo	Buy OTM (lower) put and sell OTM (higher) call.	Almost simulates going short on a stock with no or very little net debit or credit.	Same leverage as the underlying.	(diagram)	(diagram)

appendix I continued

Strategy	Execution	Benefits	Disadvantages	Component Parts	Risk Profile
Long Box	Buy one low strike call, sell one same strike put; sell one higher strike call, and buy one same higher strike put; all same expiration dates.	Create a completely hedged position where the ultimate profit is known with certainty ahead of time.	Complicated, requires many contracts to be effective. Bid/Ask spread makes it difficult to guarantee a profitable position.		

Glossary

American Stock Exchange (AMEX)	Securities exchange that handles approximately 20% of all securities trades within the USA.
American-style option	An option contract that can be exercised at any time before the Expiration Date. Stock options are American-style.
Arbitrage	Where the simultaneous purchase and disposal of a combination of financial instruments is such that a guaranteed profit is made automatically.
Ask	The price that you buy at and the price that market makers and floor brokers are willing to sell at. The Ask stands for what the market makers and floor traders ask you to pay for the stock (or options or other instrument).
ATM (at the money)	Where the option Exercise price is the same as the asset price.
At the Opening order	An order that specifies execution at the market opening or else it is cancelled.
Automatic Exercise	The automatic exercise of an In the Money (ITM) option by the clearing firm at Expiration.
Backspread	A spread where more options (calls or puts) are bought than sold (the opposite of a Ratio Spread).
Bear Call spread	A net credit spread only using calls where the trader buys a higher Strike call and sells a lower Strike call. The higher Strike call is cheaper, hence the net credit. Bear Call spreads have limited risk and reward and are more profitable as the underlying asset price falls to the lower Strike price.

Bear Put spread	A net debit spread only using puts where the trader buys a higher Strike put and sells a lower Strike put. The higher Strike put will be more expensive, hence the net debit. Bear Put spreads have limited risk and reward and are more profitable as the underlying asset falls to the lower Strike Price.
Bid	The price the trader sells at and the price that market makers and floor traders are willing to buy at. The Bid stands for the price at which the market maker will bid for your stock (options, or other instrument).
Bid–Ask Spread	The difference between the Bid and Ask prices. Generally you will buy at the Ask, and sell at the Bid. The Ask is always higher than the Bid.
Blow off Top	A large rise in price followed by a quick drop. Often accompanied with high volume. Usually a technical indicator for the end of a bullish trend.
Bond	A debt financial instrument used by governments and corporate entities in order to raise capital. The bond obliges the organization to pay its holders a fixed rate of return (coupon) and repay the principal of the debt at maturity. These bonds are traded (the CBOT is one of the major bond exchanges) and their values are directly correlated with interest rates and interest-rate speculation by the markets. The lower interest rates are projected to be, the more valuable the bond will be.
Breakeven	The point(s) at which a risk profile of a trade equals zero.
Breakout	Where a price chart emerges upward beyond previous price resistance.
Broker	A person who charges commission for executing a transaction (buy or sell) order.
Bull	Someone who expects the market to rise.
Bull Call spread	A net debit spread only using calls where the trader buys a lower Strike call and sells a higher Strike call. The lower Strike call is more expensive, hence the net debit. Bull Call spreads have limited risk and reward and are more profitable as the underlying asset rises to the higher Strike price (see Chapter 7).
Bull market	A rising market over a period of time (usually a few years).
Bull Put spread	A net credit spread only using puts where the trader buys a lower Strike put and sells a higher Strike put. The lower Strike put is less valuable, hence the net credit. Bull Put

spreads have limited risk and reward and are more profitable as the underlying asset rises to the higher strike price (see Chapter 7).

Butterfly spread	A 3-leg option strategy using all calls or all puts (see Chapter 9).
Buy on Close	An order stipulating to buy the security at the close of the trading session.
Buy on Open	An order stipulating to buy the security at the opening of the trading session.
Buy Stop	A buy order where the price stipulated is higher than the current price. The rationale here is when the buyer believes that if the security breaks a certain resistance, the security will continue to rise.
CAC 40 Index	The Paris Bourse index based on 40 stocks.
Calendar spread	A 2-leg option strategy where the trader buys longer-term options and sells shorter-term options. Use all calls or all puts.
Call option	The right, not the obligation, to buy an underlying security at a fixed price before a predetermined date.
Call premium	The price of a call option.
Capital gain	The profit realized from buying and selling an asset.
Capital loss	The loss taken from buying and selling an asset unprofitably.
Chicago Board Options Exchange (CBOE)	The largest options exchange in the world.
Chicago Board of Trade (CBOT)	The oldest commodity exchange in the USA. Known for listings in T-bonds, notes and a variety of commodities.
Chicago Mercantile Exchange (CME)	An exchange in which many types of futures contracts are traded in an open outcry system.
Class of options	Options of the same type, style and underlying security.
Clearing House	A separate institution that establishes timely payment and delivery of securities.
Close	The last price quoted for the day.
Closing purchase	A transaction which closes an open short position.
Closing sale	A transaction which closes an open long position.
Commission	A charge made by the broker for arranging the transaction.

Commodity	A tangible good that is traded on an exchange, for example, oil, grains, and metals.
Commodity Futures Trading Commission (CFTC)	An institution charged with ensuring the efficient operation of the futures markets.
Condor	A 4-leg option strategy using all calls or all puts (see Chapter 9).
Consumer Price Index (CPI)	An index measuring the change in consumer prices. An important inflation indicator.
Contract	A unit of trading for an option or future.
Correction	A post-rise decline in a stock price or market.
Covered Call	An income strategy involving the simultaneous purchase of the underlying asset and sale of call options (see Chapter 5).
Covered Put	A high-risk strategy involving the simultaneous shorting of the underlying asset and put options.
Credit spread	Where the simultaneous buying and selling of options creates a net credit into your account (that is, you receive more for the ones you sell than those you buy).
Day order	An order good for the day only.
Day trade	The acquisition and disposal of an asset in the same day.
Day trading	A trading style where positions are closed by the end of every day.
Debit spread	Where the simultaneous buying and selling of options creates a net debit from your account (that is, you pay more for the ones you buy than those you sell).
Deep In the Money (DITM)	*Calls:* where the price of the underlying security is far greater than the call Strike price.
	Puts: where the price of the underlying security is far less than the put Strike price.
Delayed time quotes	Quotes which are delayed from real time.
Delta	The amount by which an option premium moves divided by the dollar for dollar movement in the underlying asset.
Delta Hedge	A strategy designed to protect the investor against directional price changes in the underlying asset by engineering the overall position delta to zero.
Delta Neutral	Where a spread position is engineered so that the overall position delta is zero.
Derivative	A financial instrument whose value is 'derived' in some way from the value of an underlying asset.

Discount brokers	Low commission brokers who simply place orders, and do not provide advisory services.
Divergence	Where two or more indicators move in different directions indicating different outcomes.
Dividend	A payment made by an organization to its owners (shareholders), hopefully from profits.
Dow Jones Industrial Average (DJIA)	An index of 30 blue chip stocks traded on the New York Stock Exchange (NYSE). This index is often considered a bellwether of overall market sentiment.
Downside risk	The potential risk of a trade if prices decline.
End of day	The close of the trading day when prices settle.
EPS	Earnings per Share. The amount of profits of an organization divided by the number of outstanding shares.
Equity options	The same as stock options.
European-style option	An option which cannot be exercised before the Expiration date.
Exchange	Where an asset or derivative is traded.
Exchange rate	The price at which one currency can be converted into another currency.
Execution	The process of completing an order to trade a security.
Exercise	The activation of the right to buy or sell the underlying security.
Exercise (Strike) price	The price at which the underlying asset can be bought or sold by the buyer of a call or put option.
Expiration	The date at which the option's ability to be exercised ceases.
Expiration Date	The last day on which an option can be exercised.
Extrinsic Value (Time Value)	The price of an option less its Intrinsic Value. Out of the Money (OTM) options are made up entirely of Extrinsic (or Time) Value.
Fair market value	An asset's value under normal circumstances.
Fair value	The theoretical value calculation of an option using a pricing formula such as the Black-Scholes Options Pricing Model.
Fibonacci Retracement	Where prices on a chart move off their latest tops or bottoms in swings of 38.2%, 50%, or 61.8% from their previous bottoms or tops before resuming their original trend direction. The most common and easiest to spot is 50%.

Fill	An order that has been executed.
Fill order	An order that must be filled immediately or cancelled.
Fill or Kill	An order where a precise number of contracts must be filled or the order is cancelled.
Floor broker	A member of an exchange who is paid to execute orders.
Floor trader	An exchange member who trades on the floor of the exchange for their own account.
Fundamental Analysis	Analysis of a stock security based on the ability of the organization to generate profits for its shareholders. Such analysis embraces earnings, PE ratios, EPS, net assets, liabilities, customers, etc.
Futures contracts	Agreement to buy or sell an underlying security at a predetermined date at an agreed price. The difference between futures and options is that with options the buyer has the right, not the obligation. With futures, both parties are obliged to fulfill their part of the bargain.
Gamma	The speed by which delta changes compared with the speed by which the underlying asset is moving.
Gap	Where the opening bar of a price chart opens and stays beyond (lower or higher) that of the spread of the previous bar. Gaps can be lower or higher.
Good Till Cancelled order (GTC)	An order that remains active until either it is filled or cancelled specifically by the trader.
Guts spread	An expensive strategy where the trader buys OTM calls and puts to replicate the risk profile of a Strangle. Far cheaper to trade the Strangle.
Hedge	A term for reducing the risk of one position by taking other positions with options, futures or other derivatives.
Historic (Statistical) Volatility	A measure of the price fluctuation of an asset averaged out over a period of time. A typical and popular period would be 21–23 trading days.
Index	A group of assets (often in a similar class of sector or market capitalization) which can be traded as a single security.
Index options	Options on the indexes of stocks or other securities.
Interest rates	The rate at which borrowed money is charged by the lender, usually annualized into a percentage figure.
In the Money (ITM)	Where you can exercise an option for a profit.
	ITM *calls* are where the current stock price is greater than the call Strike price.

	ITM *puts* are where the current stock price is less than the put Strike price.
Intrinsic Value	The amount by which an option is In the Money.
Iron Butterfly	A 4-leg option strategy using calls and puts together.
Japanese Candlesticks	A popular method of visually depicting price bars where the open, high, low, close are shown explicitly.
	Upward moving price bars are hollow.
	Downward moving price bars are filled.
	Different looking bars and different clusters of price bars can lead to different interpretations of future price movements.
LEAPs	Long-term Equity AnticiPation Securities.
	These are long-term stock options with expirations up to three years in the future. LEAPs are available in calls and puts and are American-style traded options.
Leg	One side or component of a spread.
Leg in/Leg out	*Legging into a spread* entails the completion of just one component part of a spread with the intention of completing the other component parts at more favorable prices later on.
	Legging out of a spread entails the opposite whereby you exit your spread one component part at a time with the intention of completing the other component parts at more favorable prices as the underlying security moves in the anticipated direction.
LIFFE	London International Financial Futures and Options Exchange.
Limit Order	An *order to buy* at a set price which is at or below the current price of the security.
	An *order to sell* at a set price which is at or above the current price of the security.
Liquidity	The speed and ease with which an asset can be traded. Cash has the most liquidity of all assets, whereas property (real estate) is one of the most illiquid assets.
Long	Being long means that you are a buyer of a security.
MACD (Moving Average Convergence Divergence)	Measures the difference between two moving averages and is a measure of momentum. As the moving averages drift apart then momentum is increasing and vice versa.

Margin	An amount paid by the account holder (either in cash or "marginable securities"), which is held by the brokerage against noncash or high risk investments, or where the brokerage has lent the account holder the means to undertake a particular trade.
Margin account	An account where the brokerage lends the customer part of the net debit required to make a trade.
Margin Call	Where the brokerage calls the account holder in order for them to pay more funds into their account to maintain the trade.
	Note that strategies that involve some form of unlimited risk often require a level of margin to be determined by the brokerage.
Margin requirements	The amount of cash or marginable securities (for example, blue chip stocks) that an account holder must have in his account to write uncovered (or naked) options.
Mark to Market	The daily adjustment of margin accounts to reflect profits and losses in such a way that losses are not allowed to accumulate.
Market Capitalization	The number of outstanding shares multiplied by the value per share.
Market if Touched (MIT) order	An order that becomes a market order if the price specified is reached.
Market Maker	A trader or trading firm that buys and sells securities in a market in order to facilitate trading. Market makers make a two sided (bid and ask) market.
Market on Close order	An order that requires the broker to achieve the best price at the close or in the last five minutes of trading.
Market on Open order	An order that must be executed at the opening of trading.
Market order	Trading securities immediately at the best market prices to guarantee execution.
Market price	The most recent transaction price.
Momentum	Where a market direction (up or down) is established.
Momentum indicators	Technical Analysis indicators using price movement and volume to determine market direction.
Momentum traders	Traders who use momentum as their primary criteria to invest.
Moving Average	The average of a security's latest prices for a specific period of time (for example, 50 days). Another Technical

	Analysis tool.
Mutual Fund	An open-ended investment fund that pools investors' contributions to invest in securities such as stocks and bonds.
Naked	Selling naked options refers to a sold options contract with no hedge position in place. Such a position leaves the option seller (writer) exposed to unlimited risk.
Nasdaq	National Association of Securities Dealers Automated Quotations system.
	This is a computerized system providing brokers and dealers with securities price quotes.
Near the Money (NTM)	Where the underlying asset price is close to the strike price of an option.
New York Stock Exchange (NYSE)	The largest stock exchange in the USA.
Note	A short-term debt instrument. They normally mature in or less than five years.
OEX	Standard & Poor's 100 Stock Index.
Offer	The lowest price at which the market-maker is willing to sell.
	Also can refer to the "Ask" of a "bid–ask" spread. See Ask.
On the Money (At the Money)	See ATM (At the Money).
Open Outcry	Verbal system of floor trading still used at many exchanges (for example, the CME and CBOT).
Opening	The beginning of the trading session at an exchange.
Opportunity Cost	The risk of an investment expressed as a comparison with another competing investment.
Option	A financial instrument which gives the buyer the right, not the obligation to buy (call) or sell (put) an underlying asset at a fixed price before a predetermined date.
Option Premium	The price of an option.
Option Writer	The seller of an option (naked).
Out of the Money (OTM)	Where the option has no Intrinsic Value and where you cannot exercise an option for a profit.
	OTM *calls* are where the current stock price is less than the call Strike price.
	OTM *puts* are where the current stock price is greater than the put Strike price.

Par	The nominal value of a bond that is paid back to the bondholder at maturity.
Position Delta	The sum of all positive and negative deltas within a hedged trade position.
Premium	The price of an option.
Price bar	The visual representation of a securities price fluctuations for a set period of time. Price bars can be for as little as one minute (or less) and as much as one year (or more).
Price Earnings Ratio	The price of a stock divided by the Earnings per Share for that stock.
	The same figure can be calculated by dividing the market capitalization of a stock by the earnings of that company.
Principal	The purchase price of a bond
Put option	The right, not the obligation, to sell an underlying security at a fixed price before a predetermined date.
Quote	The price being bid or offered by a market maker for a security.
Ratio Backspread	A strategy using all puts or all calls whereby the trader buys OTM options in a ratio of 3:2 or 2:1 to the ITM options he sells. In this way the trader is always long in more options than those he is short in.
Ratio Call spread	A bearish strategy that involves the trader being short in more, higher Strike calls than those lower Strike calls he is long in, at a ratio of 3:2 or 2:1. In this way the trader will have an unlimited risk profile with only limited profit potential.
Ratio Put spread	A bullish strategy that involves the trader being short in more, lower Strike puts than those higher Strike puts he is long in, at a ratio of 3:2 or 2:1. In this way the trader will have an unlimited risk profile with only limited profit potential.
Real Time	Data which is updated and received tick by tick.
Relative Strength	A technical indicator comparing a security's price action as compared to that of an index or another stock.
Relative Strength Index (RSI)	A technical indicator which is an oscillator that combines price action with volume. Best to use with trending stocks and can be used to indicate potential tops and bottoms.
Resistance	A ceiling on a price chart which is thought to be difficult for the price to burst up through because of past price

	movements.
Return	The income profit on an investment, often expressed as a percentage.
Reversal Stop (or Stop and Reverse) order	A stop order which, when activated, reverses the current position from long to short (or vice versa).
Risk	The potential loss of a trade.
Risk Free Rate	The interest chargeable on Treasury Bills (T-Bills) is generally known as the Risk Free Rate, and it is this rate that is used as a component part of the theoretical options valuation model.
Risk Profile	The graphic depiction of a trade, showing the potential Risk, Reward, and Breakeven Points as the underlying security price deviates within a range of prices.
Seat	Membership in a stock or futures exchange.
Securities and Exchange Commission (SEC)	Organization which regulates the US securities markets to protect investors.
Security	An instrument which can be traded (for example, stocks, bonds, and so on).
Series (options)	Option contracts of the same class (underlying asset), same strike price and same Expiration Date.
Shares	Units of ownership in a company or organization.
Short	Selling a security which you don't actually own.
Short selling	Selling a security which you don't actually own beforehand. You will eventually have to buy it back, hopefully at a reduced price, thus making profit.
Small-Cap stocks	Smaller (and sometimes newer) companies associated with high risk and high potential rewards. Can be illiquid to trade with large bid–ask spreads.
Speculator	A trader who aims to make profit by correctly assessing the direction of price movement of the security. Generally distinguished from investors in that speculators are associated with short-term directional trading.
Spread	The difference between the Bid and Ask of a traded security.
	or: A trading strategy which involves more than one leg to create a (hedged) position.
	or: A price spread is the difference between the high and the low of a price bar.

Standard & Poor's (S&P)	A company that rates stocks and bonds and produces and tracks the S&P indices.
Stochastic	A technical indicator, which is an oscillator based on the relationship of the open, high, low, close of price bars.
Stock	A share of a company's stock is a unit of ownership in that company.
Stock Exchange or Stock Market	An organized market where buyers and sellers are brought together to trade stocks.
Stock Split	Where a company increases the amount of outstanding stock, thus increasing the number of shares, reducing the value per share. Generally a sign that the stock has been rising and management's way of assisting the liquidity in the stock.
Stop orders	*Buy stops:* where the order price is specified above the current value of the security.
	Sell stops: where the order price is specified below the current value of the security.
Straddle	A neutral trade that involves simultaneously buying a call and put at the same strike price and with the same Expiration Date. Requires the underlying asset to move in an explosive nature (in either direction) in order to make the trade profitable.
Strangle	A neutral trade that involves simultaneously buying a call and put at different strike prices (the put Strike being lower than the call Strike, that is, both OTM) and with the same Expiration Date. Requires the underlying asset to move in an explosive nature (in either direction) to make the trade profitable.
Strike price (Exercise price)	The price at which an asset can be bought or sold by the buyer of a call or put option.
Support	A floor on a price chart thought to be difficult for the price to fall down through because of past price movements.
Synthetic Long Call	Buying a share and a put, or going long a future and a put.
Synthetic Long Put	Buying a call and shorting a stock or future.
Synthetic Long Stock	Buying a call and shorting a put with the same strike price and Expiration Date.
Synthetic Short Call	Shorting a put and shorting a stock or future.
Synthetic Short Put	Shorting a call and buying a stock or future.

Synthetic Short Stock	Shorting a call and buying a put with the same strike price and Expiration Date.
Synthetic Straddle	Combining stocks (or futures) with options to create a delta neutral trade.
Technical Analysis	Using charts and charting techniques and indicators (such as prices, volume, moving averages, stochastics, etc.) to evaluate future likely price movement.
Theoretical Value (options)	The Fair Value calculation of an option using a pricing formula such as the Black-Scholes Options Pricing Model.
Theta (decay)	The sensitivity of an option price to the variable of time to Expiration. Remember that options only have a finite life (until Expiration), therefore theta is an extremely important sensitivity to consider.
Tick	The least amount of price movement recorded in a security. Was 1/32 until decimalization eliminated the fractions structure.
Time premium	The non-Intrinsic component of the price of an option.
Time Value (Extrinsic Value)	The price of an option less its Intrinsic Value. Out of the Money options are entire made up of Extrinsic (or Time) Value.
Treasury Bill (T-Bill)	A short-term government debt security with a maturity of no more than one year. The interest charged on these instruments is known as the Risk Free Rate.
Treasury Bond (T-Bond)	A fixed interest US government debt security with ten years or more to maturity.
Treasury Note (T-Note)	A fixed interest US government debt security with between one to 10 years to maturity.
Triple Witching Day	The third Friday in March, June, September, and December when US stock options, index options, and futures contracts all expire at the same time. The effect of this is often increased volume and volatility as traders look to close short and long positions.
Type	The classification of an option, either a call or a put.
Uncovered Option	A short position where the writer does not have the underlying security (or call option) to hedge the unlimited risk position of his naked position.
Underlying asset/instrument/security	An asset (such as a share) that is subject to purchase or disposal upon exercise.
Upside	The potential for a price to increase.

Vega	The sensitivity of an option price to volatility. Typically, options increase in value during periods of high volatility.
Volatility	The measure of the fluctuation in the price movement in a security over a period of time. Volatility is one of the most important components in the theoretical valuation of an option price.
	Historical Volatility: the standard deviation of the underlying security (closing) price movement over a period of time (typically 21 to 23 days).
	Implied Volatility: the calculated component derived from the option price when using the Black-Scholes Option Pricing Model. Traders can take advantage when there is a significant discrepancy between Implied and Historical Volatility.
Volatility Skew	Whereby deep OTM options tend to have higher Implied Volatilities than ATM options. This type of discrepancy again gives the trader the opportunity to make trades whose profits are determined by volatility action as opposed to directional price action.
Volume	The number of underlying securities traded on their particular part of the exchange.
	Where price direction and volume bars are aligned in the same direction, this is a bullish sign (it means that prices are rising with increased volume or that prices are falling with decreased volume).
	Where price direction diverges from volume bars, this is a bearish sign (that is, prices rising with falling volume or prices falling with rising volume).
Whipsaw	A short, sharp price swing that ensures a losing scenario for both sides of a position.
Witching Day	When two or more classes of options and futures contracts expire.
Writer	Someone who sells an option.
Yield	The rate of return of an investment, expressed as a percentage.
Zeta	An option price's sensitivity to Implied Volatility.

References and Recommended Reading

Appel, G. (1979) *The Moving Average Convergence-Divergence Method*. Great Neck, NY: Signalert.

Bandler, R. and Grinder, J. (1979) *Frogs into Princes*. Moaba, UT: Eden Grove Editions.

Bernstein, J. (1987) *Short Term Trading in Commodity Futures*. Northbrook, IL: Probus.

Bernstein, J. (1998) *Seasonality: Systems, Strategies & Signals*. Northbrook, IL: Wiley.

Bernstein, P. (1996) *Against the Gods*. New York: Wiley.

Cohen, G. (2005) *The Bible of Options Strategies*. New York: FT Prentice Hall.

DiNapoli, J. (1998) *Trading with DiNapoli Levels*. (www.fibtrader.com) Sarasota, FL: Coast Investment Software Inc.

Dobson, E. D. (1984) *Understanding Fibonacci Numbers*. Greenville, SC: Traders Press.

Downs, E. (1999) *The 7 Chart Patterns that Consistently Make Money*. Austin, TX: Nirvana Systems Inc.

Elder, A. (1993) *Trading for a Living*. New York: Wiley.

Gemmill, G. (1993) *Options Pricing—An International Perspective*. Maidenhead: McGraw Hill.

Graham, B. (1973) *The Intelligent Investor*. New York: Harper & Row.

Graham, B. and Dodd, D. (1934) *Security Analysis*. New York: McGraw Hill.

Hagstrom, R. G., Jr. (1994) *The Warren Buffett Way*. New York: Wiley.

Hull, J. C. (1989) *Options, Futures and Other Derivatives*. Upper Saddle River, NJ: Prentice Hall.

Kinder, G. (1999) *The 7 Stages of Money Maturity*. New York: Delacorte Press.

Kolb, R. W. (1997) *Options*. 3rd edn. Malden, MA: Blackwell Business.

Laborde, G. Z. (1984) *Influencing with Integrity*. Mountain View, CA: Crown House Publishing.

Lane, G. (1984) 'Lane's Stochastics', *Technical Analysis of Stocks and Commodities*, May/June.

Lefevre, E. (1993) *Reminiscences of a Stock Operator*. New York: Wiley.

Lowenstein, R. (1996) *Buffett—The Making of an American Capitalist*. London: Weidenfeld & Nicolson.

Lynch, P. (1989) *One up on Wall Street*. New York: Penguin.

Mackay, C. (1980) *Extraordinary Popular Delusions and the Madness of Crowds*. New York: Harmony Books.

O'Higgins, M. with Downes, J. (1991) *Beating the Dow*. New York: Harper Perennial.

Patel, A. B. (1997) *The Mind of a Trader*. London: FT Pitman.

Patel, A. B. (1999) *Trading Online*. London: FT Pitman.

Schwager, J. D. (1992) *The New Market Wizards*. New York: Harper Business.

Simmons, R. (1999) *Buffett Step by Step*. London: FT Pitman.

Thomsett, M. (2005) *Options Trading for the Conservative Investor*. New York: FT Prentice Hall.

Train, J. (1980) *The Money Masters*. New York: Harper Collins.

Welles Wilder, J., Jr. (1978) *New Concepts in Technical Trading Systems*. McLeansville, NC: Trend Research.

Welles Wilder, J., Jr. (1991) *The Delta Phenomenon*. McLeansville, NC: Trend Research.

Williams, L. (1988) *The Definitive Guide to Futures Trading*. Volumes 1 and 2. Brightwaters, NY: Windsor Books.

Williams, L. (1999) *Long Term Secrets for Short Term Trading*. New York: Wiley.

Index

Q-R

S